T0300713

The Extinction of Experience

ALSO BY CHRISTINE ROSEN

Preaching Eugenics:
Religious Leaders and the
American Eugenics Movement

My Fundamentalist Education:
A Memoir of a Divine Girlhood

The Extinction of Experience

BEING HUMAN IN A
DISEMBODIED WORLD

CHRISTINE ROSEN

W. W. NORTON & COMPANY
Independent Publishers Since 1923

For information about permission to reproduce selections from this book, write to
Permissions, W. W. Norton & Company, Inc., 500 Fifth Avenue, New York, NY 10110

For information about special discounts for bulk purchases, please contact
W. W. Norton Special Sales at specialsales@wwnorton.com or 800-233-4830

Manufacturing by Lakeside Book Company
Book design by Daniel Lagin
Production manager: Lauren Abbate

ISBN 978-0-393-24171-6

W. W. Norton & Company, Inc., 500 Fifth Avenue, New York, N.Y. 10110
www.wwnorton.com

W. W. Norton & Company Ltd., 15 Carlisle Street, London W1D 3BS

10 9 8 7 6 5 4 3

For Hugo and Sebastian

We had the experience but missed the meaning.

—T. S. ELIOT, *FOUR QUARTETS*

Contents

❧ ❧ ❧

The Extinction of Experience

Introduction

※ ※ ※

Technology . . . the knack of so arranging the world so that we need
not experience it.

MAX FRISCH, *HOMO FABER* (1957)

This is a book about the disappearance of experience.
Not every experience, of course. Every day we accumulate
new experiences that confirm or challenge our sense of self while
also transforming our working knowledge of the world.

Experiences, broadly considered, are the ways we become acquainted
with the world. Direct experience is our first teacher. As we learn to
navigate the world around us, we attach meaning to what we encounter.
These experiences and meanings differ across times and cultures but
share common threads. Different people speak different languages and
have different social customs, but the fact that we all have languages
and customs is a marker of our shared humanity.

Certain types of experience—some rooted deeply in our evolutionary history, such as face-to-face interaction and various forms of
pleasure-seeking; others more recent and reflective of cultural norms,
such as patience and our sense of public space and place—are fading from
our lives. Many of these experiences are what, historically, have helped
us form and nurture a shared reality as human beings.

Mediating technologies have been a significant force behind these changes. By "technology" I mean the devices such as computers, smartphones, smart speakers, wearable sensors, and, in our likely future, implantable objects, as well as the software, algorithms, and Internet platforms we rely on to translate the data these devices assemble about us. Technology also includes the virtual realities and augmented realities we experience through our use of these tools. Our integration of these tools into our daily lives has blurred the boundary between "virtual" things—things not grounded in physical reality that we encounter while online or via mediating technologies—and "real" things embedded in physical space.

These technologies mediate between us and our world. For now, we still have some choice in how much mediation we allow. During the COVID-19 pandemic, many people lived lives of near-constant mediation out of necessity, as work, education, and social life migrated online. Culturally we were prepared for this shift, given how much time we were already spending using screens large and small to mediate our daily lives, and our evolving preference for such forms of interaction.

That preference encourages the embrace of new forms of mediated experience that do not necessarily improve our interactions as human beings, even as they also bring greater convenience. Our understanding of experience has become disordered, in ways large and small. More and more people mistrust their own experiences. More and more people create their own realities rather than live in the world around them. We can no longer assume that reality is a matter of consensus.

We are beginning to see hints of how these new ways of experiencing the world—more mediated, more personalized, more immediate yet less bounded by the realities of the physical world—have altered our understanding of reality.

In 2018, Matthew Wright of Henderson, Nevada, drove a black armored truck to the Hoover Dam, blocked traffic, and held up a sign demanding investigation of the "deep state." He had become convinced during his reading of websites and online chatrooms related to the conspiracy theory QAnon that he needed to take action to prevent injustice. Likewise, Doug Jensen, one of the hundreds of people prosecuted for storming the U.S. Capitol on January 6, 2021, and also an avid QAnon conspiracy theorist who spent a great deal of time online, told the FBI that everything that had happened to him in real life "has been like I watched a movie. Everything that's happening now, I know it all because it's all old news to me." In the weeks and months leading up to his participation in the January 6th attack, Mike Sparks struggled with what his social media use was doing to his health and temperament. "I've noticed that my phone has been in my hand more than my Bible," he wrote. "I've been locked in on my Facebook watching all this stuff play out and I get angrier and angrier." He thought about quitting social media altogether.

Although they are extreme examples, these stories demonstrate a profound confusion and mistrust about everyday experience. Having turned to online communities for help in understanding how the "real" world works, an increasing number of people are eager to reshape that real world based on the tenets of what they've learned in virtual realms— and not always for the better. QAnon is an outlier, but the principle holds for much of our regular social media interactions that bleed into real-world behavior. One family physician writes about the disconnect he sees in many of his patients who are "less sure of the distinction between virtual and actual," particularly after pandemic-era immersion in digital worlds. "I hear more and more patients complain that they emerge from sessions online feeling tense, anxious, low mood, or with a pervasive feeling of unreality," he notes.

Our personal technologies grant us the ability to spend most of our waking hours crafting and living in a "personal reality." In the twentieth century, historian Daniel Boorstin, in his book *The Image*, coined the term "pseudo-event" to describe the manufactured media landscape that was meant to appear authentic despite its being "not spontaneous but comes about because someone has planned, planted, or incited it."

Today, many of us choose to live in a form of *pseudo-reality* governed by algorithmically-enabled individual experiences. Much of what passes for authentic experience today is vicarious and virtual.

There was no deliberate effort to incentivize this way of living, although many individuals and companies have profited from our growing enthusiasm for ever more mediated experiences. It is one of the unintended consequences of the bargain we struck in embracing the Internet, a consequence few wanted to contend with at the beginning because it seemed unduly pessimistic. Besides, the new online world was fun. It still is.

But what began as a slow bleed of reality on the edges has now become a culture-wide destabilizing force. Reality has competition, from both augmented and alternative forms. The charm of Second Life, an early alternative online world, has given way to the vastly more ambitious, live-your-life-entirely-online ambitions of the Metaverse or the implant-the-Internet-in-your-brain proposals of Elon Musk's Neuralink.

In these new worlds, we are Users, not individuals. We are meant to prefer these engineered User Experiences to human reality. This book argues that we arrived here by allowing valuable human experiences to wither or die, sometimes intentionally and sometimes unintentionally. Our continued unwillingness to account for what has been lost won't lead to a world of technology-enabled progress; rather, this inability to grapple with the extinction of fundamental human experiences creates a world where our sense of shared reality and purpose is further frayed, and where a growing distrust of human judgment will further polarize our culture and politics. Technological change of the sort we have experienced in the last twenty years has not ushered in either greater social stability or moral evolution. In fact, many of our sophisticated technological inventions and platforms have been engineered to bring out the worst of human nature. The guiding spirit of Instagram isn't Rumi. It's Hobbes.

What kind of person is formed in an increasingly digitized, mediated, hyperconnected, surveilled, and algorithmically governed world? What do we gain and what do we lose when we no longer talk about the Human Condition, but rather the User Experience?

The human condition is embodied, recognizes its fragility, frequently toggles between the mediated and unmediated, requires private spaces, and is finite. By contrast, the User Experience is disembodied and digital, it is trackable and databased and usually always mediated. It lacks privacy and promises no limits—even after death, when, as several new technologies promise, our digital remnants can be gathered and engineered into posthumous chatbots to comfort our grieving family members.

Concerns about technology eroding our sense of reality are nothing new. The philosopher Theodor Adorno decried the "false realism" created by television in 1954. He argued that we do not simply watch TV. TV also influences how we understand the world if we regularly watch it—our expectations and our common cultural concerns.

Digital technology shapes expectations on a greater scale and with more power than TV ever could. While broadcast television commercials were bound to a predetermined schedule, social media platforms feed users carefully tailored streams of information meant to nudge their behavior in real time. This makes digital technology a far more aggressive tool to shape decision-making. Features that make digital technology appealing—responsiveness and precision—can impact our sense of agency.

Even our more mundane digital tools chip away at our human skills. For example, GPS is more precise than tools such as paper maps or sextants, but it also places users in the role of spectators rather than navigators during the journey. We are placed at the center of the GPS map, but we do not know how to orient ourselves. Once, in a remote location in California, when our GPS went out, my sons and I were forced to find our way by cobbling together remembered signposts and following an out-dated map. The experience was both mildly terrifying (I was not sure we would find our way back) but also rewarding when, after many false starts, we figured out which back country road would lead us to the high-way we sought.

Technology also shapes our understanding of what is possible. Our new tools increasingly encourage us to see things as problems to be solved: waiting in line, writing by hand, remote learning, navigation, boredom.

Many of our current technologies seem to view people as the prob-lem to which devices and platforms and algorithms provide a necessary solution. If earlier technologies were an extension of our senses, today's technologies train us to mistrust our own senses and rely instead on technology. This technological approach to humanity even co-opts the words we use to describe human experiences. Consider "sensorium," a word that describes both the physiological process whereby we interpret the sensory information and stimuli we receive, and the cultural process wherein we derive understanding from our senses.

Today, Sensorium is the name of a digital entertainment company that promises to move your "real-life experiences" to the virtual world via "revolutionizing digital communications through a sense of pres-ence." The company promises you will "feel closer than ever to the people you love and the things you enjoy" not by being in their actual presence, but by transporting those interactions to a "next-generation social VR platform" that will allow you to become your "true self" and "free your-self from earthly limitations." That "true self" can even become "digi-tally immortal," according to the company.

Technology interposes itself between us and the world. It translates reality "for" us but also to its designers' ends and extraordinary profit. It has transformed many human experiences not by banning them, but by making certain kinds of embodied experiences, such as face-to-face communication and other unmediated pleasures, less and less relevant to daily life.

This book is a modest effort to encourage us to cultivate and, in some cases, recover ways of thinking, knowing, and being in the world that we are losing or have lost through our embrace of mediating technologies. It grew out of my own experiences as a child of the pre-digital era (I'm a member of Gen X) who encountered this new world as an adult and is still navigating its promises and perils. My generation, known for its cynicism, has with time become more outspokenly nostalgic for that pre-digital moment when the greatest distraction from childhood play was network television or, if your family had enough money, an Atari gaming system. But the nostalgia is grounded in a concrete sense of the loss of important things. Raising my sons, who are now nearly adults themselves, in a world saturated with digital technology has rendered those losses even more starkly visible. I am trained as a historian and have written about the impact of technology on culture for decades, but, like many people, I struggle with how to strike the correct balance between mediated and unmediated experiences and reckon daily with how much time I spend staring at screens rather than into the eyes of other human beings.

And so this effort is not driven by perverse Luddism, but by the recognition that technology has altered and continues to re-form our understanding of many of the things we have in common as human beings. We don't have to accept the replacement or end of these non-technological values and ways of knowing.

Extinction is not inevitable. It is a choice.

Author's Note

I have chosen to use the collective "we" throughout this book to signal that, given how ubiquitous and widespread is our use of technology, even people who choose not to embrace every tool described in this book are nevertheless impacted by its use by others. The use of "we" is not meant to assume that everyone has a similar experience with technology, or that they bring the same set of assumptions or values to their use of it. It is intended as a shorthand for signaling membership in a community of human beings, which, until the Singularity or other such outsourced forms of consciousness is reached, or artificial general intelligence supplants us all, includes every embodied person.

You Had to Be There

Imagine the following: The restaurant is dimly lit and a little grimy. People are eating and talking; you are given a table; it's crowded but the smells coming from the kitchen are promising. The menu's contents are foreign to you and you're forced to ask your waiter, what is a Jerusalem artichoke? Is it like a regular artichoke? What does it taste like? You order and consume a deliciously weird meal. You pay with cash and leave satisfied.

Or, over drinks, you and a friend disagree about which movie qualifies as Keanu Reeves's breakout performance and end up placing a bet (you might be a little tipsy when this occurs). You don't go to IMDb.com on your phone to review Keanu's filmography or avail yourself of apps such as YouBetMe. You simply agree that when you meet again, you will decide who has won and the loser will owe the winner another drink.

Or you hand the pedicab driver a twenty-dollar bill and beg him to get you to 34th Street in Manhattan as quickly as possible, your roller bag suitcase occupying the seat beside you. The subway is a disaster, you can't find a taxi in the middle of rush hour, and you're about to miss your train home.

You don't post to X or Instagram or Snapchat about any of this.

These are all undatabased experiences and they all happened to me on a trip to New York. At the time I didn't recognize how rare they had become. If I had used my credit card or consulted Yelp before choosing the restaurant, or summoned Google to settle the bet, I would have had a different experience, a databased experience.

Behind the power we wield with our technologies is a timidity and aversion to risk. It's much easier to go with what Yelp or Google or Amazon suggest "other customers like you" might like than to squander your time and money on a guess. But does this timidity lead to a "withering of experience," as Theodor Adorno suggested in his analysis of the modern person's mechanized and homogenized approach to culture and leisure? In a world of digital experiences, do we any longer recognize any of them as ersatz?

Experience has a history, which marks our physical bodies. The bullfighter's scar from being gored stands in for a kind of knowledge; the stretch marks left behind after the birth of child are a reminder of the miraculous things the human body can do. Our physical bodies also form the basis for metaphors: I lost my head; he broke my heart; give me a hand with that; it cost an arm and a leg; stop being so nosy. The phrase "in the flesh" is used to signal one's identity, trustworthiness, and physical presence: "Is that you?" "In the flesh!"

If the worry during the Enlightenment, as mathematician Isaac Milner wrote in 1794, was that "the great and high" have "forgotten that they have souls," then today the worry is that many of us have forgotten that we have bodies. The opportunities to play out our sense of self at a remove from our physical limitations—online and through social media—and the many new ways we can track and quantify ourselves (I walked x number of steps today!) has given us the impression that we can somehow either ignore or control our bodies, or at least escape some of their quirks.

Transhumanists such as Ray Kurzweil think we can overcome our natural expiration date. They would have us jettison what is weak, inefficient, or frustrating about our physical bodies and upload our minds to achieve the "singularity." This rejection of the direct experience of our own bodies is a hallmark of our technopositive times—and a hubristic fiction that philosophers have warned for millennia against believing.

Writing about how the clock trained people to question their own experience of hunger in order to meet its dictates, for example, computer scientist Joseph Weizenbaum noted how timepieces created a new physical reality for their users. "The feeling of hunger was rejected as stimulus for eating," he wrote, "instead, one ate when an abstract model had achieved a certain state, i.e., when the hands of a clock pointed to certain marks on the clock's face," such as noon.

With the place- and time-shifting available to us through mobile technology, what we tend to reject today aren't the signals of our own hunger; those can now be satisfied instantly with an app that delivers groceries, or, like DoorDash, a buffet of delivery food options. What we reject, as we will see, are the inconveniences and small hazards of face-to-face communication, the laborious but necessary practice of doing things with our own hands, and the non-quantifiable experience of unmediated pleasure.

When one of my sons was in second grade, I went to his classroom to watch him give a presentation about Benjamin Banneker, the freeborn African American who published a series of almanacs in the eighteenth century. After he described some features of Banneker's almanac, including its predictions of weather for each planting season, and the usefulness of written almanacs, one of his classmates asked, "Why would you get the weather from a book?"

"Where do you hear about the weather?" the teacher asked. "Television!" several of the kids answered. "My mom listens to the radio,"

another said. "You get the weather on your phone," one boy said defini-
tively, as if the rest of us were being obtuse. Most of the class nodded
their approval.

How many of us check the weather forecast on our phones or computers before we walk outside every day? I do. I have a minor weather fetish
and am an avid reader of the Capital Weather Gang here in Washington, DC, a group of meteorologists whose site boasts an actively engaged
community of fellow weather nerds. The site's daily forecast is made by
human meteorologists, which until recently was something I took for
granted. I assumed the weather app on my iPhone was the same thing.

But as one of the Weather Gang meteorologists noted, "The forecast
on many of your favorite smartphone weather apps is not created by a
human being. Instead, it is generated by a computer. It does not harness
the expertise of a local forecaster who understands a region's weather
peculiarities, has a wealth of historical knowledge, and can correct for
obvious computer errors." As a result, weather apps like the popular
DarkSky will often show clear skies when it's raining buckets.

Like my favorite meteorologist's comment about weather apps, this
book is a warning about the perils of some of our technological choices. It
is a plea to pause and consider what we are losing, as well as gaining, when
we allow new technologies into our lives, and to question the motives of
the companies so eager to have us "share" ourselves with them. As the
head of Facebook's data team, Cameron Marlow, told *Technology Review*
a few years ago, "As Facebook becomes a more integral part of people's
communication, it becomes difficult to disentangle what 'real-world
social behavior' means independent of Facebook."

I maintain we need to know what the real world looks like independent of Facebook (now Meta). And we need to be able to defend that
world from technology when it threatens things that are better left alone.
We need to defend the sensory world and remind ourselves of the crucial importance of the physical body, the integrity of physical space, and
the need for people to cultivate inner lives. From these flow things that

can't be made by machines: serendipity, intuition, community, spontaneity, and empathy. As the Trappist monk and theologian Thomas Merton observed, "It does us no good to make fantastic progress if we do not know how to live with it."

The problem isn't that technological change is happening; technological change is always happening. If X was going to destroy civilization, it would have happened long ago when Justin Bieber gained his millionth follower. The problem is our collective complacence in assuming that change brings improvement. The dating app Tinder chose as its slogan, "Tinder is how people meet. It's like real life, but better." But is it better?

It used to be that an experience was something—like a vacation— which you enjoyed (or not) in your own physical body, in a particular physical space at a particular time. You might re-experience it later by looking at pictures or by sharing stories about it with others. But your sensibility about an experience, particularly if it was dramatic or memorable and you were attempting to convey what it felt like to others, might be summed up by saying, "You had to be there." The phrase rose steadily in popularity from the 1960s until the year 2012, when its use dropped precipitously, according to Google Ngram, which measures language use over time in a broad range of published material. The year 2012 also saw the fastest year-over-year increase in Americans' smartphone use, which rose from 31 percent to 44 percent in just twelve months.

Thanks to the now ubiquitous smartphone, we feel as if we can be anywhere. We can vicariously witness countless things and experience, not merely imagine, the lives of others. We immerse ourselves in sophisticated simulations and even engage in lengthy relationships with avatars. We can see street views of homes thousands of miles away and zoom in on the world's greatest artistic masterpieces. How are these mediated ways of "being there" changing our understanding of experience?

For one thing, we now spend as much time consuming the experiences of others as we do having experiences of our own. One popular genre of YouTube videos known as reaction videos shows people reacting to . . . just about anything. A video that has received more than three million views shows a boy reacting to the scene in *The Empire Strikes Back* where (spoiler alert!) Darth Vader reveals he is Luke's father. Other related genres include gaming videos, mukbang, and unboxing videos. We love these videos because they give us something we crave: a brief glimpse of an authentic experience. "Watching a reaction video is a way of vicariously recapturing primary experience," one critic noted. It also offers a form of experience plagiarism, wherein people feel as if they, too, are "there" in the moment with the people on the screen.

Instead of "you had to be there," our current moment seems best suited to "véjà du," or, as it is described by scientists in the Virtual Human Interaction Lab at Stanford University, "the ability to see ourselves doing something [virtually] we have not done physically." Using virtual reality (VR) headsets, researchers like Jeremy Bailenson hope to use véjà du techniques to model the aging process (look how scary old you'll be in ten years if you keep smoking!). Others will likely enlist VR to create a new world of manufactured experiences, such as advertisements which, in a triumph of narcissistic marketing, use a virtual avatar that looks exactly like you to sell you products.

Technology even promises to render the school field trip extinct. Google now offers a "field-trip simulation system" called Expeditions to schools. "Imagine exploring coral reefs or the surface of Mars in an afternoon," the program's website enthuses. These once-in-lifetime experiences are free—if you don't count the data Google will hoover up while beta-testing Expeditions on children, that is.

Virtual experiences are not all uplifting narratives of seventh graders in Iowa "visiting" the Burj Khalifa on Google Expeditions. Some have less feel-good consequences. In 2010, in South Korea, a couple allowed their infant to starve to death while they raised a virtual child online in a popular game galled Prius. When Spike Jonze's movie *Her* was released in 2013, it depicted a near-future Los Angeles resident, Theodore Twombly, who fell in love with his computer's alluring operating system. Yet this fictional love story already reflected a growing reality. In 2009, a Japanese man "married" an anime character from the dating simulation game Love Plus; by 2022, the *New York Times* described a subculture of thousands of people who had unofficially married fictional online characters from games and anime. Many described these relationships as emotionally fulfilling and superior to ones they might have with their fellow human beings.

The extension of the virtual world into everyday life, whether on platforms that host Massive Multiplayer Online games or on Internet-enabled chatrooms and social media sites, has brought with it a new kind of anxiety over authenticity. We (rightly) worry about fake news, catfishing, and conspiracy theories, all of which flourish online, even while reassuring ourselves that we can still distinguish the true from the false.

Writing in the 1930s, critic Walter Benjamin wondered what would happen to a culture divorced from experience, one in which experiences were largely simulated. He worried that a "poverty of experience" would drive people to a strange kind of despair, and that they would seek relief in an existence where "everything is solved in the simplest and more comfortable way." In embracing the technologies that mediate so much of our experience, we have certainly made our lives more comfortable and convenient, but it has come at a cost.

Virtual connections bring real benefits, but we are reaching a point where we are beginning, en masse, to prefer the mediated to the face-to-face. The sheer number of people in public space who are demonstrating "absent presence" is only the most complained-about example. Walk down the sidewalk. Count the number of people who are using technology to mediate their experience in some way. Note how commonplace distracted drivers have become. We are avid texters who don't make eye contact with people. We are awash in social media but our social skills—common courtesy, patience, eye contact—are deteriorating. We lack a sense of place; we are impatient with the limitations of physical reality, whether it is the physical limitations of our bodies or the need to wait in line and perhaps experience boredom. More and more, we prefer the simulated to the real.

We now must remind ourselves that we are allowed to daydream, because our default state is to use technology to fill interstitial moments with some kind of communication, work, or microbursts of entertainment. We have found ways to control, speed up, and quantify our experiences. Once digitized, we can even fast-forward through our most pleasurable experiences, like concerts, sex, and religious devotion.

We use Google to understand everything from the fate of historical figures to obscure sexual acts. Aches and pains drive us to WebMD for reassurance, or a kind of chronic Internet-enabled hypochondria. Even our most private questions are submitted to our Internet oracles. One Google advertisement showed a young man typing, "How do I ask a girl out?" on the Google homepage. It featured the slogan, "Made for what matters." The message embedded in the advertisement is that you should ask Google these important questions, not your parents or friends, because Google's algorithms will find better answers for you. Many of us probably believe that it does.

It's not that technology is making us smarter or dumber. It does both, depending on the situation. Nor is there any use in drawing strict boundaries between the "real" and the "virtual" any longer, since so many of us spend so much time living in both worlds. If you own a smartphone, you're never truly disconnected. "Smart" appliances and "smart" speakers like Alexa are infiltrating the home. Even our most private spaces will soon be fully connected to the online world, sending out data about everything from our energy use to the contents of our refrigerators to our emotional states and desires.

I am interested in exploring the unexpected ways that today's mediated life has rapidly changed the rules of human experience. What even counts as an "experience" today? Is it the physical act of going to a place, the act of digitally memorializing it, or some combination of both?

Our current technologies, both small-scale and large-scale, persuade us that we can opt out of bodily limitations in ways that even the invention of the telegraph, telephone, automobile, and jet airplane did not. The experience of "being there" no longer means being together physically; it means interacting with limitless numbers of avatars or bots or other digital interlocutors who, their creators insist, are superior to old-fashioned face-to-face interaction. We have created technologies that so effectively extend our senses that we have started mistrusting the signals our own physical bodies give us. Areas of life that used to be off-limits to technological mediation and manipulation are now saturated by it.

And we are changed.

In a speech about the environment given in the 1990s, the naturalist Robert Michael Pyle lamented the "extinction of experience." Pyle and others worried that younger generations suffered from "nature deficit disorder"—being raised without the hands-on experience of mucking around outdoors, they argued, these children would grow up disaffected from nature and unlikely to embrace the role of environmental stewards as adults.

Twenty years after Pyle coined the phrase, this challenge—to live in the real world, with all its messy physical realities—is one we all face. Our experiences of pleasure, hands-on skills, self-reliance, relationships, and connection to nature are all threatened by mediating technology. Daily intimacy with the physical world recedes, little by little, while our attachment to digital worlds grows. More and more, we relate to our world through *information about* it rather than direct *experience with* it.

This substitution of information for experience explains why we like to eat convenient meals prepared by someone else while watching TV chefs create elaborate meals from scratch.

It's why many of our architects can't draw by hand and most of us can't write in cursive. It's why we outsource our ability to find our way to GPS devices, and why it is difficult to find public spaces without televisions and people fixated on their smartphone screens. It's why we send status updates to our friends online instead of talking to them. It's the reason public spaces have become just more WiFi hotspots.

Each of these interventions also represents a triumph of human ingenuity. It was not that long ago that you would starve if you didn't possess hands-on knowledge about the natural world; in some parts of the world this is still the case. But in the developed world, we choose to mediate nearly every experience we have with the physical world, with the possible exception of performing basic bodily functions—no one else can take a bath for you, at least not yet, although many people now bring their devices with them into the bathroom as company. In pursuing these kinds of mediated experiences so zealously, we undermine our own humanity.

"Experience" has become to the twenty-first century what "lifestyle" was to the twentieth—a catchall term, quickly co-opted by marketers, that promises more than it can deliver. In 1997, business writers B. Joseph Pine II and James H. Gilmore described an emerging "experience economy" that offers customers not merely goods and services but "memorable" and "inherently personal" experiences.

An Apple ad is representative of the trend: "This is it. This is what matters. The experience of a product. How it makes someone feel." The accompanying image featured an attractive male jogger with shaggy hair, a tasteful amount of glistening sweat, and an iPod strapped to his chiseled bicep. He is in brief repose, as if he has just paused to savor this iPod-enabled moment. The ad—a two-page spread that ran in outlets such as the *New York Times*—isn't selling an Apple product. It's selling an aspirational experience.

Social psychology research finds that we garner greater happiness from experiences like travel, dining in a restaurant, or attending a concert than we do from purchasing things—"doing" versus "having." This is why every hotel room, face cream, or soda you consume is marketed as a special experience. Not long ago I had a pizza delivered; on the box was a sticker that said, "Your pizza experience managed by [name of pizza company employee]." An advertisement from Omni Hotels featured a couple paddle-boarding on a remote stretch of water and the reminder, "Experiences are the most valuable currency." The hope is to link consumption with an unquantifiable but satisfying emotion: that ice cream makes me feel decadent, this overpriced face cream makes me feel pampered (or youthful). Target collaborates with SoulCycle to bring consumers "energizing new experiences." Airbnb offers "Experience" as a rental filter selection when you go to book a trip online.

Technology companies are at the forefront of marketing experience, and not always with subtlety; at one time, Sprint's slogan was "uploading the human experience." As Jack Dorsey, founder of Twitter and the mobile payment service Square told *Fast Company* magazine about Square's partnership with Starbucks, "It's not just the product that you end up drinking, but it's how it's served. It's the experience of walking into the store, out of the store, and everything around the store." Paul Adams, who worked in user experience design at Facebook, once praised a Huggies diaper marketing campaign for the way it reached customers. The company encouraged customers to post their favorite photos of their kids in diapers on Facebook, and then Huggies printed the most popular photos on buses and in subway stations. In other words, Huggies found a way to get people to turn their private experiences into free marketing materials.

But because they are unique to each person, experiences can't be marketed. What can be marketed are people's preferences for certain products. As critic Rob Horning has observed, "It becomes more useful to have preferences than experiences . . . and to have all 'experiences' take the form of social sparring over preferences." Only then can individuals' experiences be useful to marketers and social media companies. Horning says of this process, "My love of the band Rush becomes something with theoretically measurable impact. It's not about what I hear when I listen but what others think about the fact that I've chosen to claim I've heard something by Rush."

Christopher Lasch and other twentieth-century critics such as Daniel Boorstin critiqued our desire for spectacle and the narcissism that the pursuit of spectacle often encouraged. But what is sold to us now is more than merely the vicarious thrill of watching strangers on TV or in ads and wishing we were them. Social media gives everyone the opportunity to promote themselves, and to turn every experience into a marketing opportunity, which is why so many people aspire to become successful "influencers." We have become our own personal brand managers. And we've become the ads.

Real experiences and their digital equivalents are like the distinction between *eyesight* and *vision*. Eyesight refers to how well our eyes capture what we see. Vision allows us to use our eyesight intelligently by directing our perception. It is far more than functioning eyesight. Our technologies, which began as tools to enhance some functions—as eyeglasses correct weak eyesight—are moving more rapidly into the vision business, which is really the business of interpreting experience, not merely increasing our access to it. Given the brutally instrumental approach leaders of the technology industry take to human frailty, they might not be the best guides.

Consider the widely distributed print advertisement that featured a close-up view of the small pinhole camera lens on every iPhone 5. "A better photographer, built in," the ad's copy read. The next bit of ad-speak contained the kernel of a philosophy: "Instead of teaching people to take better photos, why not teach the camera?" it read. This captures a lot about our age and its values, as well as the technology industry's assumptions about what it means to be human. The advertisement's equation of technology with the person (the ad refers to the camera as the "photographer"), and its glib assumption that the technology is the more "teachable" of the two, should give us pause.

These platforms and tools have become our new character-forming institutions. They have invaded the private world of existing institutions such as the family and become indispensable in the public world of work and leisure. Isn't something wrong when 53 percent of sixteen- to twenty-two-year-olds around the world say they would rather lose their sense of smell than their favorite personal technology?

We need a new humanism, one that can challenge the engineering-driven scientism that has come to dominate culture. Humanism puts human beings and human experiences at its center, not engineering or machines or algorithms. As sociologist Richard Sennett reminds us, humanism "requires the embrace of chance and rupture" by recognizing that these things are a necessary part of the human experience, not problems to be wished away by a new app or more sophisticated algorithm. The very things that many of our technologies want to make seamless and "frictionless," as Meta's Mark Zuckerberg is so fond of saying, such as the awkwardness of face-to-face conversations and the quirks of our physical bodies, are precisely the "ill-fitting pieces of experience" that, taken together, make us human.

We have left behind the distractions of the twentieth century, when people dissatisfied with their lives temporarily escaped them through television, or movies, or going online. If VR and wearable technologies continue to improve along the lines their creators envision, people won't need to escape. They will *replace* their reality with one that is new and improved. "The Internet and virtual realities easily satisfy such social needs and drives," say VR pioneers Jim Blasovich and Jeremy Bailenson. They grant that "sometimes [they are] so satisfying that addicted users will withdraw physically from society," but "who is to say that a virtual life that is better than one's physical life is a bad thing?"

Palmer Luckey, founder of Oculus VR (now owned by Meta), seems to agree that such questions have already been answered by the mere existence of the technology itself. He told the *Wall Street Journal* that living in a virtual world at the expense of the real world wasn't a matter of "philosophical acceptance." "I think it's mostly a technological problem," he said.

He's wrong. We still face the same deeply-felt challenges that

humans have always faced—finding meaning in our lives, paying attention, understanding ourselves and others physically, mentally, and spiri-
tually. Our new technologies and software quantify, regulate, network,
and profit from those pursuits. And we assume that that's the only way
it can be. British philosopher Bertrand Russell once called the idea that
science and technology always bring positive gains an "illusion" and
warned, "Science is no substitute for virtue; the heart is as necessary for
a good life as the head." Right now, the head is dominating the heart. But
there's a better way, one that reckons with how technology and online
worlds have altered our understanding of experience.

Social critics of technology are often accused of inciting a misguided
moral panic. When it comes to our understanding of experience, however, we could use a great deal more moral panic—if moral is understood
as reminding us of our obligations to one another.

We have allowed many of our experiences to be engineered and controlled by others.

Social media theorist Nathan Jurgenson argues that lamenta-
tions about such things fetishize real life. "Those who mourn the loss
of the offline are blind to its prominence online," he argues, and he has
doled out especially harsh criticism to technology critics such as Sherry
Turkle, whom he claims wrongly fetishize and privilege the "real world"
over the virtual. "Our own time spent not looking at Facebook becomes
the status updates and photos we will post later," he says triumphantly, as
if this parasite–host relationship is something to celebrate. Social media
offers everyone a way "to declare how meaningful our lives are," he says.

Perhaps Jurgenson is correct that distinctions between online and
offline have been "queered beyond tenability," as he put it. But there's
something else queered as well: our perspective as human beings. It was
not that long ago that witnessing the death by suicide of another human
being would have registered as a traumatic event—indeed for most people it still would. But now we also read stories about a woman in New
York who purposely used a suicidal man on a bridge as a backdrop for

her selfie, or about commuters on a Los Angeles freeway who were frustrated with traffic and so "exited their vehicles and started snapping selfies with the cause of the delay: A suicidal man threatening to jump from an overpass."

What has turned so many of us into distracted, daily voyeurs, even of tragic events like an attempted suicide? Our technologies grant us a sense of power and control that with too much use can curdle into less attractive characteristics. "The narcissist is not hungry for experiences, he is hungry for Experience," Richard Sennett wrote. "Looking always for an expression or reflection of himself in Experience, he devalues each particular interaction or scene." Geographer Yi-Fu Tuan has noted that "experience is the overcoming of perils" and that the word "experience" shares a common root with "experiment," "expert," and "perilous." Experience, Tuan argues, is venturing into the unfamiliar and embracing uncertainty and potential peril. It's not taking a selfie with someone else's peril as a background.

When I talk to people about the encroachment of technology in their everyday lives, they don't express the fears of the Luddite confronting the machine weaver. They are both hopeful and a little baffled by how quickly the transformation of everyday life has occurred. "Sometimes I look around in the evening and all four of us are doing something on a screen," a father of two school-age children told me. "I mean, we're all doing something fun or educational or work-related but when I stop and look at it I wonder if it's all too much." This is someone who works in the technology industry; he has no phobias about the use of technology at home.

And yet such anxiety has slowly replaced some of the early enthusiasm we enjoyed about our technologies. Social media platforms, with their constant demand to collect friends and signal status, and their demands for us to perform by marketing our best selves, have made us better at exposure but not necessarily at forging lasting connections.

The Delphic oracle's guidance was "Know thyself." Today, in the world of social networks, the oracle's advice might be "Show thyself."

The disorientation many people feel after immersion online leads to questions about authenticity, and about the kinds of experiences we used to take for granted as real.

Every day our experiences are guided by what we say and do online. Anyone with an Internet connection can see more vicarious experiences in one day than previous generations witnessed in a lifetime, and on a scale far greater than television or film ever provided. Is it any surprise that it is becoming increasingly difficult to distinguish between what is real and what isn't, both online and IRL? For an increasing number of us, many of our memories are now of experiences that occurred online.

In extreme cases, such disorientation produces extreme behavior. In 2016, at Comet Ping Pong, a pizza restaurant in Washington, DC, a man showed up armed with a rifle, which he fired, to rescue children he believed were being held there by pedophiles. After his arrest, he told a reporter that he had recently installed Internet service in his home and had delved deeply into stories about a child-trafficking ring that was supposedly operating out of the restaurant and run by operatives who were allegedly tied to Hillary Clinton's campaign for president. He didn't believe in conspiracies, he told authorities. He believed this was a real threat and that children were suffering. Later, after learning that the story was false and being peddled by extreme-right-wing conspiracy theorists, he admitted, "The intel on this wasn't 100 percent."

Writing about how technologies have altered civilizations, the American philosopher of technology Lewis Mumford noted in 1934 that while the focus is often on the inventions that emerged from each era, just as important has been the *change of mind* that occurred before those inventions took hold, what he described as "a reorientation of wishes, habits, ideas, goals."

We are amid just such a change of mind. The increase in digital consumption that so many of us engaged in during the COVID-19 pandemic by necessity turned even older generations into heavy users of technology. But this was an acceleration of a growing trend.

Many children now grow up in a world where their first experiences—of the natural world, play, music, and words—are mediated through the screen or some other form of technology. Their toys talk to them and record them; their baby monitors watch them; their devices track and monitor them; their parents create online identities and Instagram pages for them from birth. They will grow up in a culture that values the digital image above all, where social media platforms that dominate the online world have made sharing almost compulsory; where competitiveness and constant performance are common, face-to-face interaction is less likely, and anonymous harassment easy. It's a world with a different understanding of history. The past is no longer another country. It's that thing Facebook reminds you about with its "One Year Ago Today" feature.

As technology companies frequently remind us, it's also a world of possibilities, where life, as the Apple ad slogan promises, is "automatic, effortless, and seamless."

This is our world. Do we want to live here?

CHAPTER 2

* * *

Facing One Another

When he pressed his face against the thick glass of the puff adder enclosure at London's Zoological Gardens, Charles Darwin reminded himself that while the venomous snake was close, it could not harm him. He was self-testing a theory about the power of the human mind to overcome reflex action by pitting his "firm determination" not to flinch against his body's instinct. His rational resolve proved as weak as his scientific hunch was strong. "As soon as the blow was struck, my resolution went for nothing, and I jumped a yard or two backwards with astonishing rapidity," he wrote. "My will and reason were powerless against the imagination of a danger which had never been experienced." His mind could not convince his body to remain calm.

Darwin's experiment with the puff adder was part of the unorthodox evidence gathering that would become *The Expression of the Emotions in Man and Animals* (1872), his exploration of the innate and often uncontrollable emotional and physical reactions that characterize the human experience. In his pursuit of the biological origins of emotional expression, Darwin, then in his sixties, dispensed snuff to monkeys to try to make them sneeze, observed the birthing pains of a cranky hippopotamus, closely watched his own and others' squalling children and difficult cats, and subjected his long-suffering friends and family to bouts of experimental tickling. He also corresponded regularly with the directors of insane asylums, who sent images of the men and women in their care in various stages of emotional distress, and he studied the photographs of French neurologist Guillaume Duchenne, who did pioneering work on voluntary and involuntary facial expression—including experiments administering mild jolts of electricity to the faces of his research subjects.

The question driving Darwin's unusual research method was this: What do our gestures and expressions reveal about us and why have we evolved to "read" one another in this way? Why do we nod our head in agreement when someone says something reassuring, or mimic a friend's frown when hearing of his bad news? For Darwin, physical movements and facial expressions were crucial, often uncontrollable means of connection. From birth we are wired to look at faces. A newborn's range of vision is about the same as the distance from its own face to its mother's breast when held in her arms, and babies only a few days old respond differently to objects in the shape of a human face than they do to other shapes. Darwin believed that our expressions form the basis for human understanding, and deciphering them is a skill evolution equipped us with long before we ever communicated with language.

Darwin was especially keen on studying the face, the "most considered and regarded" and "most ornamented" part of the body, and he was an excellent observer of its permutations. Sitting across from an older woman on a railway car, he became fascinated by the peculiar contractions of her *depressors anguli oris*, the muscles associated with frowning. Watching a young couple in animated conversation, he observed the woman's eyebrows regularly moving "obliquely upwards" and the "rectangular furrows" forming on her forehead—to him "a flag of distress" that her companion should have heeded. For Darwin, faces were the maps of human emotion, and he studied them with the care of a great explorer.

Today, Darwin's own face dominates a room in London's National Portrait Gallery. In the painting, he has a melancholic expression; he sat for the artist the year before his death, and according to Darwin's son it was the great scientist's favorite likeness. Amid the twenty-odd portraits in a room filled with British men of science, Darwin's is the least stuffy. Unlike the other scientists, with their formal white ties and starchy posture, Darwin is wearing a modest cloak and clasping a slouch hat as if he has stepped in from outdoors. His gaze stands out—direct, thoughtful, intense.

Darwin's arresting gaze and his belief in the power of unique human gestures came to mind when I read about Wifarer, a smartphone app that acts as a kind of indoor GPS, allowing people to find their way around large buildings the way regular GPS guides them along roads. According to the app's developer, the inspiration for the indoor positioning system was a visit to the same National Portrait Gallery where Darwin's likeness hangs. "I was following a tour guide," founder Philip Stanger told *Fast Company.* "He was skimming over various works. Then I overheard another tour guide walking close by, and he was much more detailed and colorful in his language . . . I thought, wouldn't it be great to standardize that, so that everyone can have the same experience?"

The app developer's impulse to offer every visitor to the museum the best possible experience is laudable, but his method tells us something about our age. An "ideal" experience eliminated the human guide and replaced her with a technology that could deliver a standardized, controlled experience. He wanted people to follow the bidding of his app rather than the whims of a museum employee. "The human interaction I had wasn't as satisfying as another I could have had," he said, in a statement that perfectly captures our ambiguous feelings about face-to-face interaction. He seems not to have registered the irony of creating a "personalized" experience that removed the possibility of interacting with another person.

———

I am a partisan for the face-to-face. As Darwin proved, we all are. The ability to read one another's faces developed over the course of our evolutionary history for a reason. The many gestures, movements, postures, and facial expressions that make up physical communication are central to what makes us human. A body's signs are among the things we know without knowing why we know them.

Evidence of the power of the human face permeates history. Reverence for the human face is the basis for warnings against "defacing" something. The potency of the face is why many cultures make use of veils and masks to hide it. The powerful put images of their faces before the public at every opportunity; the pharaohs of ancient Egypt placed theirs everywhere, and Roman emperors embedded theirs on every coin. "Seeking the face of God" is how Hebrews in the Bible referred to worshipping in public, and throughout the Scriptures believers are advised to deal with things face-to-face: "And repayeth them that hate him to their face, to destroy them: he will not be slack to him that hateth him, he will repay him to his face."

Humans have often ascribed hidden meanings to facial expressions. In ancient China, face readers devised maps that detailed more than one hundred regions of the face they believed were linked to character traits or susceptibility to illness. In the mid-nineteenth century, philosopher John Stuart Mill proposed a study of what he called ethology, or "the science of human character as deduced from human appearances," which never gained traction. The notion that physiognomy is destiny was later popularized by phrenology, a pseudoscience whose adherents claimed that certain regions of the brain (which they divined by feeling for bumps and ridges on the skull) corresponded with emotional and mental traits. By the late nineteenth century, French police officer Alphonse Bertillon had attempted to systematize the meaning of appearance by using anthropometric measurements to classify certain cranial shapes and features as inherently criminal.

We have long sought to make a science of our intuition about others' appearance, in part to alleviate fears of antisocial behavior. In earlier eras, people feared a confidence man wearing middle-class clothing might fool them into thinking he was a gentleman, or that they might become the victim of a criminal that they failed to recognize as such. Today, as our technologies offer us the ability to summon masses of information about another person in a split second, reading someone's face and body language seems quaint. The expression of our emotions can be quantified, or so claim engineers at Google and X.

These new ways of reading one another don't require attention to subtle physical signals or gestures. We trust that the text messages and emails and likes we send are honest expressions of our feelings (which they frequently, but not always, are), even as they often feel like a more muted form of communication. Has the primacy of the face and body as humans' most powerful communication tool ended? And if so, how do our interactions change when a skill evolution fitted us for—face-to-face communication—gives way to mediated forms of interaction?

Face-to-face communication includes both the physiological reactions we have as the result of our evolutionary history and the elaborate cultural rules that create a social glue for human interaction. To understand how mediated technologies have impacted our ability to communicate, we must look to three dynamics: first, what face-to-face interaction does to us physically, emotionally, and socially; second, the effects of mediation (via screen technologies) on those human interactions; and third, our efforts to create technologies that can read and understand our human expressions, such as new face-, gesture-, and expression-recognition technologies.

"Humans are a primate—really just an evolved ape—and this fact has important implications for how humans act and interact," sociologist Jonathan Turner has noted. "Interaction does not transcend biology; it is embedded in biology." We have evolved over millions of years to read faces and body language and to understand the expressions, postures, and gestures that signal our feelings. By contrast, symbolic and written forms of communication are fairly recent developments in our evolutionary history—less than 1 percent of it by some estimates, if we measure from the first appearance of cave paintings made by our ancestors.

We are meant to look at one another, and doing so triggers a host of physiological responses. Intense eye contact increases one's heart rate and triggers the release of phenylethylamine, an organic compound that functions as a neurotransmitter in the human central nervous system and serves as a mood and stress regulator. As one scientist put it, everything about our "biological apparatus," from our sensory and motor organs to the particular way our brains have developed, "must have been designed primarily for face-to-face communication." It is not a design without flaws, however; the development of the larynx deep in our throats, which allows us to make a much wider range of vocal sounds than our ancestors, also makes us more likely to choke on our food.

Facial expression is our primal language. The fact that our faces have less fur or hair than other mammals means that our expressions are more visible and our emotions can be more easily read. But reading expressions is a skill; distinguishing anger from contempt, or happiness from surprise, takes a lifetime of practice. Today's kindergarten classrooms often include a poster that asks, "How Do You Feel Today?," illustrated with images of human faces expressing over twenty emotions—an attempt to help a group of unrelated and rambunctious five-year-olds visualize and identify their feelings.

In a small way, we have psychologist Paul Ekman to thank for that poster. Following the path first traced by Darwin's work on emotions,

Ekman studied emotional expressions in cultures all around the world, in search of evidence of universal human emotions. In 1978 he devised his Facial Action Coding System (FACS). FACS is a taxonomy of the face's many possible expressions, broken down into individual "action units" that can be analyzed for their meaning. Ekman claimed to have pinpointed the specific muscles involved in the involuntary expression of emotions and argued that many of those emotions were universal, among them anger, fear, sadness, disgust, surprise, contempt, and happiness. He also identified emotions that are universally experienced but not always expressed with the same facial movements: feelings such as embarrassment, guilt, shame, envy, jealousy, and pride.

Ekman is perhaps best known as one of the discoverers of microexpressions, the fleeting, nearly invisible facial movements that occur when we attempt to conceal emotions. If you have ever encountered a person whose smile seems a little "off" or talked to a friend who reassures you that she's fine when she clearly isn't, you've picked up on microexpressions. As Ekman notes in his book *Emotions Revealed*, "We must have *automatic* appraising mechanisms that are continually scanning the world around us, detecting when something important to our welfare, to our survival, is happening."

Much of Ekman's research focused on high-stakes deception— identifying lies that might cost people their reputations or even their lives—and he advised police departments, the Transportation Security Administration, and of course Hollywood on lie detection. I met Ekman at a conference in San Francisco in 2012. Nearly eighty years old at the time and walking with a cane, he was still an energetic stage presence and was the only person on his panel who didn't lobotomize the audience with PowerPoint slides. I asked him about the future of face-to-face communication in an age of technological mediation, and he emphasized that no matter how much we mediate our interactions, emotions will reveal themselves in one form or another. "Our faces can perform over two hundred uniquely different expressions of anger," he said, "even more than the number of words we have to describe various forms of anger. We still have to learn how to read these signals."

Ekman's work has had many critics over the years, including anthropologist Margaret Mead, who argued that Ekman did not properly acknowledge significant cultural differences in emotional expression. Kate Crawford, a scholar who studies artificial intelligence, argues that there is little reliable research showing that one can "accurately predict someone's emotional state from their face." Other social scientists, including Maria Gendron and Lisa Feldman Barrett, note "the specific dangers of Ekman's theories being used by the AI industry because the automated detection of facial expressions does not reliably indicate an internal mental state."

Nevertheless, our growing preference for mediated forms of communication impacts our ability to assess the trustworthiness of others. Researchers who study computer-mediated communication have found that when we communicate via text or email and our bodily signals are muted, we alter our behavior to adapt to our new tools. Professor Jeff Hancock at Cornell University coined the phrase "motivational enhancement effect" to describe the way computer-mediated communication makes for more skilled liars. If you lie to someone face-to-face, you might be dissuaded by the fact that your nervous twitches or shifty eyes could give you away. By contrast, Hancock found, liars whose communication was mediated through the screen were immune to this effect, so much so that they became much more motivated to deceive as well as more successful in their deception.

The nonverbal signals we send when we are in one another's physical presence also help to convey trustworthiness. Social scientists have found that people are significantly more likely to agree to a request for help if it is made in person rather than over the phone, Zoom, or text. Help-seekers "underestimated the relative advantage of asking for help face-to-face compared with asking through any mediated channel," one study noted.

An experiment involving cooperation between pairs of strangers, some who met face-to-face and others who communicated only online, supports this. A person's ability to assess the other's trustworthiness was greater for the people who met face-to-face than online. "There is something the mind is picking up that gives you greater accuracy and makes you better able to identify people who are going to be trustworthy," the lead researcher noted.

We also behave differently when we're trying to impress someone online as opposed to in person. Researchers at the University of Toronto paired off people who wanted to get to know each other, then separated them into two groups: the first group was asked to talk to each other face-to-face and the other through online chat only. Later, when the researchers analyzed the quality of the conversations, they found that men and women in the online conversations asked fewer questions about the other person and referred to themselves more frequently than the couples meeting face-to-face. Face-to-face conversations—exchanges where we can read bodily cues, facial expressions, and tone of voice—offered a "deeper and smoother form of social engagement."

We know this intuitively. The sixteenth-century essayist Michel de Montaigne once described how "lovers quarrel, make it up again, beg favors, give thanks, arrange secret meetings and say everything, with their eyes." And not only with the eyes. Hands, heads, shoulders—even eyebrows tell a story. "None of their movements fails to talk a meaningful language which does not have to be learned, a language common to us all."

The exchange of unspoken signals and gestures, which anthropologist Edward T. Hall called "the silent language" and psychologist Albert Mehrabian later labeled "implicit communication," are precisely what fascinated Charles Darwin as he watched people interact on the street. They include so-called paralanguage cues such as the pitch, volume, and inflection of the voice, and the range of haptic (touch) strategies we employ to convey meaning.

Skilled politicians know how to use them all. A series of photographs taken in 1957 when Lyndon Johnson was Majority Leader of the U.S. Senate shows him leaning into and eventually fully invading the personal space of the diminutive nonagenarian Senator Theodore Green. The "Johnson treatment," as it was known, left Green backed up against a desk, Johnson's face looming mere inches from his own. Proximity matters. Proximity also reveals. A 2018 photo of German chancellor Angela Merkel confronting President Donald Trump at the G7 summit captured a particularly tense moment of negotiation. The image shows Merkel standing, hands firmly planted on a table and leaning in to look directly at Trump, who sits across from her with his arms folded, avoiding eye contact, and with a churlish expression on his face.

Research by neuroscientists on our biological capacity for connection and empathy suggests that we shouldn't underestimate our need for frequent face-to-face interaction. Scientists such as Barbara Fredrickson have shown how the vagus nerve, which ties the brain to the heart, is implicated in our ability to read facial expressions and understand tone of voice. Increases in one's "vagal tone," which is measured by studying heart-rate variability, are related to one's capacity for connection. "The more attuned to others you become, the healthier you become, and vice versa," observes Fredrickson, describing research she published in the journal *Psychological Science*.

The facial expressions and gestures we exchange when we meet face-to-face aren't crucial only to human connection, but also to our physical health. The vagal system is part of the biological system for human connection—evolution's empathy engine, if you will. And it deteriorates without use. "If you don't regularly exercise your ability to connect face to face, you'll eventually find yourself lacking some of the basic biological capacity to do so," Fredrickson notes.

———

In 2010, performance artist Marina Abramović presented a 700-hour piece at the Museum of Modern Art in New York. "The Artist Is Present" involved Abramović sitting in a chair directly opposite another empty chair, in which museumgoers could sit for any length of time and look at the artist face-to-face. People came in droves to sit with Marina. Some giggled nervously. A few cried. One person spent several hours staring at her; another spent the entire day. Nearly half a million people visited the exhibit, and each day Abramović remained, in the words of one critic, "persistently, uncomfortably there."

While most critics placed Abramović's work in the context of late-twentieth-century performance art, it reminded me of the work of sociologist Erving Goffman, who explored norms of proximity in public space by observing the everyday interactions of ordinary people in the mid-twentieth century. Like Abramović, Goffman saw a great deal more than most of us see in these small acts of ordinary behavior. "The gestures which we sometimes call empty are perhaps in fact the fullest things of all," he wrote in his book *Interaction Ritual.* For Goffman, our interactions in public space, or lack thereof, are the building blocks of social life.

Writing in a world before mobile personal technology, Goffman contended with very different rules for social interaction. Like Darwin, he was an astute observer of gestures and the messages those gestures send. When people meet, Goffman argued, they "give" information to each other consciously, usually by talking, but they also "give off" information unconsciously by the movements of their eyes, by their tone of voice, and by the way they stand or fidget. Remaining attuned to this delicate ballet of spoken and unspoken signals requires attention from both parties in an interaction. Both people must assume that the other understands the rules, "the unstated implication being that he can predict from what he sees what it is that is likely to come about, and this is not alarming," Goffman noted. These unspoken signals are "the traffic rules of social interaction," Goffman argued. We follow them because they help us authenticate our own experiences and, more broadly, our sense of self.

What happens when we ignore them? There is a German expression, *wie Luft behandeln*, which means "to be looked at as through air," similar to the English expression "he looked right through me." Both describe an unpleasant feeling of exclusion. A study published in *Psychological Science* reported the findings of a small field experiment conducted on a college campus. In the experiment, a woman walked around and when she encountered a stranger, she did one of three things: made eye contact, made eye contact and smiled, or looked through the person as if she didn't see them. A different researcher then stopped the unknowing study participants a few minutes later and asked them about their feelings of social connection. The people who had been acknowledged with eye contact or acknowledged with a smile "felt less disconnected than passersby in the air-gaze condition," the researchers found. "Humans evolved systems to detect the slightest cues of inclusion or exclusion," they noted, and looking someone in the eye is a subtle gesture of inclusiveness, a small but significant act of civil attention.

Our personal technologies, particularly the cellphone, are a massive drain on civil attention. Talk to anyone who works behind a cash register, and they will tell you stories about their increasing invisibility to customers who complete entire transactions with cellphones glued to ears or earbuds in, without a single acknowledgment of the person standing in front of them. Most of us have probably done this when we feel our attention is needed, and barely paused to consider the message we are sending to the human being ringing up our groceries. "They don't know how to deal with a human being," a Brooklyn roofing contractor told *The New Yorker*'s George Packer when Packer asked him how his work had changed over the years. "They stand there with that text shrug . . . and they just mumble. They can't talk anymore."

People have always found ways to carve out moments of privacy in public space; this is part of what makes public space tolerable for everyone. Civil attention's twin is civil *inattention*, "whereby one treats the other as if he has been seen but is not an object of undue curiosity," as

Goffman described. We nod at the stranger stepping into the elevator and then return to staring at the ceiling or look up briefly from reading when other commuters get on the bus. Civil inattention is still a kind of acknowledgment, qualitatively different from being "looked at as through air." When we focus our attention on the glowing screens of our smartphones rather than on the people around us, never granting them even brief acknowledgment, we are not practicing civil inattention but civil disengagement. This is becoming the norm in public space.

Growing up in Florida in the 1980s, I remember when our local Sun Bank got its first ATM. I thought of it as a futuristic money machine and couldn't wait for my parents to try it, but the bank's managers, worried that this new convenience might alienate customers who were used to face-to-face encounters with tellers, tried aggressively to humanize it. Beside the ATM in the bank lobby was a life-size cardboard cutout of a smiling woman and, if memory serves, reassurances about the machine's "smiling, personal service." The message was clear: convenience did not come at the expense of what Sun Bank assumed its customers valued most, human contact.

In the twenty-first century we no longer require such handholding. Every day we navigate self-service checkout kiosks, one-click our way through online purchases, and endure the spiraling purgatory of automated phone tree answering systems. As new technologies or technology-enabled services move rapidly into the mainstream, we often don't notice that those technologies replace functions once performed by a human being.

A few years ago, Clinique, the largest skin care and makeup company in the U.S., radically rethought its relationship to its customers. Before, going to a Clinique counter in a department store meant receiving solicitous service from a white-coated assistant who would offer skincare advice and even a full application of makeup. Today, Clinique booths feature a sign that says, "Carry a Clinique browsing basket and we'll leave you alone. Promise."

Clinique's new mantra became "Service as You Like It," and the company claims it made the changes in response to customers' desires. Case in point: one thirty-two-year old Clinique customer told the *Wall Street Journal* that she wants a "low-pressure environment" where she doesn't have to interact with other people when she shops. Instead of talking to a potentially officious human being, shoppers can use an iPad, one of 1,500 Clinique are placing in stores across the country, to get recommendations for lotions or lipsticks. Clinique even retrained its employees, teaching them how to read customers' body language so they don't inadvertently impose themselves. "Consumers wanted the freedom to have knowledge and service on demand," a Clinique representative told the *Journal.* During the COVID-19 pandemic, the company went a step further, introducing a "Clinical Reality" service that allows shoppers to use their smartphones to scan a QR code, take a picture of themselves, and get an immediate "skin diagnostic" and product recommendations without ever setting foot in a store.

The "on demand" experience is devoid of human interlocutors, although not, as Clinique's iPad and QR code efforts show, technological ones. And it is an experience that is finding its way into many areas of our lives. "Entered Apple store. Scanned my purchase with my phone. Paid with my Apple account and walked out. Soon we'll never have to talk to people!" a journalist for *Politico* tweeted. Why waste time interacting with people, even online, if you don't have to?

If you travel by plane, chances are your airport experience is increasingly automated. You purchase your ticket online and check in at an automatic kiosk or via your mobile phone or computer. More airlines are beginning to install self-boarding gates, removing the need for a gate agent to scan your boarding pass and wish you a pleasant flight. "A lot of our passengers are frequent fliers who really prefer not to talk with staff all the time," a Lufthansa spokesman explained to a reporter. Hotels are eliminating human-staffed concierge desks and installing tablet computers for guest check-in instead.

"Maybe it's just us," a reporter for the *Wall Street Journal* wrote, "but the idea of dragging the kids to the mall to wait in a long line and then clamber up onto a stranger's lap just doesn't bring much holiday cheer." The stranger in question is Santa Claus, and seeing him in person evidently is becoming a chore. Instead, kids can now have "a video chat with him from the comfort of home" using services such as SkypeMeSanta or Zoom. These platforms enable mediated music lessons for students who don't live near a good music teacher and offer opportunities for book clubs to "meet" authors online.

When the coronavirus began its long, deadly march through the United States in the spring of 2020 and states mandated that businesses and schools close and people stay home to limit the spread of the virus, the ability to communicate and work via videoconferencing platforms such as Zoom, Microsoft Teams, and Skype was hailed as a technological blessing. Newspaper articles set a celebratory tone, hailing the arrival of the Zoom cocktail hour and encouraging Americans who were now spending countless hours online to add preselected digital backgrounds depicting exotic beaches and other happy scenes to their calls. Here was a simple technological response to the many complicated social problems that arose during the pandemic, a solution that seemed to address a practical challenge while also proving the legitimacy of Zoom's slogan, "We deliver happiness."

But as the weeks of lockdown wore on and virtual gatherings shifted from novelty to obligation, many Americans began to confess to feelings of dread each time a new Zoom meeting appeared on their calendars. By the end of April, *New York Times* reporter Kate Murphy was explaining to readers "why Zoom is terrible." The disappointments she outlined were not technical but experiential. Murphy noted the unease she felt about her connections to others, even after hours spent talking to people through a screen, because she could not always interpret the subtleties of facial expressions and body language.

In addition, as family birthdays, weddings, bar mitzvahs, and other life celebrations all played out across the same platform, the details of each began to blur for many people. Psychologists Gabriel Radvansky and Jeffrey Zacks have described the crucial role of "event boundaries" in memory formation and cognition. "Events are at the center of human experience, and event cognition is the study of how people perceive, conceive, talk about, and remember them," Radvansky and Zacks write. But those events require clear demarcations to help us distinguish one from another and form permanent memories of our experiences.

Even before the pandemic, other shifts toward the mediation of everyday experiences happened with little fanfare. Even something as mundane as the tollbooth is disappearing from daily life, as cities and states move to EZ Pass systems that automatically deduct money from passholders' accounts or, for those who don't have accounts, simply mail bills to the address associated with the vehicle's license plate. In March 2013, after seventy-six years, the Golden Gate Bridge in San Francisco replaced its human toll collectors with an automated system. The city's transportation district will save $8 million—a quantifiable savings, to be sure—but commuters will no longer be greeted with a smile or a hello by another human being before crossing the bridge, a qualitative loss that is rarely part of the accounting when we assess the costs of automation. As one toll collector who worked at the bridge for eighteen years told a reporter, "I think what it is, sometimes we are the first, if not the only smile they get in the morning, and that's for a lot of people... You take away that human touch. I don't think a computer can replace that."

Few people miss the inconveniences of toll booths staffed by people, but their disappearance speaks to a broader cultural embrace of the idea that computers and other technologies can mediate or even replace the human touch—including in fields such as medicine where face-to-face engagement would seem crucial. The U.S. Food and Drug Administration approved the RP-VITA, a medical robot made by iRobot, the company that makes the Roomba robotic vacuum. A "human-sized tele-presence robot," it lets doctors interact remotely with hospital patients by showing the doctor's face on a screen where the robot's head would be.

Researchers at Northeastern University created a similar computer-on-wheels, named Louise, that acts as a "virtual discharge advocate" for hospitals. Louise rolls up to a patient's bedside and spends upward of forty minutes going through each patient's instructions for care before they leave the hospital. Patients evidently like her; hospital administrators told the *Washington Post* that many patients prefer Louise to "real, live nurses," who can be brusque or impatient when answering their questions. Louise never gets tired or angry or distracted with petty human worries. She is the perfect servicebot. Other "collaborative robots" such as Diligent Robotics' Moxi are in use in hundreds of hospitals across the country.

Assisted living facilities are also enlisting care-giving robots to alleviate the burdens on human employees. One such project in Canada, led by Dr. Paola Lavin, uses Grace, a humanoid robot, to help combat loneliness among seniors in a facility. "She could be working [throughout] the day without fatigue, without all the mental burden of dealing with very strong emotions as we humans usually do," she said.

Wellpoint, the second-largest health insurer in the U.S., allows its members to talk to physicians on demand via video chat, although they are required to pay the same co-payment as they would for an in-person visit. For several years, therapists in Britain's National Health Service have used online therapies to treat people suffering from panic attacks and phobias, and a new generation of medical chatbots, such as Woebot, are marketed to patients as "your personal mental health ally" and "the best listener in the business."

Such programs have undoubtedly helped many people, but mediated forms of therapy are not always best. Virtual therapy prompts questions about whether the convenience and cost-effectiveness these services promote might make in-person care, which is usually more expensive and time-consuming, difficult to defend in the future. Already, advocates of the traditional, in-person physical exam, such as Dr. Abraham Verghese, are called practitioners of a lost art. Verghese can tell just by looking at a sparse eyebrow or a bumpy ear what a patient's malady might be (thyroid problems and gout, respectively). "There are volumes one can say medically about the face," he told a reporter. And seeing those faces in person makes a difference in their treatment.

Mediated life is becoming normal life, but we don't register the transformation as revolutionary—or in many cases even register it at all. What does it matter if restaurants trade customized iPads for human waiters or Amazon replaces the shopping mall? Don't these technologies offer us more choice and convenience, two things we consider sacrosanct?

We often don't realize the cumulative effect of mediation until a situation reminds us of what real, unmediated human contact is. Consider the observations of one *New York Times* theater critic. Reviewing *Theater for One*, a Times Square performance piece from 2011 that drew on the tradition of the peep show to create a one-on-one theater experience, he wrote, "This artful production leaves you with an unsettling sense of how guarded, mediated and constrained most of our daily interactions with other people are. An intense focus on another person—even for a mere five minutes—is a more extraordinary experience than it probably should be."

Intense, in-person focus on another person is becoming less common among younger Americans. Ten years ago, the Pew Internet and American Life Project found that while 63 percent of teenagers exchanged text messages daily with people in their lives, only 35 percent spoke to others face-to-face. Only 25 percent of teenagers see their friends in person outside of school every day, a decline from 35 percent who did so in 2009. Only 37 percent of teens meet face-to-face several times a week outside of school.

Updated research in 2018 found a continuation of this trend. "When it comes to daily interactions with their friends," Pew reported, "teens are much more likely to report that those interactions take place online. Six-in-ten teens say they spend time with their friends online every day or almost every day, compared with 24 percent who spend time with their friends in person with the same frequency (not including school or school-related activities)." A Monitoring the Future Survey revealed that the number of twelfth-graders in the U.S. who saw friends in person "almost every day" dropped from 44 percent in 2010 to 32 percent in 2022.

Although large-scale studies of the long-term effects of mediated relationships on children are not yet available, a few intriguing new studies suggest that this is not a harmless transition from one form of communication technology to another. A study published in *Developmental Psychology* in 2012, as smartphone use was becoming ubiquitous among teenagers, measured the multitasking and media use of 3,461 girls ages eight to twelve. The contrast between mediated and face-to-face interaction was dramatic. Subjects in the study spent an average of 6.9 hours per day using electronic media compared to 2.1 hours per day in face-to-face interaction.

The late Stanford University communications professor Clifford Nass, an expert on media multitasking who developed the study, which used "a more granular measure of media multitasking and a new comparative measure of media use versus time spent in face-to-face communication," found a strong correlation between media use and what researchers call negative social well-being, including feelings of low confidence, not feeling normal, and even sleeping less. By contrast, he noted, "face-to-face communication was strongly associated with positive social well-being."

Professor Nass admitted that the findings disturbed him so much that he told reporters that the substitution of face-to-face interaction for screen-mediated interaction among the young could lead to "serious emotional and developmental consequences." He added, "Kids have to

learn about emotion, and the way they do that, really, is by paying attention to other people. They have to really look them in the eye." FaceTime,
Skype, and other video chatting services aren't the same, he found, especially since kids often multitask while using the services and don't give
the person on the screen their full attention. "If you eschew face-to-face
communication," Nass warns, "you don't learn critical things that you
have to learn . . . You have to learn social skills. You have to learn about
emotion." He added, "The most important message is that face-to-face
communication is just enormously important and there has been a dramatic decline in that, among kids and among families."

The decline in teenagers spending time face-to-face with friends
began around 2010, as smartphone usage increased. As Jean Twenge and
others have found, although many teens report a preference for texting
or using social media platforms to stay in touch with friends, as rates of
in-person time declined rates of reported loneliness among teenagers
started to rise. Gary Small, a professor of psychiatry and neuroscience at
UCLA, concurs. "Tech skills are great and young people obviously have
them," he told me. "But they really need those human skills as well, those
face-to-face interactions."

If you live and work in Japan, you might be subjected to the merciless
gaze of SmileScan technology. Developed by OMRON's OKAO Vision,
SmileScan is a machine that uses a small video camera to scan a person's
face, then renders it as a 3D model on the screen. After evaluating critical
points on the face, such as the eyes and the mouth, the machine delivers
a verdict on the intensity and authenticity of the smile and ranks it on
a percentage scale of 0–100. The technology was originally developed
to help advance machine reading of human facial expressions—a kind of
automated Paul Ekman, if you will. But this technology has potential as a
tool of social control. As one of OMRON's laboratory managers enthused
about potential applications for the technology, "What about a 'smile-

checker' for people working in the service industry?" In fact, SmileScan is already in use in Japan at Keihin Station, where workers must submit to a scan before they begin a shift.

Why are we asking machines to take over tasks like judging the authenticity of our smiles? By outsourcing to machines our own hard-wired "automatic appraisal mechanism," might our ability to read one another weaken as the machines' ability to read us improves? Already, computers can discern a sincere smile from an insincere one; engineers have also built a robot that always wins at Rock Paper Scissors by reading its human opponent's movements to determine which of the three gestures the human intends to play. Why cling to our analog intuitions when such techniques are available?

Apple and other technology companies are patenting eye-tracking software, and video game systems like Kinect are already equipped to watch you in real time and learn your habits and routines based on your nonverbal behavior. Jeremy Bailenson of Stanford University's Virtual Human Interaction Lab, who has studied the digital footprints left behind by players of video games, cautioned recently, "Gamers need to be informed that they can be watched, and that how you interact with a game system like the Kinect can potentially reveal a lot about you." Perhaps you are quicker to anger than you'd like others to know, or prone to anxiety? Your Kinect might "know" that, but should anyone else?

As psychologist Marianne LaFrance reminds us, smiles are "social acts with consequences." Outsourcing the reading of our emotions to machines will leave us less capable of understanding a smile's meaning in context. Would SmileScan understand why people often remarked on the weirdly unnatural timing of former British prime minister Gordon Brown's grin? Or why the former U.S. presidential candidate Herman Cain was mocked for a TV ad where his creepy smile took a full nine seconds to elapse?

Our ability to detect emotions and intent on others' faces will become even more important as technologies of manipulation multiply. In a volume of essays about communication over the Internet using video platforms, several contributors assumed that the future would bring increased manipulation of what we see when we hold meetings via platforms like Zoom. "It is plausible that the intensity of particular expressions could be modified on the fly," one contributor wrote, "In addition, expression could be augmented—for example, wrinkles around the eyes could be added to increase an impression of genuine smiles." In other words, technology will soon offer us real-time Photoshopping of the human face with the explicit intent of misleading the viewer. This kind of a "charisma amplifier" would make a killer app for a lackluster politician, for example. We already use modest forms of charisma and image enhancement through applications such as FaceTune and Photoshop, to say nothing of their more nefarious cousins, the deepfake images and videos that are increasingly challenging to identify as having been manufactured.

And what of the rest of us? People used to find opportunities to amplify their connections at professional events, but these too have been altered by mediating technologies. Breaks during a conference or meeting are now dominated by our compulsion to check smartphones, send texts, or otherwise disappear into mediated communication.

Although many office workers rebelled against employers' demands to return to the office after pandemic closures were lifted, there is strong evidence that the chance encounters that happen at work (informal chats around the water cooler, as the cliché goes) do lead to greater productivity. A study of telephone call centers found that the ones where workers had more in-person interactions with their coworkers were twice as productive as those that did not. Apple's Steve Jobs had such serendipitous interactions in mind when he installed a central atrium in the headquarters of Pixar Animation Studios which required the company's engineers, artists, and writers to cross paths. When GlaxoSmithKline rearranged the office space for 1,200 employees in Research Park Triangle, NC, to promote more in-person interactions, it not only saved money but made the employees more productive.

Physical proximity can even affect the quality of scientific research. A study published by Kyungjoon Lee at Harvard's Center for Biomedical Informatics explored physical proximity among coauthors of scientific papers and found, "Despite the positive impact of emerging communication technologies on scientific research, our results provide striking evidence for the role of physical proximity as a predictor of the impact of collaborations." The closer the authors are to each other physically, the study showed, the more their work was cited; as distance between collaborators grew, the number of citations fell.

Physical proximity isn't only important for sparking creativity; it is also crucial for awareness and safety in public space. On a crowded commuter train in San Francisco in 2013, a man shot and killed twenty-year-old student Justin Valdez. As security footage shows, before the gunman fired, he waved around his .45 caliber pistol and at one point even pointed it across the aisle. No one on the crowded train noticed because they were so focused on their smartphones and tablets. "These weren't concealed movements—the gun is very clear," District Attorney George Gascon later told the Associated Press. "These people are in very close proximity with him, and nobody sees this. They're just so engrossed, texting and reading and whatnot. They're completely oblivious of their surroundings."

Our use of technology has fundamentally changed not just our awareness in public spaces but our sense of duty to others. Engaged with the glowing screens in front of us rather than with the people around us, we often don't notice what is going on. Another attack, on a blind man walking down the street in broad daylight in Philadelphia, garnered attention because security footage later revealed that many passersby ignored the assault and never called 911, suggesting a form of the bystander effect. Commenting to a local radio station, Philadelphia's chief of police at the time, Charles Ramsay, said that this lack of response was becoming "more and more common" and noted that people are more likely to use their cellphones to record assaults than to call the police. Indeed, YouTube features hundreds of such videos—outbreaks of violence on sidewalks, in shopping malls, and at restaurants.

The fascination with capturing images of violence is nothing new, as anyone who has perused the photographs of Arthur Fellig (a.k.a. Weegee) of bloody crime scenes from the early twentieth century can attest. But the ubiquity of camera-enabled cellphones has shifted the boundaries of acceptable behavior in these situations. We are all Weegee now.

In 2019, a man charged in a New York City subway attack on a seventy-eight-year-old woman was caught after video of the event was posted online and viewed more than 10 million times. News reports noted that as the man viciously kicked the woman, "bystanders recorded the encounter and shouted but did not intervene," and that as the attacker left the train, he told the people recording, "WorldStar that!" WorldStarHipHop is a content aggregation site best known for videos of people fighting.

A compounding factor is the ease with which we can record and send images, which encourages those of us who are paying attention to document emergencies rather than address them. Sometimes, as in case of the Minneapolis police officers who detained and killed George Floyd, video evidence galvanizes mass protests and calls for reform.

But if everyone is filming an emergency, who is responsible for intervening in it? In one tragic case in New York City, a man was pushed onto the subway tracks. Struggling unsuccessfully to heave himself onto the platform, he turned, in his final seconds, to see the train barreling down on him. We know this because a freelance photographer who happened to be on the platform took a picture of the awful episode and sold it to the *New York Post*, which ran it on the front page the next day, prompting public outrage about profiting from a man's death. The photographer noted that others on the platform closer to the man made no effort to rescue him and quickly pulled out their phones to capture images of his dead body.

The brutal nighttime stabbing of Kitty Genovese on a New York City sidewalk in 1964 has become a notorious symbol of the uninvolved bystander. The well-known story was that many people heard her screams, but no one went outside to assist her or to intervene in the attack. This tidy narrative has since been debunked (most thoroughly by Kevin Cook in his book *Kitty Genovese*). Nevertheless, the incident spawned much handwringing and some intriguing social science research about why we don't always come to another's aid.

In a 1968 study, sociologists John Darley and Bibb Latané tested the willingness of individuals to intervene in various emergency situations (for example, a "lady in distress," or a smoke-filled room). They found that the larger the number of people present, the more the sense of responsibility was diffused for any given individual. When alone, people were far more likely to help. But in large groups, each person assumed that someone else would step up.

In subsequent experiments carried out by Irving Piliavin, bystanders on the subway were much more likely to help an actor on their car who pretended to be ill and asked for help. Why? As psychologist Elliot Aronson wrote in his classic textbook *The Social Animal*, "People riding on the same subway car do have the feeling of sharing a common fate, and they were in a face-to-face situation with the victim, from which there was no immediate escape."

Our collective bystander conscience might be changing, both for good and for ill. A more recent study of the bystander effect that analyzed footage of real-world violence in public spaces in Cape Town and Amsterdam in 2019 found that strangers intervened in nine out of ten incidents, and that the more people in the area, the more likely someone was to intervene.

But technologies work against intervention. Our gadgets, as the San Francisco shooting makes plain, often block out vital information about our surroundings and the unspoken obligations that attend them. Most of these duties—to be aware of others, to practice basic civility—are not onerous. But on rare occasions, we are called upon to help others who are in danger. At those moments, we should not be anticipating how many views we will get on YouTube if we film their distress; we should act. To do otherwise is to risk becoming a society not just of apathetic bystanders but of cruel voyeurs.

In the future, will more of us become mediated bystanders? We have come to prefer mediated forms of communication, with their ease and control, to the messier realities of face-to-face interaction. How will this change us? We aren't so different from Darwin, with his face pressed against the glass of that puff adder enclosure. We press our faces against a different kind of glass (mobile screens and perhaps in the near future the lenses of augmented reality technologies). But unlike Darwin, we lack curiosity and inventiveness. When he reared back from the glass of that enclosure, he set out to determine why his physical body had betrayed him and how the body mediated his experience of emotion.

By contrast, we use our screens to avoid confronting our own and others' bodies at all. Our "first impressions" of people are now just as likely to come via interaction with the screen as the body. Our tools for instant, asynchronous communication have habituated us to the assumption that we can always tell one another how we're feeling. As a result, we also assume that we don't have to make the effort to ask. And mediated communication is so much easier, anyway. As companies like Facebook integrate more sophisticated facial recognition technologies into their platforms, and technologists improve SmileScan-like technologies, it is likely that we will soon be able to buy apps that will scan and "read" a friend's face so that we can know immediately if she is happy or sad, truthful or deceitful. Clicking on and then away, scrolling, swiping, time-shifting, deleting. Face-to-face communication doesn't let you do this. So we compromise empathy for the sake of convenience.

It is a bit like the risk compensation effect—the documented reality that when people add safety precautions, they become bolder in their actions. You don a helmet and ski more aggressively, negating the added security the helmet provides. Today we are at risk of embracing an experience compensation effect. As our face-to-face experiences become more hurried, less frequent, and less satisfying, we delve deeper into mediated experiences to compensate, in a cycle that endlessly repeats itself. And while our technological skills flourish, our primal skills of embodied interaction deteriorate. "What makes performances false is not the creation of a new, false routine," Goffman wrote, "but the continuation of an old, valid one under altered circumstances."

Face-to-face, real-world experience can be unpleasant—that smelly man sitting next to you on the subway doesn't prompt enlightened thoughts, and only a moralizing prig would argue that such experiences are worthwhile for their own sake. But these daily encounters with the physical world enlarge and enrich our understanding of one another because in making ourselves open to them, surprise, discomfort, and inconvenience might occur. And so might serendipitous interaction.

"Attention is the rarest and purest form of generosity," French philosopher Simone Weil wrote. Attention to one another as embodied creatures is central to what makes us human—breathing the same air, sensing one another's unspoken feelings, seeing one another's faces, and being attuned to one another's gestures—and to give attention to others we must spend time in their physical presence. Our technologies, as brilliant as they are, cannot satisfy all of those needs.

CHAPTER 3

Hand to Mouse

H umming away in offices on Capitol Hill, in the Pentagon, and in the White House is a technology that represents the pragmatism, efficiency, and unsentimental nature of American bureaucracy: the autopen. It is a device that stores a person's signature, replicating it as needed using a mechanical arm that holds a real pen.

Like many technologies, this rudimentary robotic signature-maker has always provoked ambivalence. U.S. presidents have been using autopens to sign letters and proclamations since Harry Truman was in office, but no one publicly acknowledged doing so until Gerald Ford's administration. The military is reportedly the largest user of autopens, but a *Washington Post* journalist had trouble getting representatives from the government or military to disclose precisely how many autopens they owned and how often they used them. In congressional offices, the autopen is often sequestered in a closet under lock and key, lest anyone get ideas about using it for unofficial business.

We invest signatures with meaning, particularly when the signer is well-known. There is something unnerving about the marketing materials for automatic signature machines, which emphasize the signature's verisimilitude while acknowledging the trickery that achieves it: "The Autopen has long been a tool for the world's most influential leaders, allowing them to more effectively apply their time and attention to important issues without compromising the impact of personalized correspondence," one manufacturer's website states.

During the George W. Bush administration, Secretary of Defense Donald Rumsfeld generated a small wave of outrage when reporters revealed that he had been using an autopen for his signature on the condolence letters that he sent to the families of fallen soldiers. President Bush himself sought a legal opinion from the Justice Department about whether legislation signed by his autopen was legal (they said it was), but he never used it to sign a bill into law. Barack Obama was the first president to use the autopen to sign legislation when he authorized an extension of the Patriot Act in 2011. His political opponents criticized him in 2013 for autopenning his signature on last-minute budget legislation while vacationing in Hawaii. A CBS radio correspondent deduced that Obama had authorized the use of the autopen to sign legislation at least half a dozen times and reported that the White House was "often reluctant to admit its use."

The autopen has not lost its stigma in politics. During the 2020 election, Vice President Mike Pence invoked the autopen to criticize Senator Joseph Biden, who was running for president. "It's clear Joe Biden would be nothing more than an autopen president, a Trojan horse for a radical agenda," he said, seemingly unaware that his own running mate, Donald Trump, had angered supporters by hawking autopen-autographed merchandise on his website.

Fans of singer Bob Dylan expressed similar ire when they discovered that the limited edition of his book *The Philosophy of Modern Song*, which cost nearly $600 and came with an official certificate "attesting to its having been individually signed by Dylan," in fact had made unlimited use of an autopen.

Dylan took the unusual step of issuing a statement on his Facebook page: "With contractual deadlines looming," Dylan wrote, "the idea of using an auto-pen was suggested to me, along with the assurance that this kind of thing is done 'all the time' in the art and literary worlds." He also acknowledged that "using a machine was an error in judgement and I want to rectify it immediately."

Our mixed feelings about machine-made signatures make plain our broader relationship to handwriting: it offers a glimpse of individuality. Any time spent doing archival research is a humbling lesson in the challenges and rewards of deciphering the handwritten word. You come to know your long-dead subjects through the quirks of their handwriting; one man's script becomes spidery and small when he writes something emotionally charged, while another's pristine pages suggest the diligence of a medieval monk. Calligraphist Bernard Maisner argues that calligraphy, and handwriting more broadly, is "not meant to reproduce something over and over again. It's meant to show the humanity, the responsiveness, and variation within."

But handwriting is disappearing. A high school junior who took the PSAT confessed to the *Wall Street Journal* that "audible gasps broke out in the room" when students learned they would have to write a one-sentence honor code statement in cursive. "Cursive? Most students my age have only encountered this foreign language in letters from grandma."

The Common Core State Standards for education in the U.S. no longer require students to learn cursive writing. One assessment claimed that more than 33 percent of students struggle to achieve competency in basic handwriting, meaning the ability to write legibly the letters of the alphabet (in upper- and lower-case letters). "We're trying to be realistic about skills that kids are going to need," said one school board member in Greenville, South Carolina. "You can't do everything. Something's got to go." Children who cannot write in cursive also can't read it, and yet no one asks if we "need" kids to be able to read our country's original founding documents, such as the Declaration of Independence, which is written in cursive.

Schoolchildren are not the only ones who can no longer write or read cursive. Fewer and fewer of us put pen to paper to record our thoughts, correspond with friends, or even to jot down a grocery list. Instead of begging a celebrity for an autograph, we request a selfie. Many people no longer have the skill to do more than scrawl their name in an illegible script, and those who do will see that skill atrophy as they rely more on computers and smartphones. A newspaper in Toronto recorded the lament of a pastry instructor who realized that many of his culinary students couldn't properly pipe an inscription in icing on a cake—their cursive writing was too shaky and indistinct to begin with.

As a practical skill in the digital world, handwriting seems useless. There is a term in Chinese, *tibiwangzi*, which means "Take pen, forget character." It describes how more frequent use of computers and smartphones has discouraged the use of traditional Chinese handwriting, including the ability to write traditional characters. Chinese children pick up a pen to write ("take pen") but experience a kind of "character amnesia" when it comes to putting pen to paper ("forget character"). According to the China Youth Daily Social Survey Center, 4 percent of Chinese youth are "already living without handwriting."

What does it mean to live without handwriting? The skill has deteriorated gradually, and many of us don't notice our own loss until we're asked to handwrite something and find ourselves bumbling as we put pen to paper. Some people still write in script for special occasions (a condolence letter, an elaborately calligraphed wedding invitation) or dash off a bastardized cursive on the rare occasions when they write a paper check, but apart from schoolteachers, few people insist on a continued place for handwriting in everyday life. Those who do frequently find themselves labeled nostalgists or fetishists.

But we lose something when handwriting disappears. We lose measurable cognitive skills (as we will see), and we also lose the pleasure of using our hands and a writing implement in a process that for thousands of years has allowed humans to make our thoughts visible to one another.

We lose the sensory experience of ink and paper and the visual pleasure of the handwritten word. We lose the ability to read the words of the dead.

Like many experiences that are nearing extinction in our lives, handwriting's end was not the result of a campaign against it. It has been nudged aside gradually and has become "an option, and often an unattractive, elaborate one," as Philip Hensher writes in *The Missing Ink: The Lost Art of Handwriting.* We are far more likely to use our hands to type or swipe. We communicate more but with less physical effort, forgetting the vast evolutionary history that fitted us for physical movement and expression as a means of understanding our world. This way of understanding through the use of our physical bodies is what philosophers such as Maurice Merleau-Ponty and, more recently, George Lakoff have called embodied cognition.

Theorists of embodied cognition argue that any way of being in the world involves understanding the links between one's mind, one's body, and physical experiences. They argue that we cannot separate our understanding of ourselves from bodily experience. Our language for self-understanding is rich with physical metaphor; the direction up is equated with happiness and down with unhappiness, for example, and we associate physical warmth with affection. We may embrace new ideas, jump at an opportunity, or step back from something to take an honest look at it. When we change what we do with our bodies, even in small ways such as no longer using pens to write but instead turning to screens on which we swipe and tap, we change the way we understand our world. This is why shifting from handwriting to keyboarding is in fact a shift away from one way of being in the world to another, with consequences that are more complicated than they might at first appear.

In 2000, physicians at Cedars-Sinai Hospital in Los Angeles took a remedial handwriting course. "Many of our physicians don't write legibly," the chief of the medical staff explained to *Science Daily.* And unlike many professions, doctors' bad writing can have serious consequences, including medical errors and even death; a woman in Texas won a $450,000 award from a jury that heard the case of her husband's death after taking the wrong prescription medicine. The pharmacist had misread the doctor's poorly handwritten instructions and given the man the wrong prescription, which killed him. Even though many medical records are now stored on computers, physicians still spend a lot of their time writing notes on charts or writing prescriptions by hand.

Clarity in handwriting isn't merely an aid to communication. It yields measurable cognitive benefits. Neuroscientist Karin James at Indiana University in Bloomington published a study comparing the learning styles of a small group of preliterate five-year-olds who were instructed to type, trace, or handwrite letters and shapes. Using functional MRI scanning before and after the training, she found that a "reading circuit" in the brain that had been documented by previous research "was recruited during letter perception only after handwriting—not after typing or tracing experience."

"Handwriting is important for the early recruitment in letter processing of brain regions known to underlie successful reading," James concluded, and "may facilitate reading acquisition in young children." In some significant way, writing by hand, unlike tracing a letter or typing it, primes the brain for learning to read.

Earlier studies drew similar conclusions about handwriting's cognitive benefits. A study conducted by psychologist Virginia Berninger at the University of Washington examined 700 elementary school students in Seattle, 144 of whom were struggling with reading and writing. After dividing the students into groups and testing various remedial activities to improve their performance, the researchers found that one group was far superior: those who had spent the most time working on their handwriting.

The group with improved handwriting had enhanced word recognition and reading skills, better memory of what they had worked on, and were more successful in expressing ideas. More importantly, the students who focused on handwriting reported enjoying learning more. "Handwriting is not just a motor process," the study concluded. "It is also a memory process for letters—the building blocks of written language."

In a follow up study in 2017, Berninger updated her work by examining how writing by hand relates to the development of executive function skills in children, such as planning and staying attentive to tasks. She found once again that "handwriting—forming letters—engages the mind, and that can help children pay attention to written language." She noted the importance of one region of the brain, the fusiform gyrus, "where visual stimuli actually become letters and written words"—the "mind's eye" that allows us to visualize something before committing it to paper. And she recommended that children learn both print and cursive handwriting before learning to use a keyboard, since, as many other studies have found, "starting around fourth grade, cursive skills conferred advantages in both spelling and composing" written words.

What about the rest of us who, for the most part, have abandoned writing by hand in favor of typing on keyboards? We, too, might be impairing ourselves in significant ways when it comes to retaining knowledge.

Psychologists Pam Mueller and Daniel Oppenheimer compared students taking class notes by hand or on a laptop computer to test whether the medium mattered for student performance. Earlier studies of laptop use in the classroom had focused on how distracting computer use was for students. Not surprisingly, the answer was very distracting, and not just for the note-taker but for nearby peers as well.

Mueller and Oppenheimer instead studied how laptop use impacted the learning process for students who used them. They found that "even when laptops are used solely to take notes, they may still be impairing learning because their use results in shallower processing." In three different experiments, their research concluded that students who used laptop computers performed worse on conceptual questions in comparison to students who took notes by hand. "Laptop note takers' tendency to transcribe lectures verbatim rather than processing information and reframing it in their own words is detrimental to learning," they wrote. In other worse, we retain information better when we write by hand because the slower pace of writing forces us to summarize as we write, as opposed to the greater speed of transcribing on a keyboard.

The researchers studying how technology transforms the way we write and learn are akin to ecologists who warn of species decline or environmental pollution. We face a future without handwriting. Their authors worry that abandoning the pen for the keyboard will lead to any number of unforeseen negative consequences. "The digitization of writing entails radical transformations of the very act of writing at a sensorimotor, physical level, and the (potentially far-reaching) implications of such transformations are far from properly understood," notes Anne Mangen, who studies how technology transforms literacy. Writing on a keyboard with the words appearing on the screen is more "abstract and detached," something she believes has "far-reaching implications, educationally and practically." Like species decline, skills decline gradually. It is popular to assume that we have replaced one old-fashioned, inefficient tool (handwriting) with a more convenient and efficient alternative (keyboarding). But like the decline of face-to-face interactions, we are not accounting for what we lose in this tradeoff for efficiency, and for the unrecoverable ways of learning and knowing, particularly for children. A child who has mastered the keyboard but grows into an adult who still struggles to sign his own name is not an example of progress.

As a physical act, writing requires dexterity in the hands and fingers as well as the forearms. Before pens replaced quills, writers would select feathers from a goose or swan's right wing or left wing to get precisely the curve that suited their hand. The labor of writing by hand is also part of the pleasure of the experience, argues novelist Mary Gordon. "I believe that the labor has virtue, because of its very physicality," she writes. "For one thing it involves flesh, blood and the thingness of pen and paper, those anchors that remind us that, however thoroughly we lose ourselves in the vortex of our invention, we inhabit a corporeal world."

Handwriting is also evocative in a way the printed word is not. Literature abounds with plot twists prompted by the appearance of a handwritten letter or signature. In Charles Dickens's *Bleak House*, Lady Dedlock recognizes the unusual handwriting of her former fiancé, whom she thought dead, on a legal document, prompting the events that lead to the revelation of her greatest secret.

Our own handwriting can be a surprisingly effective prompt to memory. When American chef and cookbook author Deborah Madison stumbled upon some old handwritten recipes from the 1970s, she was transported back in time. Jotted down in brown notebooks along with notes and doodles and food stains and lists of suppliers that she used for the restaurant Greens in San Francisco, the recipes were "a record of time spent fitting new thoughts together," she wrote. "At times it looks careful and deliberate. Other times my hand gets distracted and strays, looks sloppy and tired. But mostly it conveys such a deep sense of discovery that reading through these notebooks, I am re-infected with the obsessive excitement I felt then." She doesn't think that feeling would emerge from a list written on a computer: "There's much to be said for the mark of the hand."

The mark of the hand can still thrive in a world dominated by technology if we let it. In an effort to upgrade to modern technology, a family-run bento box business, Tamagoya, switched from accepting fax orders to having their patrons order online for their daily lunch deliveries. Sales plummeted, so they switched back to fax machines to receive the "minutely detailed handwritten requests" their patrons prefer to send in. The Japanese business found a clever way to reconcile handwriting with new forms of technology.

Novelist Mohsin Hamid takes notes by hand in notebooks and tries to remove himself from the online world when he is working on a novel, although he writes his novels on a computer. "The technology is shaping me, configuring me" when he uses it, he told the BBC, and he sees danger in embracing machine-like ways of doing things. The human way of doing things imposes limits, depending on our tools. Ten fingers can fly across a keyboard, but the experience of writing with a pen or pencil in one hand requires more patience. The average American can type 40 words per minute but can only write 13 words per minute by hand. As calligraphist Paul Antonio notes, when he teaches children to write, he is really teaching them to slow down.

The pace of writing by hand, as with many embodied acts, is far slower than the tempo of tools that dominate modern life—the devices and algorithms that move at lightning speed, processing information and meeting our demands for instant gratification. The ease and efficiency of the keyboard trains us to move with efficiency, and the more we use it, the more our habits of mind reflect that use.

In this environment, it isn't surprising that working with our hands now means honing technology-friendly techniques such as swiping and tapping on screens and keyboards. "The sheer extent to which we are using our hand in this new way makes it no exaggeration to say that swiping has now become a part and parcel of our culturally inherited ways of manual dexterity, like cutting with scissors, writing with a pen, or turning a screw," one researcher wrote about the shift from pen to touch screen.

We often applaud our ingenuity in making ourselves better and faster than our predecessors. In the Information Technology world, programmers and designers use the word "deprecated" to describe software, hardware, and other tools whose failings are widely known and whose use is discouraged in favor of newer, better things. In this view, handwriting is merely a deprecated tool that might still be in use but is far from ideal.

As the IT way of looking at the world replaces other ways of knowing, we lose valuable things. Our willful de-skilling of longstanding human activities is not only happening with handwriting. Other embodied skills, also valuable, are at risk of disappearing.

———

Like writing, drawing by hand forges connections between mind and body, connections that have defined human creativity for centuries. The ancient cave paintings depicting a hunt in Lascaux and Altamira are so recognizable despite the millennia that separate the artists from contemporary viewers because painting is such a recognizably human act. We draw to make a record of our own activities and to show others what we've done. This is why drawing is so important for children, and one of the ways they learn to make sense of their world even before they can read and write. Scale, proportion, possibility—drawing images of the things they see around them helps them better understand the concrete world they are a part of.

Like handwriting, however, drawing is on the decline, even in professions that used to rely on it, such as architecture. Until the late 1990s, most architecture students learned how to draft by hand. Within a few years, however, computer-assisted design software (CAD) transformed the field. Architects experimented with innovative forms of design whose complexity was difficult to imitate when drawn by hand. The computer quickly became an integral design tool. Architect Frank Gehry, who once confessed he didn't know how to turn on a computer, was an early adopter of the technology. "I was trying to make a double curved line on a building and I didn't know how to transmit that to the contractor," he told an audience at an engineering forum. Eventually his firm partnered with a 3D software company. "The Guggenheim Museum in Bilbao and the Walt Disney Concert Hall in Los Angeles could not exist today" without it, he said.

Others in the field eagerly embraced these new digital tools. Writing in *Places,* architect and former dean of the Princeton University School of Architecture Stan Allen noted, "The computer has ceased to be a technology to be either celebrated or resisted; it is simply a fact of life. Its logic has been fully absorbed into contemporary work routines and habits of thought." This changes what it means to be an architect. My sister, who earned her architecture degree just as CAD software permeated the practice of architecture, recalls how she and other junior architects in her firm referred to themselves as "CAD jockeys," so thoroughly was their work determined by the pace of the software.

CAD's automation of the creative process has brought precision, efficiency, and new opportunities for visualization in architecture, but not without costs. As architect Witold Rybczynski has noted, the "fierce productivity" provided by a computer means "more time at the keyboard, less time thinking." Finnish architect Juhani Pallasmaa argues that drafting by hand represents a link between the architect and the "physical materiality" of the object he is designing. By contrast, computer design exists in an "abstract immaterial world" where "false precision" can mislead the designer. In his insightful critique of the encroachment of automation on our lives, technology critic Nicholas Carr argues, "Simply transferring work from the world to the screen entails deep changes in perspective. Greater stress is placed on abstraction, less on materiality. Calculative power grows; sensory engagement fails."

Even Michael Graves, a pioneer in the use of digital drafting software, argued a few years before his death in 2015 that "Architecture cannot divorce itself from drawing, no matter how impressive the technology gets. Drawings are not just end products: they are part of the thought process of architectural design. Drawings express the interaction of our minds, eyes and hands." By contrast, ideas rendered by the computer can lead to "so-called blob architecture"—or non-traditional, amorphously-shaped renderings that "lack the emotional content of a design derived from hand."

James Wines, an artist and founder of SITE Environmental Design, an architectural and environmental arts organization in New York City, is a champion of drawing by hand. Recognizing the "universal triumph" of digital graphics, he nevertheless makes a plea for the importance of hand-drawn work. "By focusing exclusively on computer-generated illustration alone, something conceptually profound is forfeited in the design process," he says. The "fertile territory of the subliminal accident is lost."

Wines notes how the "graphic musings" and "charcoal smudges" made by hand drawing became "the springboard for new ideas" in his work, and how he learned over time to spot the weaknesses of computer-assisted design. "As my eyes became accustomed to sorting out slickness from substance, I gradually acquired a highly refined aptitude for detecting mediocrity (or outright crap) lurking under the pictorial gloss," he notes. Wines is not opposed to using digital tools, but he argues that they will "always be best employed as an efficient means of confirmation . . . never a deeply resonant art experience in itself."

Even for those who don't rely on sketching for their livelihood, drawing and painting offer difficult-to-quantify creative benefits. Although he wields a scalpel for his day job, New York plastic surgeon David Hidalgo creates photorealist sketches with graphite on paper in his free time, which he says helps him better understand the "gestalt" of the human face. "Drawing shapes, shadows and lines enhances my ability to see surgical shapes, forms and lines," he told a reporter.

Science fiction writer Ray Bradbury was an avid painter in his spare time and was purported to have claimed, "Painting fulfills a need to be non-intellectual. There are times when we have to get our brains out in our fingers." This is perhaps why leaders of state from Winston Churchill to George W. Bush have found solace in painting. Churchill, who didn't begin painting until he was forty years old, felt that painting made him a better observer of the world and advised would-be painters, "Audacity is the only ticket."

While audacity served Churchill well in his own artistic pursuits, the values and habits of mind formed by working with our hands are more modest: patience, perseverance, and diligence. These are not the virtues of our technological age, which values speed and novelty, and is too quick to reward fecklessness disguised as innovation. How can we recover those more modest virtues? Working with our hands and taking time to learn a craft offers one path.

———

When I was eight years old, I decided for reasons unclear to me still that I wanted to play the bassoon. When I unpacked the four large sections of the instrument from its musty-smelling case, each part felt unwieldy and alien. Once I put the pieces together and stood it on end, the bassoon was taller than I was. My hands weren't large enough to reach all of the keys, so my band director fashioned extensions to the keys out of Popsicle sticks and masking tape. The first sounds I managed to produce from the instrument sounded like the cries of a tortured duck. I was in love.

As the years passed, my hands grew to span the width of the instrument and I learned to master scales and trills and sonatas and concertos. I played in wind ensembles and pep bands and orchestras and woodwind quintets and eventually went to university on a music scholarship. The instrument that had once felt alien and bulky now felt like an extension of my hands. I knew its quirks—which keys were likely to stick in the humid South Florida air, how its intonation varied by season, playing sharp in the dry winter and flat in the rank doldrums of summer. I knew the source of every dent and scratch that marked the varnished maple and must have glanced at the stovepipe-like bell of the instrument thousands of times.

My relationship with my instrument was both tactile and emotional—it was "mine," which is why it felt odd when I played someone else's bassoon. When I played it, I made use of all of my senses: the sound and sight of the instrument, foremost, but also the smell of the cork grease I used to treat the joints, the pulpy taste of the reed on my tongue, the creaks and clicks of the silver keys as I played. Playing that instrument was and still is a full-body experience.

"When we focus on making a physical object, or on playing a musical instrument, our concentration level is mainly self-directed," sociologist Richard Sennett argues. The act of manipulating a tool or of drawing a bow across a string forces us to feel and do simultaneously, and the more skilled we become at the act, the less we have to think about what we are doing. This form of "situated cognition," as Sennett calls it, takes time to develop. It also forces us to slow down, as we see when we study people who make things by hand. "Part of craft's anchoring role is that it helps to slow down labor," Sennett told *American Craft* magazine. "Making is thinking."

Lee Miller, a bootmaker in Austin, Texas, spends up to forty hours hand-crafting a single pair of boots using tools that are more than one hundred years old. Miller notes how the time dedicated to his craft is inseparable from what he creates. "No automated machine can do as fine work as the human hand can," he argues. His customers, who are willing to wait years for the custom boots he makes, agree.

The significance—some might say "aura"—of the handmade object derives from our knowledge of the time and effort and skill that went into making it; even the most sophisticated machine churning out identically sophisticated objects doesn't inspire the same feeling. "We are knowing as well as sensing creatures," philosopher Julian Baggini writes, "Knowing where things come from, and how their makers are treated, does and should affect how we feel about them." One need not belong to the elite to enjoy the luxury of owning handmade goods; platforms such as Etsy offer a wide array of handmade goods at every price point.

Some critics argue that our desire for handmade goods is increasing because so much of what we buy is now mass-produced, alienating us from a human connection to the objects we use. This is perhaps one reason that the revelations of horrific working conditions at the Chinese factories that make iPhones prompted outrage. The recognition that these sleek technologies emerged from overworked—even suicidal—human hands changed the way we understood them, at least until the outrage faded and the new version of the iPhone landed in stores.

Our desire for the mark of the human hand hasn't diminished. Today we satisfy it in a novel way, however. We embrace a vicarious form of craftsmanship comprised of images of well-made things rather than the things themselves. We look at perfectly prepared meals on Instagram, or the efforts of strangers on home remodeling TV shows and do-it-yourself videos on YouTube, which range in quality from highly-produced plumbing tutorials to boring, badly-lit snippets of people mowing their lawns (which still somehow garner tens of millions of views). This is in keeping with the growth of other vicarious pursuits. As it has for years, television viewing remains Americans' most popular leisure activity, according to the American Time Use survey, accounting for over half of all leisure time, on average, although time spent online watching videos or engaging with social media nearly matches that.

Some aspects of craftsmanship are clearly in decline. Critic Louis Uchitelle has argued that the Home Depot approach to craftsmanship in the U.S.—"simplify it, dumb it down, hire a contractor"—is one of many markers of that decline. "Mastering tools and working with one's hands is receding in America as a hobby, as a valued skill, as a cultural influence that shaped thinking and behavior in vast sections of the country," he argued. A blogger who writes about woodworking in the digital age wrote an only partially facetious post titled "Arguing about woodworking more popular hobby than woodworking."

New forms of hands-on making have arisen in their place, forms more in step with our technological age, such as the Maker Movement, which grew out of a late-twentieth-century hacker culture that sought to give individuals more power over how their technologies worked. Chris Anderson, who left his position as editor of *Wired* magazine to join a DIY drone-making company, argues that this new breed of DIY tech tinkers and 3D printing mavens are responding to a culture that has become too invested in the virtual. "Making something that starts virtual but quickly becomes tactile and usable in the everyday world is satisfying in a way that pure pixels are not," he wrote, predicting that the growing

HAND TO MOUSE • 71

number of "makerspaces" would usher in a new Industrial Revolution. Critics such as Evgeny Morozov argue that the movement hasn't produced a revolution but rather another form of "consumerism and D.I.Y. tinkering" sponsored by large corporations and the Defense Advanced Research Projects Agency.

Whichever man has the better of the argument about Maker culture (my money is on Morozov), both would agree that tinkering is a kind of play, one that encourages the development of both tactile and cognitive skills. And yet, like handwriting, drawing, and craftsmanship, virtual experiences and technological tools are replacing unmediated, unstructured opportunities for play and learning among the population most in need of it for their healthy development: children.

⸺

When she embarked on research into how infants and toddlers learn languages, Patricia Kuhl of the Institute for Learning and Brain Sciences at the University of Washington wanted to answer several questions: At what age do babies recognize their parents' or caregivers' native language? How open are they to the tones and tempo of a different language? At what developmental stage do their brains become efficient at storing language? Kuhl performed a series of experiments on infants that involved the children sitting in a parent's lap and listening to them talk while tracking the infants' head movements and, in some cases, images of their brains using magnetoencephalography.

Kuhl also tested whether it would make a difference if the babies heard words directly from a human being or from an audio recording or video. She and her colleagues reran their experiments using a television set rather than a human being, then ran them again with only an audio recording. "What you see here is the audio result—no learning whatsoever—and the video result—no learning whatsoever," she told an audience at a TEDx conference. Her conclusion would seem obvious, and yet, given the amount of time young children spend with screens today and how often one sees parents staring raptly at their smartphones while pushing their children in strollers, perhaps it is worth emphasizing Kuhl's conclusion: "It takes a human being for babies to learn."

For the past decade or more, educational theorists, teachers, and technologists have debated how online tools will influence education. Virtual learning, we are told by its advocates, will transform education by streamlining and personalizing the experience, as well as making knowledge accessible to all. The idea isn't new. Behavioral psychologist B. F. Skinner urged the adoption of "teaching machines" to eliminate classroom inefficiencies in his 1968 book *The Technology of Teaching.*

Skeptics question what is gained and what is lost when students spend more time interacting with a screen than a teacher, as well as the fact that many of these educational ventures are profit-making businesses rather than educational institutions. "The purpose of a for-profit that is venture-backed in Silicon Valley is to grow as quickly as possible and to exit providing a considerable financial benefit for its investors," argues video game designer and academic Ian Bogost, "and that goal may not be compatible with education."

These ongoing debates often pit teachers against technology in a version of the man vs. robot trope. Skeptics of online education praise the human touch as crucial for teaching and promoters of online education fear it for just that reason. You can't manage what you don't measure, management theorists claim, and the value of human interaction isn't easily measurable. Education "requires one mind engaging with another, in real time: listening, understanding, correcting, modeling, suggesting, prodding, denying, affirming, and critiquing thoughts and their expression," argues Pamela Hieronymi, a philosophy professor at UCLA and a critic of claims that online learning is superior.

For more than a decade, teachers have been trying to meet the challenge of holding the interest of students raised on sophisticated media and technology. Ten years ago, brain science and child development scholar Dimitri Christakis told the *New York Times* that thanks to technology use, students were habituated to a "supernatural" level of stimulation in their daily lives that teachers found difficult to match. "Reality, by comparison, is uninteresting," Christakis said.

An unwelcome form of reality-testing of the teacher vs. technology question occurred during the coronavirus pandemic of 2020–21. The closure of schools across the country prompted an immediate, large-scale experiment in distance learning for nearly 50 million K–12 students, with mixed results. Some school districts moved swiftly to online learning models, replacing in-person classes with Zoom lessons; others struggled to meet the needs of student populations who lacked access to the technology that would allow them to continue learning from home.

The results of this experiment, as the *Wall Street Journal* summarized, are not positive: "The grade from students, teachers, parents and administrators is already in: It was a failure." Preliminary research finds that "students nationwide will return to school in the fall [of 2021] with roughly 70% of learning gains in reading relative to a typical school year, and less than 50% in math, according to projections by NWEA, an Oregon-based nonprofit that provides research to help educators tailor instruction." Notably, it projects "a greater learning loss for minority and low-income children who have less access to technology, and for families more affected by the economic downturn."

Beyond the practical challenges for those who lack access to technology for learning, distance education assumes a great deal about its recipients that has not proven true. Children who expertly sift through YouTube videos and Instagram posts, or master video games like Fortnite, have honed skills that have not proven transferrable to online learning.

The appeal of such policies for political leaders and technology companies is apparent: they can claim to have solved a problem in the near term (Zoom classes for all!) while punting on planning for the problems that will emerge later (such as gaps in learning). Similarly, technology billionaires' foundations and technology companies maintain power to set policy without responsibility for any of the long-term consequences.

When students fall behind, we rarely blame technology; more often we blame the lack of availability of the technology or improper parental investment. Those peddling the technological fix are praised for their progressive thinking, but responsibility for failure ultimately rests on the population the solution was supposed to help. These outcomes are particularly stark with education, which enthusiasts of virtual learning rarely approach holistically. As a result, proponents of virtual education ignore the fact that many lower-income students rely on in-person schooling not only for education but also for crucial social support and nutrition.

As physicist and writer Ursula Franklin reminds us, "It may be wise, when communities are faced with new technological solutions to existing problems, to ask what these techniques may *prevent* and not only to check what the techniques promise to *do*." School closures during the pandemic were an extended exercise in prevention, one that also revealed serious problems with mediated education. One such problem? The shift from embodied to screen-based learning has prevented the flourishing of something we know to be educationally and psychologically beneficial, especially for young children: unstructured physical play.

Kathy Hirsh-Pasek, author of *Einstein Never Used Flashcards* and a psychology professor at Temple University, calls lack of play a crisis akin to global warming. "The science is clear," she told a reporter. Assessing the state of research on play, the *Chronicle of Higher Education* noted, "Whether children play enough isn't an obscure debate among developmental psychologists. If it's true that children who spend too little time playing struggle with executive function, then we may be raising a generation of kids with less self-control, shorter attention spans, and poorer memory skills."

Another study published in *Science* examined how preschoolers who learned using play-based learning techniques compared to preschoolers who were taught using more traditional methods. Play-based methods yielded much better scores on measures such as self-control, working memory, and other traits linked to executive function. "Although play is often thought frivolous, it may be essential," the authors concluded. Brian Sutton-Smith, author of *The Ambiguity of Play*, goes so far as to call play, like religion and sex, "a major method of becoming reconciled with our being within our present universe."

Play, both at home and at school, is the early proving ground of embodied cognition. Its decline, like the decline of handwriting, has happened gradually, but as children's engagement with screens both at school and at home increases, it is worth asking what we are giving up in this new world of virtual, rather than embodied, learning. Many experts are offering evidence that we are giving up the very thing that allows children to learn at all. As Erika Christakis, education expert and author of *The Importance of Being Little*, warns, "When we deny young children play, we are denying them the right to understand the world."

On a beam in the library of sixteenth-century essayist Michel de Montaigne's home near Périgord, France, is carved a liberal paraphrase of a passage from the New Testament book of Ecclesiastes: "You who do not know how the mind is joined to the body know nothing of the works of God." Montaigne embraced the human body in all its glorious and alarming incarnations (his essays contain gleeful descriptions of his own and others' bouts of flatulence) and he criticized the hypocrisy of those who deny their corporeality. Our bodies are one of the central ways we understand ourselves, Montaigne believed. They are a reminder of our frailty and a check on the ego. "And upon the highest throne in the world, we are seated, still, upon our arses," he wrote.

The physical requirements of everyday life in Montaigne's time were fundamentally different from our own, and far more difficult, prompting greater humility. Such humility is rare in our technological age. The mundane tasks we perform every day with our bodies seem insignificant compared to the powers available to us when midwifed by our new technologies. It's easier, physically, to send a message to the other side of the world than it is to tie your own shoe.

But our instruments and tools remain extensions of our bodies in crucial ways. As computer scientist Joseph Weizenbaum observed in his book *Computer Power and Human Reason*, we must "internalize aspects of [our tools] in the form of kinesthetic and perceptual habits." Our tools become part of us. In a similar way, our bodies help us find our way in the world. "The body is our first and most natural technical object," the French sociologist Marcel Mauss observed.

Our choice of tools and the way we use them facilitate not only habits of hand but also habits of mind. Our embodied experiences shape not only how we learn to do mundane things, but also how we understand the world around us. In Wallace Stegner's novel *Angle of Repose,* one of the characters describes the mores of an earlier generation: his grandmother, who grew up on a farm, "could kill a chicken, and dress it, and eat it afterward, with as little repugnance as her neighbor." Her generation had a different relationship to the physical world, which was reflected in the way they understood its challenges. "When animals died, the family had to deal with their bodies; when people died, the family's women laid them out."

Today, we experience less discomfort and don't confront our bodies' failures as often. Our increased comfort may mean that we struggle more with our bodies' inevitable decline, often using technology to prolong life for as long as possible. We also struggle to care for the failing bodies of others, outsourcing the problem to professionals including, increasingly, to the care of robots that their makers promise will provide the companionship that human beings are too busy to offer. That struggle is the logical conclusion of the habits of body and mind we are embracing at the very beginning of life, when we avoid tackling the physical and mental challenges of skills such as handwriting and other activities that require patience, repetition, and the coordination of our minds and bodies. As we make every effort to live lives of seamless ease and comfort, eliminating inefficiencies with the use of technologies, the unavoidable limitations and challenges of our own and others' bodies become all that much harder to bear when they do, inevitably, appear.

Some of our disappearing habits, such as handwriting and drawing, might not seem important. They are modest skills whose benefits are experienced privately, cannot easily be monetized (unless you are that rare thing, a professional calligrapher), and whose use in daily life no longer makes sense for an increasing number of people.

Yet the quiet disappearance of handwriting from our lives shows how the extinction of certain experiences happens: experiences recede gradually, not through some top-down edict or bottom-up populist campaign. And we rationalize their obsolescence not as a loss but as another mark of progress and improvement. A skill fades, and with it a human experience that spans millennia. Even those experiences leave a trace, like the cave drawings in Altamira and Lascaux, painted some 40,000 years ago and hundreds of miles apart, which both contain images of the same thing: the human hand.

Handwriting's rapid decline in a world dominated by screens is also a symbol of how thoughtlessly we've settled between the old and the new. New technologies don't have to destroy old ways of doing things. The printing press didn't destroy handwriting. There is no reason to assume the triumph of the keyboard and touch screen over pen and paper is inevitable, or that software spells the end of drawing by hand, or that the encroachment of technology in the classroom need force out more traditional embodied forms of learning. We can achieve some form of coexistence, even if it is likely to be an uneasy rather than a peaceful one.

"For our flesh surrounds us with its own desires," the poet Philip Larkin wrote. It also surrounds us with opportunities—to learn, to understand, to feel in a way that our vicarious, screen-based experiences do not. As our world becomes ever more saturated with images and virtualizations, we shouldn't let our desire for alluring technologies eclipse the human need to see, touch, and make things with our hands.

CHAPTER 4

❧ ❧ ❧

How We Wait

"There's hardly a wait at all!" said the Walt Disney World cast member who greeted me at the entrance to the Buzz Lightyear Space Ranger Spin in Tomorrowland. The display board gave an estimated wait time of ten minutes for the ride, and I had only a moment to register the low lighting, cold air, and promising pings of cartoon weaponry before I was tracking back and forth along a zigzagging line, passing television screens showing battle scenes between Buzz and his large purple nemesis, Zurg. As I moved along at an unhurried pace, the environment remained dim and muffled except for brightly colored images of Buzz and the excited murmur of expectant children. Soon I shuffled onto the moving sidewalk that delivered me and my kids to our rocket ship for the ride. Had it only been ten minutes? Everything about the experience of waiting for my turn had been designed to prevent me from experiencing the real passage of time.

If you want to understand the future of waiting, stand in line at Walt Disney World's Magic Kingdom in Orlando, Florida. It doesn't matter if the line is for food, a ride, or even for the bathroom; the structure and psychology of the wait is the same. When Disney opened his first theme park in Anaheim, California, in 1955 he inaugurated the modern era of queue psychology—crafting lines that would transform the experience of those waiting in them by making time seem to pass more quickly.

You can fault Disney for many things, but the man understood human nature. And he (and the behemoth company that now bears his name) knew that people hate to wait. In addition to the relentless "imagineering" the company pursues across Disney's many square miles of family fun, the company's employees spend a great deal of time trying to alleviate the stubborn human experience of waiting. "It's our number-one guest complaint," Dale Stafford, then Vice President of Development and Planning for Walt Disney Attractions, remarked in a popular travel forum.

To create a more efficient leisure experience, Disney World initiated the FastPass system in 1999. FastPass, whose logo is a frantic-looking Donald Duck, is a virtual queuing system that allows visitors to get carefully timed tickets to the park's most popular rides. With a FastPass ticket appointment for noon at the Haunted Mansion, for example, you stroll right into the ride, avoiding the crowds and the hours-long wait. FastPass's clock-driven directives and strict rules is the second coming of Frederick Winslow Taylor's nineteenth-century principles of scientific management—applied to your vacation rather than the factory floor.

Contributors to Disney forums debate the FastPass system with religious fervor, trading tips on how best to maximize its use. I didn't consult these forums before my own trip to Disney World in Orlando, but I did see the stark dichotomy of the pre- and post-FastPass era at the popular log flume–ride Splash Mountain. Having secured FastPasses for myself and my family a few hours earlier, we muscled our way through the humid crowd to the FastPass line and walked briskly for about five minutes, shortcutting past people whose collective torpor was broken only by flashes of annoyance as we breezed by—if they noticed us at all, that is. Most of them were fiddling with their smartphones. These hundreds of hapless visitors penned between the serpentine ropes of Splash Mountain's "standby" line were doomed to spend the next few hours broiling in the sun in Disney's equivalent of purgatory. One of my sons expressed a kind of horrified pity for their situation. "They shouldn't have to wait so long," he murmured. "It's not fair to have to wait in such a long line!" Later, after an hour inching along the line for the non-FastPass-enabled It's a Small World, the ride's upbeat theme song chirruping away relentlessly, I had to agree with him.

As a child growing up in Florida in the days before FastPass, I went with my family to Disney World many times and I remember the seemingly endless waits for rides. My sisters and I would peevishly whine to our parents as we shuffled along, waiting and waiting. Occasionally a lackadaisical Disney employee dressed as Goofy would wander by, but distractions were minimal. The physical experience of that kind of boredom was like an itch.

Today, instead of standing outside for an hour to ride Dumbo the Flying Elephant, children frolic inside a circus-themed play area while their parents clutch pagers that ping them when their wait is over. The Dumbo attraction is no longer merely a long wait followed by a few minutes whirling around in an elephant-shaped gondola, as it was when I was a kid, but an "experience" that lasts "an immersive fifteen minutes," as a Disney vice president described to the *New York Times*. Disney's last-generation waiting technologies (turning points in lines to disguise their length, a few entertaining distractions along the way) are no longer sufficient.

Waiting isn't what it used to be. Today we expect a great deal more distraction and control over the experience of waiting, and not just when we are spending a day at a theme park. We turn to our smartphones to check email, text a friend, or play Candy Crush or FreeCell any time we experience a wait. Nearly every moment of interstitial time can be filled with entertainment or communication. Disney refers to the areas where visitors wait to board rides as "scene ones"—as in, the first scene of the performance. As more of our lives resemble a perpetual performance, every person's experience of waiting becomes a potential "scene one." In a short span of years, unmediated waiting has become the exception rather than the rule. We have, in effect, Disneyfied every waiting experience.

It is alluring to remove oneself mentally from the inescapable physical reality of waiting. Checking your phone to escape the tedium can feel like a micro-revolution against the tyranny of time. But the problem with revolutions is that they sometimes devour their children.

When new technologies such as the train, the telegraph, the telephone, the airplane, the computer, imposed new tempos on life, these technologies alleviated or ended a certain kind of waiting. These tools changed our expectations about what is and is not worth waiting for. We have also long been worried about what speed and acceleration will do to us. As Henry David Thoreau claimed, "We do not ride on the railroad; it rides upon us." At every stage of innovation people have fretted, yet life has nevertheless moved on at a quickened pace.

Modern people tend to see speed as an improvement, a boon that eliminates the bane of "wasted time." We embrace what speed has wrought and count ourselves better for having it. And yet, how we wait tells us something about who we are, about what we expect from one another and how, both individually and as a society, we understand time and plan for the future. Our willingness or unwillingness to wait reveals our feelings about patience (and impatience), our acceptance of things such as idleness and boredom, and our need for a sense of control. How we wait reveals our attitudes about silence and reticence, reflection and daydreaming. The question today is how and why the experience of waiting has changed and how, in turn, it is changing us.

And there is an "us" to this story. Any individual experience of waiting might be unique, ours to cope with as we choose, but our attitude about waiting has a public effect—on our families, friends, neighbors, communities, and even on our broader political culture. Unlike an animal's unreflective instincts or a machine's finely calibrated algorithms, we are not programmed by nature or engineers to wait, at least not yet; we must choose it. If, as writer Frank Partnoy has observed, "Our ability to mute our hard-wired reactions by pausing is what differentiates us from animals," then the way we wait differentiates us from other animals and machines. Recalling mankind's impulsive consumption of the fruit of the Tree of Knowledge of Good and Evil in the Garden of Eden, poet W. H. Auden wrote, "Perhaps there is only one cardinal sin: impatience. Because of impatience we were driven out of Paradise, because of impatience we cannot return." Waiting has always been a part of our everyday lived experience. But how we understand it and how we cope with it has changed. If patience is a virtue, it is one we are happily eviscerating.

Lines have their own logic. Leaving from Ronald Reagan National Airport near Washington, DC, I found myself in a long security line. Unlike the sinuous and amiably autocratic herding at Disney World, this line was barely controlled chaos. It stretched haphazardly all the way into the baggage claim area. No signs marked the entrance to the line or even signaled what the line was for, which meant that every person who approached the line had to question the people already in it. "Yes, this is the line for security. No, I have no idea how long it's going to take." No airport employees advised the increasingly agitated public. People regularly bolted the line, or, muttered about how they were going to miss their flight and tried to jump the line, to no avail. The scene thrummed with thinly veiled mass anxiety.

One week later I queued for the train at Amtrak's Union Station in Washington, DC. Two police officers enforced line rules, refusing to let people jump ahead of others. The beginning of the line—the entrance to the train platform—was visible to everyone. And almost everyone was texting or talking on a mobile phone, including, eventually, me, when after five minutes of standing around looking at people I felt the familiar urge to check my email. Surveying the sea of hunched torsos busily tapping at tiny glowing screens, I was both relieved and alarmed by our collective passivity, as just above our heads television sets periodically blared Orwellian terrorism reminders: "It doesn't hurt to be alert! See something? Say something!" We were saying plenty—to the people on the other end of our digital devices. But few of us would have seen anything had it happened.

Daily life is studded with waiting rooms—waiting for a train, a bus, for traffic to move. In *Oh! The Places You'll Go!*, Dr. Seuss advised his young readers that one day they would encounter the Waiting Place, for "people just waiting" for a pot to boil or the phone to ring or the fish to bite. According to one estimate, Americans spend a combined 37 billion hours waiting in line every year.

Our everyday experience of waiting is thoroughly subjective; ten minutes spent waiting for a medical diagnosis will feel longer than the same amount of time spent in line at the grocery store. Researchers who study queue psychology have found that two things govern our perceptions of waiting: the amount of information we have about the wait, and its fairness. An unexplained wait will feel longer than an explained wait, and uncertain waits feel longer than certain ones, which is why all Disney World attractions include wait times at the entrances. Purgatory isn't purgatory merely because you're uncomfortable there. You are uncomfortable because you are uncertain about when it will end.

Unfortunately, external realities such as the clock that tells us how much time has passed do not always square with our internal perceptions. In one experiment, researcher Jacob Hornik observed and timed 640 people who were waiting in an average-length grocery checkout line. After asking them how long each of them thought they had waited, he found that they perceived their wait to be about 30 percent longer than it was. A survey performed by retail consultants Envirosell revealed that for the first two to three minutes of waiting, we have an accurate perception of time passing, but after three minutes we begin overestimating the time we are waiting. Women are slightly more patient than men; they will wait three minutes before abandoning a checkout line, for example, while men bail after two minutes.

Strongly-held beliefs about fairness are also implicated in queuing. More than twenty years ago, Richard Larson, a professor at MIT, began investigating the relationship between queues and social justice. After he and his graduate students fanned out to study fast food lines and other waiting places, they noted that, consistently, "first come, first served is the socially just queue discipline and first in, first out the socially just system discipline," even if that structure leads to longer wait times for everyone in the aggregate. Of course, human nature being what it is, vague feelings of social justice only extend so far. We rarely pity those behind us in line. In fact, we tend to feel superior. Queue researchers writing in the *Journal of Consumer Research* note, "Consumers in a queue make downward comparisons with others behind them" and "derive some comfort from looking back on a large number of people behind them and thinking, 'I bet you all wish you were here where I am.'"

How we perceive fairness depends on the way our wait is structured. Larson also conducted research at Houston International Airport, where passengers were complaining about having to wait too long at baggage claim. He discovered that the average wait, including a one-minute walk from the plane to the baggage claim area and a seven-minute wait for bags to appear, was well within the industry standard. Why were passengers experiencing the wait as unfair? Their perception of the wait was skewed because they spent most of their time waiting for bags to appear rather than doing something (like walking) that passed the time. The solution was simple and brilliant: the airport moved the baggage claim area further away so that passengers had to walk for six minutes to reach it but wait only a minute or two for their bags to appear. The time they spent waiting was the same, but their perception of their "empty" or wasted time was altered. Complaints plummeted.

As the war against waiting evolves, however, the principle of fairness is under attack. Today, with enough money, you can buy your way out of waiting in many lines. There has always been a small market for line-standing services such as linestanding.com, which operates in the

Washington, DC, area and specializes in finding surrogates to stand in line for seats at congressional hearings and U.S. Supreme Court arguments. But the notion that it is socially acceptable to buy one's way out of waiting is expanding into the restaurant reservations business and many entertainment venues. For a fee, airlines now offer passengers priority queues for security and boarding (and of course, for those privileged enough to fly by private jet, there is no waiting at all). For an extra cost, ski resorts offer visitors access to shorter lift lines, and many cities sell passes or offer toll roads that allow access to less congested lanes on the interstate. Many theme parks offer passes similar to Disney's Fastpass, with various gradations—gold, platinum—so guests can pay to skip lines. Universal Studios Hollywood is at least honest in its marketing of privilege; its Front of the Line Pass has been enthusiastically received by visitors such as the media and entertainment executive who told the *New York Times*, "If Universal didn't offer a VIP option I wouldn't go . . . I just don't have the time to wait in a line, and I want a certain level of service." In an age of entitled, time-conscious consumers, paying for the privilege of avoiding a wait doesn't seem like a privilege at all; it seems like common sense.

This sense of entitlement, combined with an unwillingness to wait, has social consequences. In 2013, Walt Disney World announced that it was changing its policies for families with children with special needs. In the past, those families could go to the front of the line at the theme parks' attractions. But given extensive "abuse of this system," including an increasing number of people who were paying tour guides to rent a wheelchair so they could avoid waiting in line, Disney decided to initiate a more restrictive policy. Now families of guests with special needs use a FastPass-like system for Disney's rides; many of them took to forums to decry the new rules. What really rankled was the fact that a corporation like Disney, master of queue management, would kowtow to the impatience and unethical behavior of a growing number of its customers. We are not just more willing to accept the idea that we should be able to buy or cheat our way out of waiting; we seem increasingly less tolerant of waiting at all.

On a warm August evening in Hammond, Indiana, twenty-three-year-old Montrell Moss was driving his girlfriend and their three children to the Horseshoe Casino to eat dinner. Somewhere along a stretch of Indianapolis Boulevard, a gold Chevrolet van cut in front of Moss's car. Angered, he threw a plastic cup of water out his window, hitting the van. The van's sixty-one-year-old driver responded by pulling out a handgun and shooting Moss to death.

In Orange County, California, a woman gave the middle finger to a driver who had cut her off on the interstate. Someone in the other car pulled out a gun and shot at the woman's car, killing her six-year-old son, whom she was driving to kindergarten. And in Lumberton, North Carolina, a couple from Pennsylvania who were traveling to the beach for an anniversary trip angered another driver while trying to merge onto the highway. That driver shot at their car, killing the wife, a mother of six, who was sitting in the passenger seat.

Ten years ago, the *Washington Post* polled people in the Washington, DC, area about road rage and found that "the number of people who admit they feel 'uncontrollable anger toward another driver' has doubled since 2005." One in ten drivers (and one out of six younger drivers) admitted to feeling road rage, and that was probably a low estimate since many people will not answer honestly about their own behavior even as they eagerly highlight the bad behavior of others. In the years since, the problem has increased. According to the AAA Foundation for Traffic Safety, in 2019, "nearly 80 percent of drivers expressed significant anger, aggression or road rage behind the wheel at least once in the previous 30 days."

Nationwide, according to the most recent statistics from the National Highway Traffic Safety Administration, road rage was responsible for 446 crashes that led to 502 deaths in 2019 alone. Many of these incidents involved guns; according to Everytown for Gun Safety, in 2020, "42 people a month on average were shot and killed or wounded in road rage incidents," nearly double the rate only four years before.

Many road rage incidents are queuing disputes played out at high speed on busy roads: someone in one car cuts in front of another driver or refuses to allow someone to merge into traffic. Anger and aggressive behavior and sometimes death ensue. A sense of anonymity and invulnerability lowers people's inhibitions about behaving aggressively while driving, like the sense of impenetrability that can dictate our online behavior. University of Wisconsin–Green Bay psychologist Ryan Martin, who studies road rage, notes of driving, "Everyone is anonymous to us and we are to them. We do things we wouldn't normally do—give people the finger, yell at them, cut them off."

At its root, road rage is about impatience—impatience with other people who are as flawed, tired, and distracted as we are. Like the growing frustration with having to wait in line in daily life, the often deadly overreaction to perceived slights while driving speaks to a broader shift in our expectations.

How did we get here? Some of this is a consequence of the relentless acceleration of everyday life. As our daily pace increases, our expectations for what we can and should wait for change. Over a short period of time, we have become habituated to *not* having to wait to be in touch with one another. Our inability to wait to communicate when we are behind the wheel—and the increase in accidents caused by distracted driving— prompted AT&T Wireless to launch "It Can Wait," a campaign to discourage drivers from texting and driving. States have passed numerous laws banning phone use while driving or requiring hands-free use of devices only. New cars feature integrated dashboards meant to make hands-free interactions easier, while discounting the continual distraction such features pose to drivers. Highways now offer pull-off spots where drivers can rest and text without risking their own or others' lives.

Of course, the technology AT&T is now urging us to use responsibly—the mobile phone—is the same one the company boasts about introducing into cars in the first place. On its website, AT&T describes how, in 1946, "a driver in St. Louis, Mo., pulled out a handset from under his car's dashboard, placed a phone call and made history." As important as AT&T's public service campaign against distracted driving is, this campaign is unlikely to curb our expectation of swift, instant communication, even when we are driving. Safety is not a powerful enough motivation for people to reject connection in the moment.

The novelist Milan Kundera once described speed as "the form of ecstasy that technology has bestowed upon modern man," and he is correct about its pleasures. What he might not have predicted is how quickly we raise our expectations for speed. We expect things to happen more quickly than they once did. We live in the era of the QRC—the Quick Response Code, the smartphone-scannable symbol now seen on everything from food packaging to bus stop schedules to restaurant menus. Online, users are given estimated "reading times" for articles they might peruse; these estimates are beginning to appear on books as well, ostensibly so we can avoid wasting too much time on any given subject. Amazon claims that for every 100 milliseconds of time saved loading its pages, the company increases revenue by 1 percent. A millisecond is a thousandth of a second.

Google's engineers are engaged in a race against that millisecond; they have found that even a delay of 400 milliseconds (about the time it takes the eye to blink) is too long for people to wait for search results. A lead engineer for the now-defunct Google Glass project once told reporters that one of the major goals of the wearable technology was to dramatically increase the speed with which we get what we want. "What may take 30 to 60 seconds on a phone will instead take 2 to 4 seconds on Glass," he said. As smartphone use became nearly ubiquitous, businesses struggled to increase loading speeds on mobile platforms as well. Forrester Research studied how long online shoppers were willing to wait for a page to load and found two seconds was the magic number; three years earlier people had been willing to wait four seconds.

Even over the course of the Internet's short lifespan, our expectations for how long something should take to get to us have changed dramatically. Nearly all of us (four out of five users) will abandon an online video if it loads slowly. Most online shoppers ditch their shopping carts in eight seconds if a website begins to slow. One study found that if a site operates merely 250 milliseconds slower than a competitor's site, we stop visiting it as often.

A granular study of online video use by Ramesh Sitaraman and S. Shunmuga Krishnan suggests that this habituation process is likely to continue. After analyzing the viewing habits of 6.7 million unique viewers from around the world who watched a total of 23 million videos, they found that viewers abandoned a video if it didn't start playing within two seconds. But they also discovered that the least patient viewers were the ones most habituated to speed: "Viewers with better connectivity are less patient and will abandon a slow-starting video sooner, while mobile users have significantly more patience than others," they found, although that gap is also narrowing, as more of us use our smartphones as all-in-one consumption devices for shopping, summoning cars, making reservations, and communicating. The acerbic nineteenth-century writer Ambrose Bierce once described patience as "a minor form of despair, disguised as a virtue." He probably never thought that one day we would be measuring it out in milliseconds.

As our habituation to speed continues, we become more impatient about everything, including the interactions of daily life. Not long ago, *New York Times* technology reporter Nick Bilton wrote a screed against what he called "time-wasting forms of communication." For Bilton, who confesses that his preferred method of communication with his mother is Twitter, this includes most of the things that used to be called pleasantries. "In the age of the smartphone there is no reason to ask once-acceptable questions: the weather forecast, a business phone number, a store's hours. But some people still do," he wrote. They take up band-width writing "Dear" and "Yours sincerely" in emails and placing land-line telephone calls rather than sending text messages.

Others share Bilton's exasperation. "I have decreasing amounts of tolerance for unnecessary communication because it is a burden and a cost," said Baratunde Thurston, who, ironically, is cofounder of something called Cultivated Wit. But as technology scholar Evan Selinger noted of this trend, "We're sacrificing attention and care for the type of expediency that turns maintaining important relationships into mere to-do list items."

The problem isn't that Bilton and others prefer a world without pleasantries; such people have always existed. It's their expectation that efficiency in human interactions is innately superior, an ideal that society should embrace. This expectation encourages the misguided notion that we should each act like technicians of our private lives, mimicking the technological virtues of efficiency, predictability, and repeatability in our interactions with one another. The attitude is reminiscent of Isaac Asimov's 1975 story about a networked supercomputer, "The Life and Times of Multivac." As Multivac's artificial intelligence grows, it becomes "chary, somehow of its time," Asimov wrote. "Perhaps that was the result of its ever-continuing self-improvement. It was becoming constantly more aware of its own worth and less likely to bear trivialities with patience."

Efficiency does not improve all rituals of everyday life. Consider the family meal. According to the National Center for Substance Abuse at Columbia University, 32 percent of families in the U.S. spent 20 minutes or less eating dinner together. Efficient conviviality is becoming a more common experience around the American dinner table, with some unfortunate results. In one study that examined the link between family dining rituals and childhood obesity, researchers videotaped 200 family mealtimes and found that when the family dinner lasted on average only 16.4 minutes, children were at greater risk of becoming overweight when compared to families whose dinners lasted an average of nearly 20 minutes. Three and a half minutes made a difference.

In a letter Aldous Huxley wrote to George Orwell in 1949 he argued, "I feel that the nightmare of *1984* is destined to modulate into the nightmare of a world having more resemblance to that which I imagined in *Brave New World*." What did Huxley believe would bring about this dystopia? Not a global world order or a charismatic despot: "The change will be brought about as a result of a felt need for increased efficiency."

Texting Mom instead of calling her will not usher in the apocalypse. But Huxley's warning has merit. The speed of computer processing power can be measured quantitatively. But the transformations in a culture's tolerance for delay are experienced qualitatively. It is only when we step back—or, more likely, when we are forced into a situation where we *must* wait without distraction—that we are reminded of other ways of doing things. We enjoy the efficiencies and distractions technology brings, but they leave us less skilled at patience. They also falsely promise to eliminate forever an age-old human experience: boredom.

———

"Shepherds do it, cops do it, stevedores and merchants in their shops do it," technology critic Marshall McLuhan observed in *Understanding Media*. He was talking about Greek men's use of *komboloi*, or worry beads. The beads, which look like amber-colored rosaries, are used throughout the day to pass the time, a secular version of praying the rosary. "More aesthetic than thumb-twiddling, less expensive than smoking, this Queeg-like obsession indicates a tactile sensuousness," McLuhan wrote. It is also an example of the deeply felt human need to fill interstitial time. We all engage in these weird little rituals. Some people doodle or fidget, others knit, a lot of people used to smoke. One study of college-age students who smoke occasionally found that cigarettes were a way for them to "structure ambiguous social situations" and to "accomplish interactional goals"—that is, smoking eased moments of awkwardness. Psychologist Mihaly Csikszentmihalyi calls these "the 'microflow' activities that help us negotiate the doldrums of the day." These "small automatic games woven into the fabric of everyday life help reduce boredom," he notes, "but add little to the positive quality of experience."

The experience of boredom is deeply human, but what we reach for when we experience it is socially structured, unique to our particular moment in time. Increasingly we are choosing mediated methods for alleviating our boredom. Unmediated interstitial time is going extinct. The worry beads and cigarettes of previous eras have given way to portable technologies; as the advertisement for a new smartphone app recently asked, "How in the world did we wait in line before smartphones?" Ours is a less carcinogenic but more commodified distraction, the long-term impacts of which we're only beginning to fathom. Do we have a diminishing tolerance for boredom, and if so, how does that change us?

According to the Pew Internet and American Life Project, nearly all adult Americans (97 percent) own some kind of cellphone; since Pew first began measuring smartphone ownership in 2011, the percentage of Americans who own one has risen from 35 percent to 85 percent. An extensive survey of phone users by Pew revealed that 72 percent of people aged eighteen to twenty-nine "use their phones to beat boredom," a number that has surely risen as smartphone adoption has increased and ever younger children use them. People accustomed to speed, including those with wireless Internet access and broadband and those living in urban areas, are more likely to use their phones to alleviate boredom than others.

One could view this as a brilliant coping mechanism, and in many ways it is. As philosopher William James once argued, "Stimulation is the indispensable requisite for pleasure in an experience, and the feeling of bare time is the least stimulating experience we can have." But James was writing when stimulations were far less sophisticated than even the most rudimentary games and distractions available on a smartphone. It begs the question: Might boredom have a purpose?

Although the experience of boredom is nearly universal—Peter Toohey, author of a history of boredom, reminds us, "There's Latin graffiti about boredom on the walls of Pompeii dating from the first century"— the science of boredom has come into its own only in the last decade or two. Now a flourishing academic subfield (there is even a Boredom Studies reader), scholars have studied the science of boredom, the psychology of boredom, and pondered its place in modern life. Assessing the state of the field, *New Yorker* writer Margaret Talbot noted how, "for all their scales and graphs," these researchers do "engage some of the same existential questions that had occupied philosophers and social critics," the qualitative as well as the quantitative changes in our experience of boredom. Some researchers point to a lack of meaning in modern life as fueling boredom, while others frame it as a problem of attention in a world of constant distraction.

We know boredom disrupts our experience of time; researchers have likened it to being trapped in an endless present. Designers of smartphones and apps know this. There is no single, killer app to combat this peculiar feeling of dissatisfaction; *every* app aims to do that, whether it catapults you from waiting at the bus stop into a quick game or fills your screen with information about the weather or your friend's most recent Instagram post. Online we can jump from website to website until we find something to hold our attention, "boredom on the installment plan, one click at a time," as novelist Benjamin Kunkel described it. Lately I've seen more people in their cars thwarting stoplight boredom—that is, unable to sit unmediated for even the few moments that it takes a red light to turn green, they reach for their smartphones. Kids tweet about boredom throughout the school day (#bored). The space between the time when they experience boredom and when they broadcast it has disappeared.

Clinical psychologist Dr. John Eastwood of York University, a leading researcher of boredom, argues that boredom is best understood as a matter of attention. Writing in the journal *Perspectives on Psychological Science*, Eastwood and his colleagues noted the connections between distractions and feelings of boredom. In an interview, he expressed concern about the way we can alleviate boredom instantly by turning to the stimulations of our screens. "We're very used to being passively entertained," he told *Smithsonian* magazine. "We have changed our understanding of the human condition as one of a vessel that needs to be filled."

Coping with boredom involves self-regulation. We must decide what to do with the feeling, so we counter desultory everyday experiences by reaching for technologies with assiduous abilities to distract us—so many distractions, each one a siren's island where attention might founder. In effect, our devices eliminate boredom not by teaching us how to cope with it but by outsourcing our attention so that we *don't* have to cope with it. In the oft-cited observation of economist Herbert Simon, "What information consumes is rather obvious: it consumes the attention of its recipients. Hence a wealth of information creates a poverty of attention." It also creates a poverty of self-regulation when it comes to coping with boredom.

What happens when we replace boredom with constant distraction and stimulation? Warnings about the harmful effects of too much stimulation are nothing new. "For a living organism, protection against stimuli is an almost more important function than the reception of stimuli," Sigmund Freud observed. But given the range and speed of stimuli at our disposal, we might need a new way of thinking about their effects. *Stimulation* seems too quaint a word. Some researchers who study schizophrenia have hypothesized that schizophrenics are more susceptible to "stimulus overinclusion," or "difficulty in attending selectively to relevant stimuli." People with schizophrenia pay attention to everything rather than selectively ignoring what isn't relevant. But overinclusion occurs in all kinds of people. Given the extent to which we mediate our everyday experience, it might be more apt (although less perky) to call our information age the "age of stimulus overinclusion."

There are many books that explore the erosion of human attention, but perhaps the question is less of attention than of the challenge of being alone with one's thoughts, what philosopher Blaise Pascal described long ago when he observed that all miseries derive from not being able to sit in a quiet room alone. Why do we feel entitled never to experience boredom? What does it say about our age that we fear idle time so keenly? No one admits to enjoying boredom, but our current anxieties about attention suggest that we aren't entirely comfortable with a world where distraction is ubiquitous either.

When psychologist Mihaly Csikszentmihalyi wrote more than twenty years ago about "flow"—that state of being in which someone is so involved in an activity "that nothing else seems to matter"—he argued, "Attention is our most important tool in the task of improving the quality of experience." We might believe that our attempts to fill our interstitial time with mediated distractions qualify as an effort to optimize our experiences under less than optimal conditions. But the concept of flow needs to be revisited in an era of smart machines.

A fascinating study of machine gambling in Las Vegas notes that flow is precisely the state gamblers seek and attain at the machines, and precisely what machine designers seek to exploit when people initiate play. Gamblers are experiencing flow, but they are not having the kind of optimal long-term experiences psychologists had in mind when they advocated pursuing activities that put you "in the zone." In a less intense way, we all enter "the zone" when we turn to our devices to alleviate the experience of waiting. The distractions we seek don't only consume our time, however. They consume the habits of mind that require time and patience to form, such as empathy. As our experience with social media platforms suggests, we get used to receiving mediated forms of feedback, recognition, and acknowledgment from our technology. We begin to prize these mediated interactions above more inefficient forms of interaction because they are more immediately rewarding.

A culture without boredom undermines the act of daydreaming, something interstitial time used to be given over to. Daydreaming seems a fusty term in an age when productivity and usefulness are prized. But as psychologists and neurologists have found, a wandering mind, often the first signal of impending boredom, is also a creative mind. In the 1960s, psychologist Jerome L. Singer, the grandfather of daydreaming studies, identified three kinds of mind-wandering: the productive, creative "positive constructive daydreaming," obsessive "guilty–dysphoric daydreaming," and "poor attentional control." Singer believed daydreaming was a positive adaptive behavior—a bold departure from the conventional wisdom at the time, which linked daydreaming to other psychopathologies such as excessive fantasizing. As one student of Singer's noted, Singer's work found strong associations between daydreaming and the personality type "openness to experience," which demonstrates sensitivity, curiosity, and willingness to explore new ideas and feelings.

Since then, researchers have found numerous positive effects of a wandering mind. Psychologist Scott Barry Kaufman summarized them: "self-awareness, creative incubation, improvisation and evaluation, memory consolidation, autobiographical planning, goal driven thought, future planning, retrieval of deeply personal memories, reflective consideration of the meaning of events and experiences, simulating the perspective of another person, evaluating the implications of self and others' emotional reactions, moral reasoning, and reflective compassion."

Anecdotally, history provides many examples of scientific breakthroughs—"aha!" moments—that arose during moments of daydreaming or downtime: René Descartes in bed staring at a fly on the ceiling and coming up with coordinate geometry; Albert Einstein's glimpse of the Bern tower on a streetcar ride prompting the theory of special relativity; the walk in the woods that prompted Nikola Tesla to devise alternating electrical current. Novelist and technologist Robin Sloan noted in an interview that when he realized his use of the iPhone was encroaching on his interstitial time, he stopped using it when he was standing in line or on the train. "I've been daydreaming more, jotting down scraps of stories again," he said.

Unstructured, unmediated time is especially important for the development of creativity in children. "In the space between anxiety and boredom was where creativity flourished," note Po Bronson and Ashley Merryman in their examination of declining scores on the Torrance Test for creativity among American children. They hypothesize that one of the reasons creativity scores might be declining is children's increased use of screen-based technologies during downtime. Rather than being left to their own imaginative devices, their wandering minds are often captured *by* devices—smartphones and other screens that grasp their attention and, in the process, occlude other possible uses of those moments of idle time.

Today you rarely see the word "idle" except when used as a pejorative; to be idle is to be wasteful, and several of the most popular Internet startup companies have targeted underutilized resources such as idle cars (Turo, ZipCar), household equipment (SnapGoods), or empty bedrooms (Airbnb), allowing people to make use of them by renting them out when they aren't in use. These services monetize idleness.

Some technologists have set their sights higher. Max Levchin, a cofounder of PayPal and investor in many Silicon Valley technology companies, gave a speech at a conference in Munich in which he lamented, "The world of real things is very inefficient." Harnessing the network effects of big data, he foresees a future where we can more efficiently do many things: "We will definitely see dynamically priced queues for confession-taking priests and therapists," he said. This is not an original idea; computer pioneer Joseph Weizenbaum once mused about a future with telephone booth–style therapists dotting the landscape, although, unlike Levchin, he did not welcome this as an improvement.

Of course, these new businesses will also make judgments about how we use our idle time. A bank might infer "that a particular college grad is financially responsible by looking at their tweets," Levchin notes. He is untroubled by the potential for abuse or bias. "I believe that in the next decades we will see [a] huge number of inherently analog processes captured digitally. Opportunities to build businesses that process this data and improve lives will abound." Indeed, Levchin launched one—Glow, a fertility-tracking app that aims to eliminate the inefficiencies of getting knocked up (while also introducing new challenges to privacy for women who live in places where reproductive rights are not guaranteed). "We use data science to help you create your tiny miracles," the company's website states. In Levchin's vision, technology should exploit idleness and repair the inefficiencies of the analog world—all while making a tidy profit. One wonders if Marx might have rethought his theories on the alienation of labor if he knew that one day we would be selling the idle time of our toasters and tracking our menstrual cycles via apps that profit people like Levchin.

Moments of idleness and daydreaming used to be prized for the unexpected pleasure they brought. As Wordsworth wrote, "For this one day we'll give to idleness . . . One moment now may give us more than fifty hours of reason." He advocated straying about "voluptuously" through rural fields, asking "no record of the hours given up to vacant musing." We might not spend our free time lolling about rural glens, but idleness of this variety is the opposite of the instrumental, practical use that our culture encourages us to make of our time. Technologists like Levchin would have us hire out our voluptuous time on TaskRabbit. To borrow an image from Wordsworth's rural fields, we should embrace this fallow time. To be fallow is not the same thing as to be useless; it is to let rest so that cultivation can occur in the future. When mediated experiences co-opt our idle time, it leaves us with fewer and fewer of these fallow moments, moments that are central to the experience of being human.

———

Located about one hour south of Louisville, Kentucky, past bourbon distilleries and restaurants with names like Biscuit World, the Abbey of Gethsemani was once the home of Catholic writer Thomas Merton and is still home to a small community of Trappist monks. There is something both weirdly instrumental and wildly cliché about writers visiting monasteries. As Brother Benet Tvedten of the Blue Cloud Abbey in South Dakota has noted, "Very few people want to enter monasteries these days, but it seems more and more people want to visit them." It is not unlike the motivation that takes one to Disney World, although instead of seeking stimulation you're trying to escape it.

I went to Gethsemani to gain a different understanding of time, but I came away with a greater appreciation of patience. On our first evening at the abbey, Father Carlos, the monk who served as our guestmaster, greeted us by stating, "What is the main cause of our sins? Convenience. Seeking for ourselves convenience. Ease. Seeking to make things easier. Or entertaining."

There is nothing easy or entertaining about life in the monastery. The prayer schedule that guests are invited to follow (which I did), is rigorous and begins with Vigils at 3:15 in the morning; 5:45 a.m. is Lauds, 6:15 a.m. Eucharist, 7:30 a.m. Terce, 12:15 p.m. Sext, and so on through 7:30 p.m. Compline. The monks of the Abbey sing the prayers. As each day passed and I continued to follow the prayer schedule, I realized: There is little beauty in the way they sing. It is the fact that they come together so many times a day to do it that is beautiful.

This rigorous routine is precisely what protects the monks from the distractions, conveniences, and other entertaining escapes that surround the rest of us in everyday life. The monks keep to the same routine, every day, every year, until death. They dress in the same clothes and eat the same food and share the same largely unadorned space. Much of the literature of monastic life emphasizes that this way of living forces you to confront yourself—your inner demons, restlessness, and wayward thoughts. But this lifestyle also fosters a completely different experience of time, and a different understanding of what it means to wait.

To be kept waiting is generally viewed as a negative experience. Behavioral science research has shown that making someone wait is often used to denote hierarchy, dominance, or power in a relationship. And in many ways, this is the form the monks' waiting takes; they subordinate themselves and their time to God's work. The monks wait because they are listening for the voice of God, and they accept that it might take a lifetime before they hear it. Other religious traditions have waiting built into their rituals of worship; Quakers practice "expectant waiting" during silent meeting, for example. At the heart of these practices is the inculcation of patience and the creation of the habit of *listening*—whether it is for the voice of God or to the concerns of others in your community.

During my week at Gethsemani, I briefly suspended my silence to talk to the very patient Father Carlos. I asked him how he and his fellow monks balanced the demands of daily life, which for everyone at the monastery includes manual labor and other service to the community, with time for contemplation. "Make time every day for silence," he said. "And don't make it a chore. Just sit in silence. This allows you to listen to God." In *Thoughts in Solitude*, Thomas Merton noted that being comfortable with silence and waiting gave one "interior freedom." Although he was writing in the twentieth century, Merton's advice is suitable for our own age: "It is not speaking that breaks our silence," he wrote, "but the anxiety to be heard."

Our anxiety to be heard and liked and retweeted also undermines another human experience inherent in waiting: anticipation. The monks at Gethsemani are not merely waiting to hear the voice of God. They are joyfully anticipating it, and so their wait isn't painful but pleasurable. What happens to anticipation in a world where a second is too long to wait for a video to load and a minute feels like an eternity?

Each of us has a temporal bias—some people look to the past, others always ahead to the future, and still others are more present-oriented. These tendencies influence our behavior, making us more or less likely to delay gratification, for example, or to save for the future. Whatever our individual temporal quirks, our use of personal technologies introduces a new kind of temporal bias, something more extreme than present-orientation: *nowness*.

Years ago, cultural critics began noting and at times lamenting changes in the ways we talk about time. As the digital world began to encroach on analog reality, being "in sync" replaced being "on time." Concerns about instant gratification gave way to demands for speedy anticipation of our needs, and "time-shifting" (for example, recording a TV show to watch later using technologies such as TiVo) became a regular practice. Today our time horizons have shrunk even more, and real-time and live-streaming are the norm. Everyone from Rihanna to the Pope uses real-time social media. Twitter (now X) is, in effect, an enormous experiment in time-use exhibitionism.

The next frontier is technology, fueled by artificial intelligence, that knows what you want before you even ask for it. These anticipatory technologies, such as Google Assistant, employ sophisticated algorithms and old-fashioned data mining of your email, calendars, location, and web browsing habits to show you helpful things "before you even ask," as Google's website says. Much has been written about the trade-off of privacy for convenience inherent in modern technology. Less has been said about what these anticipatory tools portend for the future of waiting. "The right information at just the right time" is what Google promises users. But how much should we trust an algorithm or AI to determine something as amorphous and personal as the "right time" for things to happen?

Consider planning a vacation. There are mundane details to attend to—flights, hotels, places to visit—and then there are qualitative questions about the kind of vacation one wants to have. Adventurous? Relaxing? Most of us would probably use Google for both kinds of tasks, and Google Assistant users would appreciate a brief notice about an upcoming flight delay, for example.

But would you want Google to recommend tourist destinations to you based only on your past habits and consumption? If you purchased books about atheism in the past year, perhaps Google would avoid recommending a visit to a cathedral. And what about once you're on that vacation? Would you want Google to continue to anticipate what you might like to eat, or see, or buy when you are exploring a new place? If you often order Chinese food, Google might helpfully flag every Chinese restaurant for you during your trip—even if you're in Tuscany. An increasing number of people would enthusiastically embrace this kind of algorithmic nudging. Fear of undatabased experiences—experiences not managed or massaged by sophisticated algorithms on platforms processing and managing your preferences in real time—is the unacknowledged phobia of our connected age.

It's worth noting that in the first experience (Googling flights and hotel availability) you are using Google as a means to an end (vacation planning). In the other scenario, Google is using you as an end itself (gathering more information about you that in turn will help its advertising revenue). It's also worth recognizing that the goal of these applications isn't merely your convenience. Google emphasizes personal assistant-style information (reservations, weather reports, flight delays), but if you listen to what Google executives say about their vision for the future, those practical capabilities are merely a foot in the door of far more expansive anticipatory technologies. As a VP for Search at Google told the *New York Times*, "You can just imagine several years down the road, if that personal assistant was an expert in every field known to humankind" (every field except humility studies, evidently). As more people introduce "smart" speakers into their homes, such as Google Home and Amazon's Echo speaker with its Alexa assistant, and smartphone users rely on voice assistants like Apple's Siri, outsourcing planning to digital assistants is becoming normalized, like the fictional assistant voiced by Scarlett Johansson in Spike Jonze's film *Her*, who does everything for her lonely owner including persuade him that she really cares about him. Or, in a darker iteration, the robot-doll companion in the horror film *M3GAN*, which takes its responsibilities toward its human to deadly extremes.

Google and other technology companies want their algorithms and AI, which can take no pleasure in the experience of anticipation, to nevertheless take over more and more of it in the name of convenience. This, they argue, will allow them to engineer anticipation, as Google already claims to do with serendipity. No one is compelled to use these anticipatory services, but given Google's ubiquity, as well as Amazon's leading market share in "smart" speakers, it is worth considering how societies where most people outsource these tasks to technology companies will understand waiting. By outsourcing anticipation to Google, we miss experiencing its pleasures ourselves.

Consider a study of more than 1,000 Dutch subjects that examined the links between happiness and vacations. Researchers found, not surprisingly, that "vacationers displayed greater pre-trip happiness than non-vacationers." That is, the people looking forward to taking a trip were happier than those without vacation plans. More intriguingly, however, they also found that "post-trip happiness did not differ between vacationers and non-vacationers." The positive effects of going on vacation faded quickly for most travelers, even if they reported having a relaxing and enjoyable experience. The researchers theorized that anticipation played a crucial role in explaining this difference; planning, reading about, and arranging the details of a trip was a pleasurable experience for most people. Ultimately, it wasn't the vacation itself that made people happy; it was *anticipating* the vacation that made them happy. Why do we want to make that pleasurable experience more efficient?

Perhaps we are becoming more inclined to outsource anticipation for the same reason we scour reviews on Yelp before we eat at a new restaurant. We love surprises, but not unpleasant surprises. Anticipation is a close cousin of surprise, and when it yields a pleasurable experience our pleasure is heightened by the wait. But when anticipation and surprise yield disappointment, we tend to view the time we spent on it as wasted.

Now that we have so many ways to fill even the smallest increments of time, however, a subtle shift in our psychology of expectation follows. We are more likely to experience waiting as *delay* than *anticipation*. Waiting has become a problem to be solved, rather than a normal human experience. When we are accustomed to easily filling time, opportunities for anticipation, like opportunities for daydreaming, disappear.

Delay is a word that today has largely negative connotations (flight delay, delay of service); it no longer suggests virtue (such as exercising willpower or patience) or opportunity (for reflection or anticipation). It means inconvenience. As a comment on our culture's infatuation with speed and convenience at the expense of delay, Julian Bleecker, cofounder of the Near Future Laboratory, built Slow Messenger, "an instant messaging device that delivers messages exceptionally slowly"—as in, one letter at a time based on how long you hold the device in your hand. Talking to *GOOD* magazine about his device, Bleecker cited as inspiration handwritten love letters of the pre-digital era that often had to cross the globe to reach their intended readers. "I wanted to revisit that experience of anticipation and uncertainty," he said.

Even if we don't embrace Slow Messenger, we can learn something about ourselves when we embrace anticipation. Evolutionary psychologists have noted that the ability to think ahead and prepare for future events confers significant perceptual and cognitive advantages. Anticipation is a kind of preparation for the future. Actively embracing anticipation is also important for one's emotional health. Neuroscientist Antonio Damasio calls this practice the "imagination response," and in many ways it resembles daydreaming in its power to prepare the mind for new experiences. Damasio describes an unusual patient, Elliot, who could rationally think through positive and negative likely outcomes for his behavior, and could experience happiness or disappointment once something happened to him. What Elliot couldn't do was imagine or preview those future feelings. Without a functioning imagination response, he could think about the future rationally, but he couldn't feel it emotionally. As a result, he was usually indecisive or impulsive, which caused him unhappiness.

The experience of waiting forces a negotiation between what philosopher Derek Parfit described as our present and future selves. Our present self wants immediately to devour that Cinnabon pastry we smell wafting through the airport. Our future self needs us to resist it because it will upend our healthy eating goals. This individual struggle has broader social implications. Consider a report in the *Journal of Biosocial Science* which found a link between an increase in American impatience and an increase in obesity. John Komlos of the University of Munich and his colleagues proposed a link between time preference ("a measure of the rate at which a person is willing to trade current pleasure for future pleasure") and obesity. "Individuals with high rates of time preference will consume more high-calorie foods and non-physically active leisure pursuits at the expense of lower levels of health and utility in the future," they concluded. Later studies confirmed this, including a study by researchers at Georgia State University that noted, "Even after controlling for well-known determinants of BMI [Body Mass Index] such as gender, race, education and income, impatience stands out as a major contributor to obesity."

When people experience their time as a valuable and fleeting resource, they become less likely to patiently pursue long-term goals, such as maintaining a healthy weight. Alongside impatience, the Georgia State researchers noted how "technological advances" have "raised expectations for quick satisfaction." Other researchers have found proxies for societal impatience by looking at the decline in personal saving rates, the increase in personal debt, and an increase in gambling.

A society that cannot delay gratification or exercise the patience to plan will have very different approaches to the consumption of natural and human resources, to institutional and professional expertise, and to politics than one that does. On-demand works well for video, but not always for democracy.

Might some of the decline in our society's trust in experts and institutions also stem in part from impatience? Our new technologies encourage us to value the new and the now, which is why, in the realm of public discourse, we value reaction more than deliberation. Like deliberation, expertise takes time to develop and mature, and time to share in the form of experimentation, criticism, scholarship, and teaching. Scholarly websites and online publishing have vastly expanded the reach of expertise, of course, but in a culture habituated to immediate, brief responses, this form of expertise is often drowned in a chorus of louder, less informed voices.

By contrast, a culture that knows how to wait might have an easier time cooperating to solve social problems. Some evolutionary biologists even argue that the evolution of patience was a necessary condition for the emergence of reciprocal altruism. In one study, which examined cooperative and altruistic acts among test subjects with different time-discounting preferences, researchers found that "patient people are indeed more cooperative," something your grandmother might have told you but that is still nice to see endorsed by contemporary social science. Debates will continue to rage among social scientists and evolutionary psychologists about the origins and usefulness of patience in human behavior. But in everyday life, we can all try, however modestly, to shift our individual perceptions and behavior by embracing a more generous sense of anticipation and a healthier attitude about delay, by reframing waiting as an opportunity for daydreaming and idle time rather than an excuse for distraction, and by trying to be more patient with one another. Such advice does at least have a long pedigree. Aristotle is said to have warned, "Patience is bitter, but its fruit is sweet."

If you go to Disney World today, there is one ride you will never have to wait in line for: the Carousel of Progress. Personally designed by Disney for the 1964 World's Fair in New York, this audio-animatronic contraption highlights the technological innovations of the twentieth century. The carousel is a revolving theater that moves around a central stage at a stately pace; on the stage, animatronic robots depict scenes of family life from the early twentieth century through to the "present." Judging by the robots' clothing in the final scene, the present seems to end somewhere around 1983.

During the performance I experienced, the carousel rattled, creaked, and groaned, and it was clear that my iPhone has more computing capacity than the cheerfully aging robots on stage. But this paean to past technology—gramophones and iceboxes, radio and television are all celebrated—suggests a kind of gee-whiz optimism about the future, one captured by the song with which the robots serenade you: "It's A Great Big Beautiful Tomorrow!"

The Carousel is not the most scintillating of attractions at Disney World. As one reviewer on Yelp put it, it's "recommended for people who like to kick-it old school." When I was there, within five minutes of the start of the performance, many people, impatient at the plodding pace of the ride, began trying to find their way out of the darkened, rotating theater. The carousel came to a heaving halt, followed by a gruff announcement over the loudspeaker: "You may not get up during the performance! Please stay seated during the performance!" The would-be escapees grumbled but obeyed. Clearly this celebration of twentieth-century technology could no longer hold the attention of the technologically savvy denizens of the twenty-first century. Among the audience members not trying to leave I saw many celebrating our great big beautiful tomorrow by checking their phones.

Does it matter that we no longer like to wait? Our demand for immediate answers is voracious, and not entirely a bad thing. It drives innovation and commerce and has allowed for communication on a scale barely imaginable a century ago. But being human means coping with the liminal, those in-between moments of life when we must endure uneasy or uncomfortable experiences, from boredom during a meeting to bearing witness to another's illness, to simply being stuck on a bus.

We're used to ticking the tiny box before we download something— the one that reminds us that "terms and conditions apply"—without ever reading the fine-print specifics. But we would do well to explore more thoroughly how those terms alter the conditions of everyday experience. "Every man rushes elsewhere and towards the future, since no man has reached his own self," Montaigne warned many centuries ago. Arriving at oneself, figuring out who you are, what you love, what you think about your world and the people in it—these are experiences that require time, patience, boredom, daydreaming, and anticipation to discover. Without those things, we're just killing time.

CHAPTER 5

* * *

The Sixth Sense

uman beings are adept at imitation. We copy things we like, whether we find those things in the natural world or among our fellow human beings, and after copying them we tend to share them with others, which spreads ideas around to even more people. In the 1970s, evolutionary biologist Richard Dawkins gave this practice a name, the neologism *meme*, which combined the word "gene" with the Greek word *mimeme*, which means an imitated thing. It's an idea passed around socially (like a virus) in the way our genetic material is passed around reproductively.

Today the word "meme" conjures something slightly different, and entirely grounded in online culture: an ironic, or nihilistic, or sometimes absurd take on a recent cultural or political moment ("OK boomer," Dark Brandon) that inexplicably catches on and spreads across the Internet. It can be a phrase, or an image, or a word, but in every case it is the distillation of a powerful emotional response to something; even thoroughly overused memes ("Yaaaas queen!") retain traces of their original emotional appeal.

Memes also capture and comment on complicated feelings:

depression, anxiety, and other unwelcome emotional states that have become increasingly more common among Gen Z, who also happen to be some of the Internet's most avid users and its most creative cohort of meme-generators.

Today many of us (well, old people) also still use the more rudimentary emoji to express our feelings as frequently and unthinkingly as we use Google to answer our questions. The international group that approves new emojis, the Unicode Consortium, approved thirty-one new emojis in 2022, with thousands already in circulation.

Emojis have spawned a subgenre of odd research, such as the study of more than five thousand users of the online dating site Match that found, "Single people who use emojis have more sex than those who abstain." The study included a helpful "emoji-to-intercourse" graph and fun facts, such as that men are more likely to use the "kiss" and "heart eyes" emojis while women prefer the more traditional "smiley." Similar research by the Kinsey Institute later confirmed these findings. The "2022 U.S. Emoji Trend Report" from Adobe revealed how younger generations of Americans are even willing to let emojis do their emotional dirty work: The study found that "32 percent of Gen Z'ers have ended a relationship with someone by using an emoji."

Both memes and emojis are forms of emotional punctuation, a creative attempt to translate one aspect of the human experience—our emotional lives—to the screen, and in this they have been successful. But they are also a symptom of our broader struggle to reconcile human emotions with the limitations of the technologies through which we express them.

Emotions are wonderful, perverse, messy things. Scientists, psychologists, and philosophers have been arguing about their definitions for centuries and still can't agree. Emotions are intensely subjective and thus notoriously difficult to measure; what makes you laugh might make me cry. As well, we are only moderately successful at identifying our own feelings. Self-deception is one of the constants of human nature.

Increasingly, we mediate the expression of our emotions through the devices and software we rely on. Email, text messages, social media, video chat—each platform demands of us different expressions of ourselves, and also encourages us to present and perform different versions of ourselves. Soon, we will have a new range of technologies at our disposal—sensors, monitors, and software—that will make use of what technologists know about human emotion to track, nudge, persuade, and sometimes even coerce us. Instagram now nudges users with prompts, popping up "Can we help?" if the algorithm detects a user spending too much time marinating in self-harm or other worrisome images and videos. (Whether or not such prompts are effective is debatable.) We are performing emotion constantly, both online and IRL. Those performances can have the unintended effect of leaching meaning from strong expressions of emotion.

Describing the constant, digitally-mediated "lovefest" with others, writer Caitlin Macy noted, "These days a text to, say, my dog walker, saying that I'll be home by 5, is promptly hearted. The exterminator 'loves' having my business and cares about me." Clicking on a friend's post to "love" it is now "an act that we often perform automatically and that can conceal very different emotions—envy or fear, or perhaps, a tepid approval with the hope of the same in return," Macy writes. These new rituals of emotional expression clearly serve a social function, but do they make us feel more connected to one another?

Considered through the prism of emotion, our new technologies are starkly different from our old ones; their intimacy and persistence in our everyday lives is genuinely new. Your television couldn't take your pulse, but your Kinect gaming system can now track your heartbeat, and a sensor embedded in your employee ID badge can monitor the inflections of your voice when you speak to a colleague. Perhaps we should demand an emotional impact statement from designers of technologies such as affective computing, persuasive technologies, and sensor-based software applications, akin to the environmental impact statements developers must submit before they break ground on a new building. Then we might have a better grasp of how their encroachment will impact our emotional landscape.

What the clock did to time technologists hope to do to emotion—regulate and regiment it, measure and monitor it. But taming the temperamental beast that is human emotion might prove a challenge contemporary technology cannot—or perhaps, should not—try to overcome.

I once attended a conference at a university in Southern California that included a motley group of architects, urban planners, scholars of community, and historians. We debated how technology is transforming public space and sociability and agreed on the importance of cultivating a sense of place in a world defined by mobility and instant communication.

An encounter with a student from the audience left a deep impression on me. This friendly, thoughtful young man told me about a female acquaintance who had been a Facebook friend of his since freshman year. He had never really thought about categorizing their relationship; she was one of hundreds of social connections in his vast network, a person he might see in passing on campus but never engage in conversation.

One day on his way to class he bumped into her, and she recognized him. "We started talking," he told me. "And after a few minutes I realized I was just sweating like crazy. I had no idea why. It wasn't even hot. I was just sweating. It was so weird." He paused and with a rueful look said, "It wasn't until much later that I realized maybe I was sweating because I kind of liked her and was off my game because she was right in front of me." He hadn't recognized his body's signals when they flooded him, and it surprised him when he figured out what they meant.

As we saw in chapter 2, with our need for face-to-face communication, we are physical animals, and we express our emotions in physical ways. We sweat, flinch, and grin. We send unspoken messages during the most fleeting interactions—"naked little spasms of the self," as sociologist Erving Goffman called them. Many things which our bodies understand we would find difficult to articulate, and these physical responses are a crucial part of our emotional repertoire. Some say these feelings are the basis of intuition. We will always be able to "know more than we can tell," as philosopher Michael Polanyi wrote of this form of "tacit knowledge."

Such knowledge is difficult, if not impossible, to measure, which is why so much mystery surrounds the question of what emotion is. René Descartes attempted to define emotion in terms of basic passions common to all human beings; for Descartes these were gladness, sadness, love, hatred, and desire. As we saw in chapter 2, Charles Darwin devoted a great deal of time to studying the expression of emotions in men and animals through his observation of facial expressions and bodily movements. More recently, psychologists including Jerome Kagan have noted how we infer our emotional states and the emotions of others through actions, biological reactions, and verbal descriptions.

Neuroscientist Antonio Damasio draws a useful distinction between *feelings*, which are "inwardly directed and private," and *emotions*, which are "outwardly directed and public." Our feelings, Damasio argues, are "mental experiences of bodily states" and require a level of consciousness that other animals lack. Feelings require a sense of identity or self. "Only with the advent of a sense of self do feelings become known to the individual having them," Damasio writes. Emotions can be consciously acknowledged and unconsciously experienced (that vague feeling of annoyance whose source you can't identify). They vary in range and intensity depending on the individual (the Stoic shedding a single tear vs. the hyperventilating diva).

We are adept at ignoring our own emotions. "Life is the art of being well deceived," essayist William Hazlitt remarked, and the greatest deceptions are the ones we perform on ourselves. Failures of self-knowledge are commonplace, which is perhaps a factor in why we tend to elevate "reason" over "feelings" when assessing our own and others' actions. The heavily used Myers–Briggs personality test places feeling and thinking on opposite ends of the spectrum in its typology.

Our sometimes skeptical reaction to displays of emotion is linked to a fear of manipulation. Emotions can be faked—indeed, entire industries rely on it—and part of being human is navigating others' emotional signals to distinguish truth from fiction. We all perform this emotional labor, whether at work or among our social peers, smiling at something we might dislike to fit in or offering a white lie to soothe a distressed friend. As part of its broader "science" of "guestology" (Walt Disney World's term for "the study of the people for whom we provide service"), Disney employees—or cast members, as Disney calls them—train in the art of delivering happy feelings to visitors. Cast members are supposed to remain relentlessly cheerful while performing their duties and are equipped with an arsenal of tactics gleaned from a weeklong training session.

But forced happiness and force-feeding happiness to others has consequences. A study on emotional labor found that most Disney employees engaged in "surface acting," faking feelings of happiness while suppressing genuine feelings of anger and resentment, which, not surprisingly, leads to "emotional exhaustion." This hasn't deterred other companies from adopting Disney's strategy.

Disney is on to something. We experience our emotions as unique, but they are also socially influenced. In an experiment conducted by psychologists Stanley Schachter and Jerome L. Singer, test subjects were dosed with an unnamed substance (it was epinephrine, a form of synthetic adrenaline) and either told that heart palpitations were a possible side effect or told nothing at all. The researchers then placed the subjects in a room with actors who were scripted to act either angry or euphoric.

The results suggest the power of emotional influence. Subjects who were not told of the side effect of the drug and were in the room with the angry actor reported feelings of anger; those in the room with the happy actor reported feelings of euphoria, whereas those told of the side effect were largely unaffected by the actors' behavior. Schachter and Singer concluded that when people experienced "a strong physiological response, the origins of which were not clear, they interpreted their own feelings as either anger or euphoria, depending on the behavior of other people who supposedly were in the same chemical boat." In other words, they took their cues from those around them. Contemporary technology provides countless, compelling opportunities for such emotional contagion, but on a vast and virtual landscape.

If emotions use our bodies as their theater, as Antonio Damasio puts it, what happens when that theater becomes virtual?

As the late Stanford University psychologist Clifford Nass found, spending a lot of time in mediated environments undermines our ability to read others' emotions. When Nass showed heavy technology users (those who reported above-average use of the Internet on a questionnaire) pictures of human faces or told them stories about people, they had trouble identifying the emotions being expressed. "Human interaction is a learned skill," Nass concluded, "and they don't get to practice it enough."

As more of our emotional experiences occur when we are online, we expand the quantity of our connections, more easily finding like-minded people with whom to share our feelings. At the same time, we lose the physical cues that define face-to-face interaction and so risk undermining a crucial skill: how to read another's intentions and understand another's feelings. This leads many of us to assume the worst about other people's motives.

Although we all recognize rationally that there is another human being on the other side of the screen, it's becoming clear that our use of technology privileges certain emotional responses over others. A study published in the *Journal of Computer-Mediated Communication* explored whether insulting comments influenced people's perceptions of an article, which was a neutral explanation of emerging technologies such as nanotechnology.

The results were startling. Rude comments didn't merely polarize readers; they changed their perception of the story. The researchers noted how "social reprimands such as nonverbal communication and isolation can curb incivility in face-to-face discussion." By contrast, "the Internet may foster uncivil discussion because of its lack of offline, in-person consequences." They argued that this form of bad manners online, which they call "the nasty effect," may impede the "democratic goal" of public deliberation online.

Contagion of this sort spreads rapidly. The swift punishment of supposed villains meted out on social media platforms like X is a particularly virulent form. Our new "digilante" justice provides instant, global retribution for the mistakes that people used to be shamed for only by their close peers. Public shaming on social media has even trickled down to children. A white cheerleader in Virginia lost her college acceptance and scholarship after a classmate, who is biracial, posted a years-old Snapchat clip in which she used a racial slur. She was fifteen years old at the time and apologized to her classmates when the video resurfaced. Nevertheless, as the classmate who launched the social media mob boasted "with satisfaction" to the *New York Times*, "I'm going to remind myself, you started something . . . You taught someone a lesson."

Or consider the emotional impact of anonymous apps such as Yik Yak, which allow users within certain geofenced areas, especially college or high school campuses, to post hyperlocal jokes about the dining hall or recent parties, all anonymously. Not surprisingly, Yik Yak, initially launched in 2013 and relaunched in 2021, creates challenges for institutions. Although many of the posts are mundane, others are sexist, violent, racist, and demeaning. One university professor discovered that students had been using Yik Yak to message back and forth during her lectures, trading sexually degrading insults about her. "Ourself behind ourself concealed—Should startle most," the poet Emily Dickinson wrote, long before the rise of anonymous apps. We have granted our concealed selves great power to demean.

As we saw in the discussion of waiting, some of this change in behavior is the result of the way we as a culture understand time. Bodies process different emotions at different speeds. A study by researchers at the Brain and Creativity Institute at the University of Southern California used brain-imaging techniques to examine how feelings such as admiration and compassion arise. After participants in the study read real-life stories meant to evoke compassion and admiration, it took participants between six and eight seconds to respond to narratives of others' pain or expressions of virtue. As one of the researchers noted, "If things are happening too fast, you may not ever fully experience emotions about other people's psychological states." Technology favors one velocity: now. If we spend most of our time mediating our emotions online, we lose opportunities to reflect on our feelings. "Our study shows that we use the feeling of our own body as a platform for knowing how to respond to other people's social and psychological situations," one researcher said. "These emotions are visceral, in the most literal sense."

The lives we live on Facebook, Instagram, Yik Yak, or Twitter are virtual, not visceral; they favor immediacy while often encouraging more negative than positive feelings. One study in Germany found the "rampant nature of envy" and other "invidious emotions" among heavy users of Facebook. "The spread of ubiquitous presence of envy on social networking sites is shown to undermine users' life satisfaction," the researchers found, creating a "self-promotion–envy spiral," where users were "reacting with even more self-promotional content to the self-promotional content of others." We hear many stories about the positive effects of social networking (of which there are many); only recently has research begun to show that the effects are more complicated when it comes to our emotional responses to social media.

Coming to grips with these complications is crucial at a time when technology companies are becoming more adept at manipulating our emotions. In an interview with *Technology Review*, Cameron Marlow, then head of Facebook's Data Science Team, said, "For the first time, we have a microscope that not only lets us examine social behavior at a very fine level that we've never been able to see before but allows us to run experiments that millions of users are exposed to." More recent revelations made by former Facebook employee turned whistleblower Frances Haugen detailed how the company's engineers designed its algorithms to favor content that exhibited more heightened emotions, particularly anger. "Anger and hate is the easiest way to grow on Facebook," she told the British Parliament in 2021. Only after years of granting more weight to angry reactions did Facebook change its algorithms to deemphasize anger in favor of reactions such as "love" and "sad."

Engineers at the dating website OKCupid programmed the site to send its users matches that it claimed were "exceptional" but that were in fact weak—all for the purpose of finding out if you would believe the assessment and pursue the match. Not surprisingly, most users did. We are nothing if not suggestible when it comes to love, even if Cupid's arrow has been replaced by OKCupid's algorithm. That algorithm knows a lot about your emotional life. Some OKCupid users were horrified to learn that the site kept every single message they sent to a potential date. The users felt, well, *used*. OKCupid founder Christian Rudder was unmoved by such concerns; as he boasted on an OKCupid blog, "We Experiment on Human Beings!" The company announced in 2023 that it would be using ChatGPT to create "match" questions for the dating app, hinting of a future where AI might run experiments on human users as they search for true love online.

Facebook and other social media are like the now-banned pesticide DDT. DDT killed disease-carrying mosquitoes (a good thing), but it also weakened the shells of birds' eggs, rendering them so fragile that baby birds could no longer survive inside them. Platforms like Facebook give us an efficient way to keep in touch with far-flung connections (a good thing), but they weaken other things in the process, such as our accountability for our behavior and our willingness to take emotional risks. Writing about her gradual estrangement from talking to people on the telephone, writer Caeli Wolfson Widger noted, "It's an instinctive preference, seemingly shared by everyone I know, for the low emotional risk of communicating via words on a screen."

Empathy, by contrast, is an act of imagination and will. It demands that we try to see the world from another person's point of view. Empathy is grounded in our physical bodies—our observations of others' movements and facial expressions. "When we see a stroke aimed, and just ready to fall upon the leg or arm of another person, we naturally shrink and draw back our own leg or our own arm; and when it does fall, we feel it in some measure, and are hurt by it as well as the sufferer," the economist Adam Smith wrote. This is not the same action as consuming another person's experience when they post it online. That feeling is more akin to sympathy or pity or envy or, in some cases, *Schadenfreude*.

Today we practice a cunningly efficient form of "click-here" empathy. A few weeks before Christmas one year, I overheard (eavesdropped on, actually) a conversation at a nearby restaurant table. "Oh, it's really easy," one woman was telling another. "You just go to Target's website and you can gift socks to the homeless." I have no idea if this was true, but it seemed plausible. One-click charity and other fundraising platforms such as Kickstarter have raised a lot of money for many good causes. But we should acknowledge that these technologies foster different levels of emotional engagement than going to a homeless shelter or other charity organization and spending time, face-to-face, talking with people and dedicating one's time to a cause.

As we spend more of our waking hours online, there is growing evidence that we need to encourage this kind of offline engagement. Studies such as one from the University of Michigan Institute for Social Research found, "College kids today are about 40 percent lower in empathy than their counterparts 20 or 30 years ago," and the steepest decline coincided with the rise in adoption of smartphones. "The ease of having 'friends' online might make people more likely to just tune out when they don't feel like responding to others' problems, a behavior that could carry over offline," one of the researchers noted. The COVID-19 pandemic exacerbated these trends. A 2022 study of college students found even greater decreases in empathy, as well as increases in anxiety and depression, in the aftermath of the pandemic.

Professor Jeff Hancock of Cornell University, whom we met in chapter 2 describing the "motivational enhancement effect" of communicating online versus face-to-face, has spent years studying how our online behavior impacts our offline behavior. He tests whether the tenets of social learning theory, which posits that practicing certain behaviors and actions can lead to their performance in real life, also apply to the behavior we practice online. One of his studies asked participants to pretend to be extroverted either in a Word document, which researchers told them would not be made public, or on a live blog that would. The bloggers were far more extroverted, leading Hancock to conclude that acting in certain ways online reinforces the behavior and thus makes it "more likely to be followed in real life."

The question of how our online activities influence our offline behavior is a subject of considerable (and controversial) research; there is a vast subgenre of studies investigating the effects of violent video games on behavior, for example. Much of this research wrestles with the question of whether or not exposure to simulated violence desensitizes people to its expression elsewhere. A consensus is beginning to form that although playing violent games doesn't lead people to commit acts of violence (indeed, the violent crime rate has declined even as more people play violent video games), it does lead to something less easily measurable than violent crime: an erosion of empathy. "The research is getting clearer that over the long term, people with more exposure to violent video games have demonstrated things like lower empathy to violence," Dr. Jeanne Brockmyer, a clinical psychologist, told the *New York Times*. Brockmyer found that the regions of the brain linked to empathy "become muted by violent images when teenagers are exposed to them over long periods of time."

Do these new, higher levels of exposure to often violent images make us less thoughtful overall? Do our heavily mediated lives distance us from the emotional impact of our actions? Such questions are already being asked about professions that rely on their employees to practice a certain amount of thoughtfulness and empathy in their work. Consider nursing. In 2012, four students in a college nursing program in Kansas thought it would be funny to post pictures on Facebook of themselves holding a human placenta. All four students were expelled, but later reinstated. In California, two nurses were disciplined for posting images on Facebook of a dying man in their care. And two Wisconsin nurses were fired after posting a patient's X-rays on Facebook showing "a sexual device lodged in a man's rectum."

Most nurses are not posting highlights of their patients' emergency room visits online, but it is worth examining the environment and culture in which nurses have been trained for clues to the behavior of these outliers. The literature about nursing features an increasing number of articles admonishing nurses to be cautious in their use of social media, and organizations such as the American Nurses Association have developed social media principles and guidelines for nurses.

At the same time, nursing schools have begun substituting simulations for the real-life clinical experiences that nurses used to receive during their training. Rather than tend to real patients, nursing students use video games, screen-based simulations, and in some cases sophisticated medical mannequins to hone their skills. Massachusetts General Hospital in Boston has a Sim Man as well as simulated birthing and simulated infant training centers, for example.

The Laerdal Company sells Nursing Anne, a "patient care manikin" with interchangeable genitalia and an "articulating IV training arm" to hospitals and medical schools across the country. Although useful for training, the manikin looks nothing like a real person. Its "skin" is unblemished and hairless, its eyes permanently closed and its mouth permanently agape. It is an eerily perfect patient. As more and more nursing students spend more time with simulators and less with human patients, however, we need to assess the impact such training has on their ability to empathize. The real-life patients are people who squirm and smell and yell and are rarely entirely hairless.

Simulation technologies have led to some measurable educational gains for nurses, but a scholarly review of simulation techniques used in nursing noted the lack of evidence of its impact on *patients*. "I get worried when I hear about nursing programs that want to replace the person-to-person clinical experience with increased hours of simulation," Jennifer Elison, chairwoman of the nursing department at Carroll College in Montana, told the *New York Times*. Today's nursing students grew up using Facebook and other social media, spending their free time in simulated worlds on the screen. Their nursing training offers them ample opportunity for technology use and sophisticated simulations, all of which ideally improve their technical proficiency. Such proficiency aside, nursing is a profession that also demands a great deal of empathy—the "care" part of "health care professional." Face-to-face experience with other human beings is central to developing a healthy respect for and empathy toward others.

Of course, we live in an era that has embraced the outsourcing of emotional labor just like we've embraced the elimination of social pleasantries in the name of efficiency. For a small cost, we can hire people to manage our children's birthday parties and care for elderly relatives. We can delegate even the smallest domestic jobs to people on TaskRabbit. When sociologist Arlie Russell Hochschild, who has studied outsourcing, interviewed an executive assistant about her job the woman told her, "My boss outsources patience to me." (It is perhaps worth noting that professions that often require more emotional labor are female-dominated, and that the digital assistant programs now in widespread use, such as Alexa and Siri, originally featured a woman's voice as the default choice.)

Emotional efficiency can be had in the form of ToneCheck, a software program that acts as a kind of "emotional spell-check" for your email messages, alerting you to "excessive displays of anger, sadness, or insensitivity." In a highly competitive and unstable economy, where workers feel pressure to squeeze productivity out of nearly every hour in the day, we begin to measure emotions in terms of their efficiency and usefulness.

Technology companies are keen to have us embrace this new digital-emotional experience. At a technology industry conference in 2015, Abigail Posner, Google's Head of Strategic Planning, outlined early efforts in this area. She described our human ancestors sitting around a campfire trading stories. "YouTube is our global campfire now," she declared. "Brands have tapped into this!" Then she cued up an advertisement for a Toyota minivan that she claimed distilled the essence of humans' need for "deep play." In other words, she sees no problem with commodifying crucial human interactions and experiences, especially deeply meaningful or emotional ones, and is eager to enlist technology in this effort. More recently, Think with Google featured an interview with Mary Beech, an executive from the fashion brand Kate Spade, who boasted that the company's efforts to craft more empathetic marketing spots had increased consumers' viewing time of Kate Spade ads on YouTube by thirty-nine seconds, with a 500 percent increase in their earned views. Google's understanding of people's emotional states was central to this effort. "We worked with our partners at Google to learn that confidence, love, happiness, and success are key emotional need states for beauty fans on YouTube," Beech enthused. "When someone in our target audience was searching for something like 'How do you build self-esteem?' we could respond with a relevant and meaningful ad."

Technology companies discovered that the "elegant instruments of their mutual estrangement," as the British economist E. J. Mishan described new technologies of mediation more than forty years ago, don't just give us *access* to new kinds of behavior; they *create* new behaviors and new emotional connections, from low-level mimicry like TikTok dances to new group formations, not all of which are beneficial to society, like social media-organized flash mobs that engage in mass retail theft.

Technologists are also creating devices to enact emotional experiences in the physical world that initially occur online such as Like-a-Hug, the "wearable social media vest" designed by students at MIT. As Melissa Chow, one of the inventors, described it, the vest "allows for hugs to be given via Facebook, bringing us closer despite physical distance." When someone "likes" a photo or status update on the wall of a person wearing the vest, it squeezes him or her in a hug. This allows us to "feel the warmth, encouragement, support, or love that we feel when we receive hugs," Chow says.

Even those of us not eager to don a Facebook-enabled hugging vest have strong emotional connections to our technologies. A study conducted by the University of Maryland's International Center for Media and the Public Agenda examined college students from ten countries, including the U.S. and China, about their feelings when they abstained from all technology and media use for twenty-four hours. A student from Argentina said he "felt dead" without his normal diet of media; another from Lebanon described the experience as "sickening"; and an American claimed she was "itching like a crackhead" for her phone. The researchers found that the craving students expressed wasn't only for the information their technologies provided, but also for the physical device itself. A Credit Suisse Youth Barometer report found that among people in their teens and twenties, smartphones were "more important to them than anything else—even 'meeting friends,' 'Facebook,' or 'vacationing abroad.'"

Emotional attachments to technology are not new. As Luke Fernandez and Susan J. Matt describe in their book *Bored, Lonely, Angry, Stupid: Changing Feelings About Technology from the Telegraph to Twitter,* an early Bell telephone ad promised, "There is no need to be lonesome with a telephone in the house" since the technology "banishes loneliness." The difference today is that much of our technology is ubiquitous but often hidden and untethered to place or time.

Given our love of (or is it our addiction to?) our devices, our acceptance of emotional outsourcing, and our embrace of mediated experiences, it's possible that we are moving away from a world that values empathy toward one where many of our emotional experiences are vicarious. After all, it's so much more efficient to figure out how other people feel by scrolling through their feed than it is to talk to them.

In the opening scene of Ridley Scott's 1982 film *Blade Runner*, two men sit in a room, one the focus of a futuristic lie detector machine. The questioner is trying to determine if the man is a human being, like him, or a dangerous off-world replicant that must be destroyed. The interrogator's questions are "designed to provoke an emotional response," he tells the man being questioned. The man seems nervous and defensive; he gets twitchy when asked if he would help right a tortoise that had been flipped on its back. Then he's asked how he feels about his mother. "Let me tell you about my mother," he says, and shoots his human interrogator.

The movie was set in the year 2019 and played on anxieties about a future where it might be difficult to distinguish between the human and the nonhuman. The replicants' inability to experience genuine empathy or remorse was the mark of their inhumanity (and the justification for their lives as slave laborers). But the movie also featured a newer, experimental female replicant named Rachael; her designers implanted false human memories in her so that she could express emotions. As a result, she was more successful at eliciting sympathy from humans, even from the Blade Runner whose job it was to hunt down and "retire" replicants.

Early efforts to enact machine intelligence, such as the eighteenth-century Mechanical Turk, which delighted audiences worldwide with its creator's claim that the machine played chess (when in fact there was a human hidden inside the contraption), put people inside machines to awe and inspire, and in many cases fool, others. Today we put machines on ourselves to better understand our own feelings. Enlightenment scientists urged people to know the world using their five senses. Contemporary technologists think those five senses are no longer sufficient and that in many cases they lead us astray; with new sophisticated technology, we can extend our senses. Ours is the era of the "digital sixth sense," as the CEO of Qualcomm, a smartphone chip manufacturer, described it. The enthusiasts of this new world embrace ubiquitous computing, where technologies aren't merely smart but also emotionally aware. "Ubiquitous computing: has to embrace emotion as an essential element in pursuing its next level of development," argues scientist and AI researcher Egon L. van den Broek. In this future, technology is less an extension of man than an invasion of him.

For people who fret about the deterioration of face-to-face human interaction and other human skills, researchers like Alex Pentland at MIT have a simple solution: stop worrying and let the machines do the work. Network science and complementary devices make concerns about deteriorating social skills obsolete, they argue. Our devices will soon read our own and others' signals for us—and they will do it better than we ever did ourselves. "The ability to continuously and universally measure human behavior will provide us with the ability to engineer our lives to an extent never before imagined," Pentland wrote in his book *Honest Signals.* Indeed, what Pentland and his colleagues want to create is a kind of Freud Machine that would make the id ever visible, a technology that allows people "to monitor the flow of information within their group, thereby transforming unconscious and tacit knowledge into open, conscious information." Pentland and his ilk believe the Enlightenment's emphasis on individual rationality might have flattered us for a few hundred years, but it was misguided. We like to think of ourselves as rational individuals, Pentland says, but we are in fact "typically dominated by social network effects"—which is to say, we're a herd of the irrational and easily cajoled.

To measure our emotions, technologists are devising a host of gadgets and sensors that track our behavior. Pentland's lab at MIT examines

the data from sociometric badges that track individuals' physical movements using an embedded location sensor, accelerometer, proximity sensor, and microphone to record what the wearer is saying at all times, as
well as information on people's consumer purchases and their posts on
social media. "Just from data such as how much a subject walks around,
who they call and when, and how much and when they socialize face-to-
face, a user's personality type and disposable income can be estimated,"
Pentland notes. "We can also see when someone is coming down with the
flu or is depressed."

Most smartphones already or will soon feature the same capabilities
for behavioral capture. One of Samsung's Galaxy smartphones included
a built-in heart rate monitor. Students at Stanford University developed
a modified gaming controller that uses signals from the body's autonomic
nervous system, which controls breathing and heart rate, to determine
players' emotions. Working with professor Gregory Kovacs, and under-
written by corporate sponsors such as Texas Instruments, students are
also developing sensors for cars to monitor the alertness and emotions
of drivers—a boon for vehicle manufacturers and insurance providers.
As for the privacy implications of driving a car that is monitoring your
emotional state, Kovacs, like most technologists, isn't troubled. "While
some might see it as an invasion of privacy, I think operators of such vehicles should give up some privacy in exchange for the trust of human lives
placed in their hands," he told a reporter.

Bank of America, an early adopter of sensor technology, gave its
employees sociometric badges to study their interactions at work.
The sensors "measure actual behavior in an objective way," a human
resources executive at the bank told the *Wall Street Journal.* Other
companies have performed similar studies measuring employees'
movements, tone of voice, and conversational patterns with coworkers; ironically, given the high-tech nature of these experiments, companies tend to discover that their most productive teams are the ones that
engage in the most unmediated, face-to-face communication.

Even employees who work from home can be subjected to moment-by-moment monitoring. In 2020, London-based *New York Times* reporter Adam Satariano described an experiment he performed on himself, by downloading employee-monitoring software from an Indiana company called Hubstaff. "Every few minutes, it snapped a screenshot of the websites I browsed, the documents I was writing and the social media sites I visited. From my phone, it mapped where I went, including a two-hour bike ride that I took around Battersea Park with my kids in the middle of one workday." The amount of detail available to measure an employee's productivity is considerable. "Broken down in 10-minute increments, the system tallies what percentage of time the worker has been typing or moving the computer mouse," wrote Satariano. "That percentage acts as a productivity score."

Such systems are already in widespread use. A 2021 study published in *Organizational Behavior and Human Decision Processes* estimated that "organizations are expected to introduce over 83 million wearable behavior-tracking devices. A recent survey of 239 large corporations indicated that, in fact, 50% were tracking non-traditional employee metrics like their emails, social media activity, biometric data, and with whom they met and how they used their workspaces."

When Pentland first started his sensor-based research more than a decade ago, he referred to his work as "reality mining." Forget how people say they feel on surveys or what they claim they will do in interviews, he said; track their behavior. His ambitions for the data he would glean from these patterns were vast. "You can really see things in a way that you never could before—a God's-eye view," he told a reporter about his work. As for privacy, we have to "come to a new deal," he said. "It doesn't do any good to stick your head in the sand about it."

The "new deal" has been struck by many employers. Under the guise of "wellness" and improving workers' happiness, companies monitor Slack messages and employee emails, send daily surveys requesting information about employees' moods and emotional states, and issue sensor-laden badges that monitor things like heart rate. "We've moved beyond just, 'I want you to get 10,000 steps every day,'" the director of health and wellbeing for Blue Cross Blue Shield Michigan told the *Wall Street Journal*. "I want you to have an improved mental state." The Toronto-based software firm Receptiviti sells its product to numerous companies in Canada and the U.S., who use it to scan workers' communications for signs of emotional distress. "These intangibles can be measured," Receptiviti's CEO told the *Wall Street Journal*; he describes the software as integral to the development of "corporate mindfulness."

It's appealing to think that micropatterns of our behavior, once captured and measured, can give us insight into ourselves. We are understandably eager to believe that sensors can objectively measure our highly subjective emotional experiences and teach us about ourselves. But like horoscopes, sociometers and other sensor technologies offer just enough vaguely specific information to seem plausible, and like good astrologers, the technologists who translate that information offer us reassurance about our emotions and their source.

What kind of world will this be once we have outsourced the job of emotional reflection? Pentland says this will be a "sensible" society where "everything is arranged for your convenience." No need for the inefficiencies or embarrassments of a bad second date. One day soon, perhaps, with sensors embedded on our bodies or phones, they will signal us within moments whether our affection is likely to be returned or not, and we can move on. As a representative from Google told a reporter, "We like to say a phone has eyes, ears, skin, and a sense of location . . . It's always with you in your pocket or purse. It's next to you when you're sleeping. We really want to leverage that." Eventually the sensors will take on the work of emotional awareness for us, if we let them.

But this outsourcing of awareness might also make it more difficult to deal with the things we can't control, like the passage of time and the physical infirmities that attend it. We cannot control our circumstances like we control the images on our screens, and by growing to rely on technologies to tell us how we feel, we could experience a kind of mass emotional deskilling. Already we're outsourcing our memories to Facebook, our curiosity to Google, and our sense of direction to the GPS embedded in our phones. Should we also accept the idea that these technologies provide us with a more rational opinion of ourselves, one that promises certainty about our emotional lives?

The question isn't hypothetical. Consider the Moodies app, which uses the built-in microphone on your computer or smartphone to analyze "the full spectrum of human emotions" based on its analysis of the tone and inflection of your voice. You can leave the app running all the time, and it promises to deliver a new emotional analysis right to your smartphone every fifteen to twenty seconds. Its developers foresee a future where everything from iPhone's Siri assistant to your Internet-connected car uses "emotional analytics" to figure out how you're feeling in real time. The Moodies app might not be entirely reliable; one mischievous user, reviewing it on the Google Play store, claimed that when he fed it a recording of Hitler's speech announcing the invasion of Poland, the app interpreted Hitler's mood as "friendliness."

The popularity of wearable technologies like the Oura ring, a "smart" device that uses sensor technologies to monitor body temperature, blood oxygen levels, heart rate, breathing, and sleep, promises improved health but has also changed our understanding of how we experience and perform emotion. The "Oura Experience," as the company's website promises, offers "deeply personal guidance" for its wearers. "Feel the *magic* of self-care," the website claims. A new feature, Oura Circles, allows you to share your data with your social circle. "Caring is the new sharing," Oura's website declares, likely an unintentional homage to Dave Eggers's dystopian novel *The Circle*, about a rapacious technology company whose motto is "Sharing is Caring."

We need to consider how much of our emotional lives we are prepared to reveal. These technologies are potentially digital wolves in sheep's clothing; marketed as servants of self-awareness, they may just as easily become technologies of unwanted exposure. There is a "gotcha!" quality to their findings that has the potential to disrupt social interaction. You didn't realize you disliked that colleague until your sociometric badge picked up your increased heart rate and shallow breathing every time he spoke at a staff meeting. Your wife told you she loves you, but your smartphone registered her tone as nervous and possibly dishonest. "We are measuring more than ever and are not far off from continuously tracking our emotions," says Gary Shapiro, president of the Consumer Electronics Association and someone who has a keen interest in convincing us this technology is necessary and imminent. But as Shapiro also acknowledges, technologies that promise to reveal emotions will almost certainly prompt the development of technologies that can conceal them—"emotion-cloaking devices" that would turn every day into a hall of emotional mirrors or screens.

Writing in the 1950s, philosopher and writer Alan Watts noted, "In each present experience you were only aware of that experience. You were never aware of being aware . . . I can feel what is going on inside my own body, but I can only guess what is going on in others." Tomorrow's technology might eliminate the guesswork behind what others are feeling. Another person's sensor data would reveal how they felt; your own data might reveal that you often misidentify your own feelings.

But leveraging that goes well beyond giving you feedback on your own feelings in real time. It has also been the focus of so-called persuasive technologies: software and devices that aim to prod us into performing certain behaviors.

The unacknowledged patron saint of persuasive technology is twentieth-century psychologist B. F. Skinner, whose theory of operant conditioning, which emphasized the causes and consequences of observable behavior, presaged much of the rationale behind today's persuasive technologies. "It is not enough to 'use technology with a deeper understanding of human issues,' or to 'dedicate technology to man's spiritual needs,' or to 'encourage technologists to look at human problems,'" Skinner argued. "What we need is a technology of behavior."

He meant technology that could make the private experience of being human available for others to observe. Skinner was writing at a time when the most technologically sophisticated device for doing this was a mood ring. Today, however, we have technologies that allow us to engage in what persuasive technology pioneer BJ Fogg calls "mass interpersonal persuasion." These persuaders range from the sensor-based technologies like sociometers that we've discussed to features of websites that encourage consumers to act in particular ways, to persuasive games that aim to help people quit smoking or eat healthier food.

Arguably, our technologies are better persuaders than people because they are devilishly persistent, can manage large volumes of information, can offer anonymity—or at least the illusion of it—and have long memories. But these persuasive technologies also pose new challenges for social norms, privacy, intimacy, and our emotional lives.

A health insurance company, for example, would find persuasive technology's ability to influence individual behavior appealing. Certain behaviors such as smoking and engaging in unprotected sex have health risks. Theoretically, access to this kind of information about people's behavior could help an insurance company provide customers with tailored services to improve their overall health. But what if you fancy smoking a few cigarettes now and then and don't want your insurance company knowing about it?

Now, consider the power of technologies that persuade us to do things that *aren't* good for us. In her study of the machine gambling industry, cultural anthropologist Natasha Dow Schüll notes how the "enchanting perceptual distortions" that designers program into gambling machines keep gamblers playing long past the point of good sense. "Industry designers actively marshal technology to delude gamblers," she writes, and the designers themselves confess to getting hooked quickly even though they designed the manipulations themselves. When Schüll asked an executive from the company International Gaming Technology why some machines seemed to compel users to keep playing more intensely than others, he suggested she read B. F. Skinner's textbook on operant conditioning.

As any good politician or salesman knows, tools of persuasion—repetition, invocations of authority, and appeals to emotion—have always been available to us. But today's persuasive technologies pose ethical challenges that old methods of persuasion did not.

For one, they lack transparency. A politician kissing a baby is clear about his efforts to convince you of his trustworthiness. Persuasive technology, by contrast, has embraced opacity. A contributor to an early persuasive technology conference noted how sensors that monitor heart rate and speech are ideal because they can be made ubiquitous and unobservable. "The proposed processing scheme enables the design of persuasive technology of which the user is not even aware that it is there," the writer noted with approval, and the design and marketing choices made by most persuasive technology companies reflect the preference for keeping such technologies hidden.

Persuasive technologists also want to create "electronic environments that are sensitive and responsive to the presence and mood of people." This ambition seems innocuous enough when it means giving your local coffee shop permission to read the mood signals from your wearable sensor so management knows you prefer low lighting and soft music. Such "ambient intelligence," as technologists call it, is also anticipatory and personalized, a seeming boon for users.

But as some ethicists have noted, these technologies have already enabled the rise of "persuasion profiling," wherein technology companies compile individual profiles based on people's responses to certain persuasion strategies. Do you tend to buy books recommended by critics or ones recommended by your friends? Amazon knows—and so it understands how to subtly tweak its recommendations for you. Should governments, insurers, and other corporations have access to information about your vulnerability to specific emotional appeals?

In 1999, technology ethicists Daniel Berdichevsky and Erik Neuenschwander challenged designers of persuasive technologies to voluntarily adopt a golden rule of persuasive technology: "Ask yourself whether your technology persuades users to do something you wouldn't want to be persuaded to do yourself." They developed eight further principles for persuasive technology design, including, "Persuasive technologies must not misinform in order to achieve their persuasive end." Facebook ignored this principle when it manipulated its users' news feeds, and OKCupid trod on it when it altered the romantic matches it sent its users. Berdichevsky and Neuenschwander also urged creators of persuasive technology to "consider, contend with, and assume responsibility for all reasonably predictable outcomes of its use."

As Bran Knowles of Lancaster University, a technologist who has worked on persuasive apps in the UK, noted, "The issue of whether the techniques of so-called 'persuasion' are indeed manipulative has escaped serious scrutiny within the computing community." Knowles calls out various leaders in the field, whose approach to the ethics of their work amounts to: Trust us. "Users are expected to accept the basic premise of the 'correctness' of the designers' chosen end behavior; and the designer is not expected to have rigorously debated the preferability of this end behavior," Knowles noted. For a field that claims to care about the outcomes of its "end users"—that is what they call us—persuasive technologists' approach to ethics is highly unpersuasive.

Persuasive technologies could just as easily be viewed as subversive technologies—subversive of human intention and manipulative of human emotions. In *Man's Search for Meaning*, Holocaust survivor and psychiatrist Victor Frankl argued, "Everything can be taken from a human being but one thing: the last of the human freedoms—to choose one's attitude in any given set of circumstances, to choose one's own way." Increasingly we use technology to mediate not only our choices but also our emotional experiences and feelings. The companies that make these technologies don't want you to just smile and hum along to an ad that urges you to "buy the world a Coke," as an old television commercial once did. They want to know when you are thirsty. Once they know that, as Antonio observed in Shakespeare's *The Tempest*, you will "take suggestion as a cat laps milk."

We express emotions in many ways, but when we speak of our deepest feelings, we locate them in our hearts. As the previous section's description of sensor technology notes, your heart rate can reveal how you really feel about the people you spend time with. A smartphone app called PPLKPR (short for "people keeper") promises to track and "auto-manage" your relationships using GPS and a heart rate-monitoring wristband that computes "when you're feeling emotional." The app claims to be able to measure subtle changes in heart rate that signify stress or anxiety; it then uses that information to "determine who should be auto-scheduled into your life and who should be removed." PPLKPR will defriend and unfollow those annoying acquaintances and people who cause stress in your life. "We only have so much emotional bandwidth, and limited time," the app's promotional materials state. "Let PPLKPR find the ones that work for you."

The app's creators, Lauren McCarthy and Kyle McDonald, are artists whose previous work explored the limits of technology use, and they acknowledge both the utopian and dystopian elements of their work. The app could be useful for people on the autism spectrum, they noted, giving them feedback about their own and others' behavior, but it could also hasten the commodification of friendship if it makes our feelings for others available to third-party advertisers.

When McCarthy and McDonald tested PPLKPR on undergraduates at Carnegie Mellon University, the responses were enthusiastic. One young man told *Fast Company* that he was thrilled to have an excuse to ignore people who stressed him out, while another woman, assessing the data, remarked, "Maybe I shouldn't hang out with Mark. Maybe he's kind of a dick."

When we outsource the emotional labor of everyday life to apps and algorithms and bodily sensors, we are making technologies that effectively act as emotional mercenaries. This is the logical conclusion of a trend that has already replaced empathy with "click-here" charitable efficiency, emotions with emoticons, and the self with the selfie.

And yet we remain emotionally hungry, perhaps because of the wealth of virtual alternatives rather than despite them.

When our feelings become data, and our world is guided by sensors rather than sensitivity, our experience is no longer unique; it is mere information. Our emotions can be made *useful* to others when transformed into data, but at what cost? And at what risk to the standardization of emotional experience? In the 1950s, French novelist Albert Camus observed of his contemporaries, "A single sentence will suffice for modern man: he fornicated and read the papers." Today we might say, "He fornicated and checked his phone." And his phone could have predicted the fornication.

Rather than grapple with the meaning of emotions or why we experience them, our technologists seem eager to understand them so that they can exploit them. Consider the field of affective computing, described by one of its founders, Rosalind Picard of MIT, as computing that "relates to, arises from, or influences emotion." Affectiva, a company that grew out of work done at the MIT Media Lab by Picard and her former collaborator Rana el Kaliouby, is building emotionally aware machines that can recognize facial expressions related to emotions. As Kaliouby told *The New Yorker*, "I think that, ten years down the line, we won't remember what it was like when we couldn't just frown at our device, and our device would say, 'Oh, you didn't like that, did you?'"

Affectiva's original mission was to develop programs that would help people who had trouble reading facial expressions, such as those on the autism spectrum, better understand others' emotions. But they quickly pivoted to marketing to corporations that were eager to use the software to test the effectiveness of their advertisements. "Every time you pick up your phone, it gets an emotion pulse, if you like, on how you're feeling," Kaliouby said in an interview. "In our research, we found that people check their phones ten to twelve times an hour—and so that gives this many data points of the person's experience."

These data points are lucrative, which is why many technology companies have already applied for patents for a range of emotion-sensing technologies, from gaming devices to sensor-enabled ATMs. These emotion-sensing machines won't get us any closer to understanding what emotion is, but they will facilitate the monetization of emotion. As Kaliouby observed, businesses want to capture and utilize our "positive moments." "So if you set a goal to run three miles and you run three miles, that's a moment," she said. "Or if you set the alarm for six o'clock and you actually do get up, that's a moment. And they monetize these moments. They sell them. Like Kleenex can send you a coupon—I don't know—when you get over a sad moment."

Technology companies treat our emotions like the law used to treat wives—as property, a kind of digital coverture. But the things technology encourages—efficiency, predictability, repeatability—are not the things we necessarily value in our emotional lives. Our technologies monitor our emotions, ostensibly to give us greater control over them, but this is part of a larger shift in the way we are choosing to see the world and live in it: more like machines. Your computer keyboard is a guide to this way of understanding our feelings. There is always a *control* button; we issue *commands*; we can *delete* what we no longer want; we *escape* when we mess up. We always have an *option*.

Many of our new technologies and software platforms elevate sensation over emotion, immediate reaction over patient reflection. At times this is precisely what is needed—live blogging a severe storm or exposing cruel bullying to the swift, harsh light of the online world can be useful. At other times, our use of these technologies seems more like a replacement for feelings than an augmentation of them, a search for affirmation and convenience rather than an opportunity to connect and express empathy. Living in a world where we "like" everything but emotionally connect to nothing is akin to the difference between a clammy handshake and a warm embrace.

Many years ago, computer scientist Joseph Weizenbaum warned of the dangers of trying to make computers do the things that humans ought to do. "It has nothing to do with what computers can or cannot be made to do," he argued. Some things were simply not suited to the worldview that computers created. "Respect, understanding, and love are not technical problems," he wrote.

They are feelings.

Our technologies shape our styles of feeling, just as language shapes our way of understanding the world. The poet W. H. Auden said that poetry was the clear expression of mixed feelings. Sensors, software, and sophisticated technologies promise a world where the confusions of human emotion are more smoothly resolved, where a data-driven, tech-enabled "sixth sense" seamlessly eliminates the ambiguity and self-deception that has so long ruled our emotional lives, and where our emotions can find clear, instantaneous, and global expression. This world of emotional transparency has a cost: the flattening of depth and complexity in our lives. That is the troublesome thing about human emotion: sometimes, we like our feelings mixed.

CHAPTER 6

＊ ＊ ＊

Mediated Pleasures

Sarai Sierra's wanderlust came on suddenly. Until she decided to embark on a solo trip to Turkey, the thirty-three-year-old married mother of two sons had never traveled abroad. She lived in the Silver Lake neighborhood of Staten Island, NY, where she was a part-time receptionist at a chiropractic clinic, and she had recently completed a photography class at the College of Staten Island. She joined Instagram, where she posted images of the urban skyline, bridges, and sunsets, and quickly formed friendships with other users.

Sarai Sierra wasn't particularly intrepid. She didn't need to be. It was absurdly easy to plan a trip from Staten Island to Istanbul. Sierra booked places to stay on Airbnb and arranged to meet in person with people she had been following on Instagram. Once she arrived in Turkey, she messaged and video-called friends and family back in the U.S. and posted a stream of updates to her various social media accounts. One friend later told a reporter it was like Sierra had never left home.

Sarai Sierra traveled alone, but in the twenty-first-century sense. She could constantly connect to everyone she knew back home. Like many travelers today, Sierra communicated as much or more with family and friends as she did with local people in the places she visited. She traveled happily within a digital bubble that seemed to grant her a degree of safety. Even when she was physically alone, her iPad and cellphone ensured she was never truly disconnected.

But Sierra never boarded her return flight home on January 21, 2013. Eleven days later she was found near the crumbling walls of the Sultanahmet, Istanbul's old city, bludgeoned to death. Many months later Turkish police arrested a vagrant and sometime paper collector who confessed he was high on paint thinner when he encountered Sierra. When he tried to kiss her, she bloodied his nose with her cellphone and continued to fight him off until he bashed her head repeatedly with a rock. He took the brown leather jacket she was wearing and sold it at a secondhand market nearby. He threw her cellphone and iPad into the sea. Her friends and family were left grieving her death and wondering if the technologies Sierra relied on to enhance her travel experience had fostered a mindset—a false sense of security—that might have inured her to the risks that face a woman traveling alone.

Sarai Sierra's violent, tragic fate was unusual, but her experience of travel was not. Like many of life's pleasures, travel is now often mediated through the technologies we use to plan, document, and remember our experiences of it. The benefits of mediated adventures are undeniable: convenience, ease, and a democratization of travel. Technology tames the "elsewhere"—and makes more vivid the places we see when we do travel to them. At Yellowstone National Park visitors can view the wonders of *Yellowstone*, an IMAX movie that features close-ups of grizzly bears, an eagle's-eye view of the park, and a majestic soundtrack. As the theater advertises, "Until you've been to Yellowstone IMAX Theatre, you haven't had the complete Yellowstone experience." The real park is prosaic by comparison. You might spend days in it without spotting a single large mammal other than your fellow tourists.

The way we experience pleasure—whether that pleasure is travel, food, sex, art, music, or literature—has changed dramatically in a short time. The extent to which technologies of mediation—cellphones, tablet and laptop computers, and the software and apps we use with them—saturate our lives and interpose on our daily decision-making marks a new moment in human experience. We don't use these technologies merely to find the nearest coffee shop, museum, potential sexual partner; we use them to make judgments about what is and isn't worth experiencing at all.

When we do decide to pursue pleasurable experiences, we document them relentlessly. Park rangers in Lake Tahoe, California, had to issue an official warning to tourists to stop trying to take selfies with the bears feeding on spawning kokanee salmon at Taylor Creek. "It's becoming a safety issue," a spokesperson said about the many people rushing toward the bears to capture an image of themselves. A survey conducted by Ford Motor Company revealed that a significant number of people admit to doing things for the sole purpose of posting them to social media. When asked "Have you ever, even once, done something just so you could post about it on social media?," 16 percent of the respondents said, "Yes, more than once" and 13 percent said, "Yes, once."

In the airline industry, "delethalization" is the term given to the complicated process of reducing risk in an aircraft through modification of the materials and construction—making seat cushions out of nonflammable fabric, for example, or adding emergency lighting in the aisles. Pleasure in the digital age has undergone a similar process of delethalization. Our individual pleasures have never been so widely shared, distributed, and displayed. We can vicariously witness ever more intense and risky acts, as videos on YouTube attest. The stream of images available has facilitated the mass consumption of private experience. This creates feelings of connection, but it is a false intimacy.

Mediation also homogenizes pleasure; it makes it more conformist, as if every experience has passed through the same handful of filters, as if everyone is doing, filming, and sharing the same challenge or stunt. As we increasingly seek to publicize our pleasure and invite others to scrutinize our experiences, the platforms we use encourage us to sanitize them to meet the expectations of viewers. Your celebration of pleasure is filtered through the same apps and platforms as everyone else's and consumed in the same way, as a constant flow of curated ephemeral moments. This is a timid form of pleasure, and its rise suggests a collective retreat from experience that might be too intense, too real, too risky, too uncontrollable, too physical, or too nonconformist. Pleasure is delethalized so that it can be more easily digested and shared in digital form. This transforms pleasure; it becomes, sometimes unwittingly, a more engineered experience, one that elevates control over risk, search over serendipity, algorithms over whim, convenience over privacy. Or, to put it another way: the greatest transformation of pleasure, compared to past eras, is our willingness to allow so much of it to become data.

———

Pleasure is a peculiar beast. Jeremy Bentham declared it one of mankind's "sovereign masters," and Sigmund Freud believed pleasures were the "watchmen of life." For Freud, the pursuit of pleasure, or "pleasure principle," as he called it, is the driving force of the id, tempered only in time by the development of the ego, which enforces and tames the pleasure principle with a "reality principle" that recognizes limits to one's appetite.

Today we are governed by a *virtual* reality principle, as many of our daily pleasures are filtered through, monitored by, and governed by our use of technologies and software and driven not by a hidden id but by the ego's desire for approval and attention. Basic human needs and pleasures—food, shelter, sleep, sex, amusement—now take analog and digital forms. People who self-track can monitor their sleep and sex lives with apps such as Sleepcycle and Bedpost; food enthusiasts post pictures of their latest meals on Instagram; and users post images of their own and others' aspirational homes on sites such as Pinterest. Pleasure—our own and others'—has become a form of mass entertainment.

It has also become a means to an end; the end is "sharing" with the platforms that sell our data to the highest bidder, which in turn becomes a marker for future assumptions about us that will be made and acted upon by businesses, advertisers, governments, researchers, and countless other data brokers. These are new highwaymen along a road that used not to have interlopers. In every era pleasure coexists with efforts to control it. Historically the control of pleasure was done (and still is) by religious institutions, the state, and the family, among others. Our pleasures are still monitored and controlled by these traditional regulators, but we have added digital platforms including Meta and Google.

Our pleasures are reduced to data that become a digital portrait of the human urges Freud was so keen to understand. You might understand yourself as a loyal Midwestern sports fan and friend with a healthy libido, but to the companies that track your pleasures you are merely a twenty-five-year-old man from Dubuque who enjoys streaming porn on Saturday afternoons and sharing sports news with your fantasy football friends. You are the pleasures you consume—and the data trail you leave behind.

As the time we spend moving in and out of the virtual world increases, so much so that many people have ceased even to acknowledge the distinction, we've embraced a new pleasure principle. Today's pleasure principle is governed by the pleasure of technology use itself—the sleek devices and clever apps that make so much of what we want instantly available—and the feelings those technologies foster. Buying these devices and using their software makes us feel like we are part of the progress that technology companies are always promising us in their advertisements. Owning the latest device offers us a feeling of knowingness, belonging, and connection—and who doesn't want that?

But pleasure doesn't exist in a vacuum. Time and place shape what we decide to want and how we decide to meet those desires. A good bear-baiting isn't much appreciated these days, although it was popular in Shakespeare's time. Doubtless, future generations will view our binge-watching of television shows on streaming platforms as similarly odd or masochistic. And even those pleasures considered universal—the satisfactions of a good meal or great sex—are in their particular and often peculiar fulfillment unique to each age.

Our acceptance of mediated pleasure brings with it a growing reluctance for and mistrust of undatabased experiences and an anxiety about things that haven't been recommended, rated, or ranked by others. If a restaurant meal is eaten but not reviewed, a purchase made but not rated, do we remember it differently from other pleasures? In a short span of time we've come to trust the aggregate "wisdom" of millions of strangers weighing in on a favorite restaurant, even as we know that many of those reviews are paid for, or generated by bots, or posted by people who never set foot in that restaurant. Yet there is something satisfying about having our own preferences vicariously, virtually, endorsed.

And an increasing number of our pleasures are vicarious. The screens through which we consume an increasing amount of our pleasurable experiences elevate vision and sound over touch, smell, taste, and place. It's as if the injunction we give curious toddlers around breakable objects—"Look with your eyes, not with your hands"—has become the slogan of pleasure in our age. Perhaps that's why we've embraced the phrase "touch screen" to describe our technologies, invoking that deeply felt human desire to touch and feel things to understand them. We still crave tactile connection, even in our mediated pleasures. But as Stanford University neuroscientist Robert Sapolsky has argued, "Unnaturally strong explosions of strong synthetic experience and sensation and pleasure evoke unnaturally strong desires of habituation." As we get used to such "artificial deluges of intensity," Sapolsky argues, we may weaken our ability to notice less intense—but no less important—moments of everyday experience, those "fleeting whispers of pleasure" about which poets and novelists have written for centuries.

Pleasure—and our memory of it—is more intense when it is connected not only to sight but also to sound, taste, and smell. It is the difference between feeling your lover's hand on your skin and looking at your lover's naked selfie. Today we can do both. How does having that option change the way we understand either experience? And what happens when we no longer bother separating the pleasure we experience from the devices and databases through which we filter it?

To understand a new place, you must smell it. One of the great pleasures of travel is experiencing the weird odors and new sounds of a foreign land: the sharp scent of a new city's tap water, telephones whose rings sound odd to your ears or police sirens whose syncopated wails seem off-key, coffee that feels unusually thick on the tongue. Even small sensory experiences yield long-term memories, like the ones that led Henry James to describe the city of Venice as a "repository of consolations" for those who love it.

Today our repository of consolations isn't our sense memory, but the images on the smartphones we carry with us wherever we go. We don't need consolation; we have Instagram. With GPS-enabled phones and constant access to social media, we are never alone while traveling. We can text a relative from halfway across the world and update our status while climbing Mount Kilimanjaro. Our technologies alleviate the anxiety of exploring new and unfamiliar places, something captured in an advertisement from United Airlines. The ad features a business-man, jacket and briefcase flung aside, earnestly taking a selfie with an exotic island destination in the background. "Faraway. Friendly," reads the tagline.

Of course, the faraway isn't always friendly, which is what gives travel its special thrill. Or at least, it did. Most of what counts as travel today is in fact tourism, a different sort of beast. "Whereas travel is about the unexpected, about giving oneself over to disorientation, tourism is safe, controlled, and predetermined," write Amherst College literature professor Ilan Stavans and *Habitus* editor Joshua Ellison. Contemporary technology is tourism's ideal handmaiden; it promotes control, convenience, and safety and promises to alleviate anxiety. It places the safety net of contact in the traveler's hands if the adventure goes awry. An overeager climber trapped on a mountain is no longer abandoned to his wits and the elements; he summons a rescue helicopter with his satellite phone. Adventurer David Roberts views the "epidemic" of such search-and-rescue operations for inexperienced backcountry explorers (or "yuppie 911s," as some rescue workers refer to the distress calls) as evidence of a profound shift in attitudes about exploration. Dilettante day-trippers now view dangerous rescue not as a rare luxury but as "an inalienable right."

The tourist craves predictability and convenience; the traveler understands that, like a grace note in music, anxiety is a small but important part of travel, and that being removed from one's regular routine is precisely the point of getting away. "In the best travel, disconnection is a necessity," writes novelist and travel writer Paul Theroux in *The Tao of Travel.* "It is a good thing that people don't know where you are or how to find you."

Theroux cites the example of twentieth-century explorer Peter Matthiessen, who, in his quest to see the snow leopard on the plateaus of Tibet, went weeks without any contact with friends and family back home. Even when letters did reach him, he refused to read them, reasoning that whatever message they contained risked "spoiling this chance to live moment by moment in the present . . . encouraging delusions of continuity and permanence just when I am trying to let go." Contrast this sensibility with a survey by Royal Caribbean cruise lines, which found that the average family on vacation for a week made more than two hundred social media updates; some people admitted to posting on Twitter and Facebook more than fifteen times a day during their vacations.

"Cyberspace intercourse vitiates general escapism," British adventure traveler Dervla Murphy wrote in the *Guardian.* Murphy has explored nearly every continent and believes a sturdy pack animal is far more useful than a laptop computer or smartphone; the pack animal creates the need for extra food and water and securing them forces you to get to know the locals. By contrast, technology creates the temptation to remove oneself to more familiar pleasures or entertainments from home rather than immersing oneself fully in a new place. "Concentrate on where you are, deriving your entertainment from immediate stimuli, the tangible world around you," Murphy urges. That is: stop staring at a screen or you'll miss out on what's right in front of you.

Long before screens mediated travel, airplanes, trains, and automobiles offered the opportunity to accelerate and tame the experience. In many ways the car has transformed the travel experience more thoroughly than wireless Internet connectivity has. Journalist Paul Salopek, who is currently on a decade-long, 21,000-mile "Out of Eden" walk retracing the path of the earliest human explorers, has noted the inescapable presence of cars across the globe and the way they transform the experience of walking. By contrast, he finds something "mesmerizing" about "traveling through the world at three miles per hour—the speed at which we were biologically designed to move." Walking puts him in a "meditative trance that must be primordial." An advertisement for a Chevrolet Traverse SUV encourages a different form of contemplation of the natural world. Amid a backdrop of rugged mountains, the ad reads, "Explore the great outdoors from the comfort of the great indoors," advice that suits well the images of the car's plush interior and large built-in GPS screen.

This paradoxical impulse to explore the wild outdoors in comfort and safety dovetails nicely with technology companies' desire to eliminate the unpredictability of unmapped space. Technology companies are eager for us to embrace the worldview those platforms foster, a worldview that values efficiency and a seamlessly engineered experience of travel. As well, companies such as Google and Apple make maps not only to provide information to us but also to glean information *about* us as we travel. As cartographer Lucy Fellowes reminds us, "Every map is someone's way of getting you to look at the world his or her way." Technology companies' maps are a way for them to get a good look at us; consider the sometimes bizarre images of people captured by Google's Street View cameras as they map the world's roads.

Or consider the Findery app. Founded by Caterina Fake, who was also one of the founders of Flickr, Findery allows people to leave virtual notes about physical places they have visited. Fake credits a particularly languorous hike through the Northern California redwood forests for inspiring the creation of the app. "It was a beautiful moment," Fake told the *New York Times*, so beautiful she wanted to "leave a note in this place, so whenever I come back here, and for other people who are here, this moment will be preserved." She wanted to make a public scrapbook of her feelings about her experience, and she views Findery as a way to "fill in that sense of wonder" that people are eager to experience in new places. "I'm sitting here in the courtyard of this conference center in San Francisco," Fake said. "Make San Francisco interesting to me."

Encouraging people to experience wonder in new places is surely a good thing, but Findery's sensibility is different from the one that has guided travelers for centuries, which couldn't exist in a world without on-demand digital technology. It is a sensibility notable for its self-centeredness and entitlement and profit motive more than for its desire for exploration. "Make this city interesting to me" places the burden of exploration on someone or something other than oneself. Findery's ethos suggests that one's hopes should never turn into disappointments. If the city isn't interesting, it's not because you weren't intrepid enough to explore it; you were simply using the wrong app.

Like many Silicon Valley companies, Findery cloaks its purpose as a moneymaking enterprise in the gauzy rhetoric of self-fulfillment: "These are real people, these are real places, these are real stories," Fake told *Entrepreneur* magazine in 2013. "It's got a lot of soul." Of course, these things were real before Findery tried to monetize them, and we are not told how the app verifies that the people and stories it promotes are real.

Findery is perfectly suited to our age. Our understanding of search is driven by web-crawling algorithms and sophisticated technological surrogates such as Google's maps and GPS. The pursuit of adventure for national glory or even for its own sake is nearly defunct, the expeditions of explorers such as Peter Matthiessen and Ernest Shackleton now historical footnotes or Wikipedia entries.

Now that travel is so rigorously self-documented, the bar is set quite high for calling something an adventure. Wandering around Tibet for months hoping for a glimpse of a snow leopard is too tame. To be a real adventurer, you must be the first American tween to kayak the Amazon or the first octogenarian librarian to summit K2 and you have to document the experience in real time on social media. As the tag line for one of GoPro's wearable digital cameras urges, "Be a hero."

Most of us aren't "heroes," nor do we want to be. So we don't explore. We pose. We prove that we have been there. We make "photograph-trophies," as Susan Sontag once described, or GoPro videos we post to YouTube. Our relentless documentation leads to a world where selfies at Machu Picchu are as ubiquitous on Instagram as McDonald's is on American highway exits.

Today we admire adventurers such as Felix Baumgartner, who perfectly combined the pursuit of real-time adventure, commercial endorsement, and fame in his 2012 Red Bull–sponsored jump from space. Baumgartner had a GoPro digital camera strapped to his head as he skydived from space so that we could all experience his stunt, and in crucial ways this tiny technology represents much of what has changed about our pursuit of travel and adventure. As a GoPro founder told the *New York Times*, "We realized the bigger opportunity wasn't just making wearable cameras for photographers. It was making wearable cameras for people to photograph themselves." Instead of looking out and capturing what the traveler's eye sees, the GoPro shows the traveler an infinitely more interesting site: himself. YouTube hosts thousands of GoPro videos of skiers, surfers, skateboarders, and cyclists, their grunts and frequent incantations of "Awesome!" forming a leitmotif. One GoPro user filmed himself proposing to his girlfriend at 10,000 feet while skydiving over San Diego.

Technology companies continue to encourage us in this self-documentation with ever more sophisticated editing and filtering features. Kevin Systrom, a cofounder of Instagram, described the site as a "stage" where "you want the tools to be able to put your best foot forward." Indeed, for years now, hotels and restaurants cater to the Instagram aesthetic with signs and design choices meant to appeal to social media users. As *Fast Company* noted a few years ago in an article describing "How Instagram Is Eating Dining," these "experiences [of dining out] are becoming tied up in and formed by the influencer economy" of social media platforms. The trend is also evident in museums and public art displays, such as the Color Factory in New York and the many pop-up art installations (like the Museum of Ice Cream in multiple cities) that seem to exist almost entirely to serve as striking backgrounds for people's social media posts.

Capturing an experience while you are having it alters the way you experience it, as Wendell Berry's poem "The Vacation" describes. It tells the story of a man who films his entire vacation with an older technology, the video camera. On a boat in a river, "He showed the vacation to his camera, which pictured it, preserving it forever: the river, the trees, the sky, the light." Berry pinpoints the man's motivation to preserve the experience: He filmed "so that after he had had it he would still have it. It would be there. With a flick of a switch, there it would be." The poem ends with a sharp reminder of the cost of this documentation: "But he would not be in it. He would never be in it."

When we become habituated to viewing new places through the shrunken images on the screen rather than through our own eyes, we tie ourselves to the mundane world and its devices instead of the new experiences in front of us. A kind of visual fatigue takes hold because of our relentless consumption of such images, the "reality disappointment" many writers have described. Writer Henry Shukman admitted to being disappointed when he first saw the Grand Canyon: "It was so vast, and so familiar from innumerable pictures," he wrote, "it might just as well have been a picture." Many of us have felt this sense of ennui when confronting a landmark familiar to us only through images, an uneasy realization that the reality before us was somehow more diluted, less "real," than we had expected.

After a trip to Pisa, Italy, where she saw hordes of tourists photographing the Leaning Tower from the same few angles, Swiss artist Corinne Vionnet scoured photos on public photo-sharing sites such as Flickr and found that this unintended visual conformity was common at tourist destinations. "I wondered if we were trying to reproduce the image that we already know," she told the *British Journal of Photography*. "Are we trying to reproduce the image of an image?" Her work, "Photo Opportunities," merges hundreds of these tourist photos in transparency layers, producing a surreal montage of recognizable destinations across the globe to question this conformity.

Observers have long worried that images might replace people's desire to experience travel. In *Soundings from the Atlantic*, published in 1859, Oliver Wendell Holmes found the new technologies of stereoscope and stereophoto magical enough to make travel obsolete. Looking at the images, Holmes described traveling "over the vast features of Rameses, on the face of rock-hewn Nubian temple; I scale the huge mountaincrystal that calls itself the Pyramid of Cheops . . . I stroll through Rheinish vineyards, I sit under Roman arcades."

Today, travel writers have noted how in places like Heidelberg, Germany, tourists are eager for a photo of the city's famous castle but too tired to take the steep walk up to its pinnacle. Instead of trekking up, they hand their cameras en masse to their bus driver, who makes the journey himself and takes pictures for the tourists while they wait below. And for those who want the pictures without moving at all, there are new options for high-tech armchair travel. "Virtual armchair travel has never been easier or more satisfying," one writer claimed in a story in the *Wall*

Street Journal about "digital wandering" programs such as Street View on Google Maps.

As we saw in chapter 1, Google's Expeditions field trip programs, available on its Arts & Culture app, claims that "distance doesn't matter" and promises to "whisk your students away to museums, Mars, and more, without leaving the classroom." Meta advertises its QuestPro VR headset by promising that "people will be able to use augmented reality to explore Viking era settlements" and "see, feel and fully experience what life was like" then.

When we do venture forth from our living rooms to travel, we are making our trips more like our everyday lives—saturated with screens. Every item on Royal Caribbean's recent list of "Ten things you've never been able to do on a cruise ship until now" involves some form of technological mediation, from robot bartenders to embedded Xbox Live kiosks to watching "dancing robotic screens" in one of the ship's many WiFi-enabled lounges.

As with any pleasure we choose to mediate, the image begins to seem more satisfying than the unpredictability and hassle of the real thing. And as our technologies become more adept at evoking the sensations created by travel without the inconveniences of actually traveling, we are left with the challenge Elizabeth Bishop posed in her poem "Questions of Travel":

> *Think of the long trip home.*
> *Should we have stayed at home and thought of here?*

A few years ago a friend and I went to the National Gallery of Art in Washington, DC, to see an Andy Warhol exhibit. We were standing in front of one of the displays when a woman gently but insistently nudged us aside so that she could put her cameraphone at eye level with what we were looking at. "Sorry," she said briskly, as she snapped a quick picture before moving on to the next display to do the same thing. As she worked her way through the gallery, snapping images of everything in it, she seemed oblivious to the irony that the exhibit's theme was the manic, perverse world of tabloid newspapers.

Impatient viewers of art are nothing new. In an essay in 1920, the artist Paul Klee lamented, "And the beholder, is he through with the work at one glance? (Unfortunately, he often is)." Research shows that the average person visiting a museum today spends between fifteen and thirty seconds with a work of art. That patron hustling her way through the Warhols is the norm, not the exception; the difference is that in Klee's time, she would not have been able to document the art so relentlessly.

Art is one of the most compelling ways of documenting human experience. As Aldous Huxley observed, "good art possesses a kind of super-truth" because good artists are "endowed with a sensibility and a power of communication, a capacity to 'put things across,' which events and the majority of people to whom events happen, do not possess." Art historian David Joselit calls paintings "time batteries" and "stockpiles" of human experience, and countless works of art immortalize pleasurable human activities such as feasting, bathing, and play. But art also requires something from us. It challenges us to see human experience in a different way.

New technologies prompt novel ways of seeing as well. The telescope brought us closer to the stars and the microscope made the invisible details of our world visible. The stereoscope and daguerreotype and camera and television screen and computer have all aided our insatiable visual curiosity. But in our enthusiasm for the latest ways of seeing with these technologies, we overlook the more subtle ways they disrupt the context of what we see. When you view a painting on your computer screen instead of in a museum, your view is mediated not just by the technology but also by your surroundings—not just the electronic incursions of other programs running on your computer but the tchotchkes on your desk and the pile of dirty laundry sprawled just beyond it. As critic John Berger, writing in the age of television, remarked of this experience, "The painting now travels to the spectator, rather than the spectator to the painting."

Most of us assume that such convenience is an improvement on the past, another chapter in the story of the democratization of art. And in many ways, it is. After seeing an exhibit of Paul Klee's work at the Tate Modern in London, I emailed a friend back in the U.S. about one of the pieces, *Ghost of a Genius*. She was unfamiliar with it but was able to summon its image in a moment online.

And yet, no less an authority than the painter Pierre-Auguste Renoir observed, "The only way to understand painting is to go and look at it. And if out of a million visitors there is even one to whom art means something, that is enough to justify museums." This kind of understanding requires something that many of us claim not to have: time. As Philippe de Montebello, the former director of the Metropolitan Museum of Art, observed, "Most works of art yield their secrets slowly." Art doesn't beckon like a movie screen, videogame, or smartphone app; it must be "approached and given time."

Harvard University art historian Jennifer L. Roberts makes her students spend three hours examining a single painting or work of art before they attempt to analyze it. Skeptical students usually return to tell her that they are "astonished" by how much is revealed when they invest time in patiently looking. "Just because you have *looked* at something doesn't mean you have *seen* it," Roberts notes. She believes that patience is crucial for navigating the modern world. "Where patience once indicated a lack of control, now it is a form of control over the tempo of contemporary life that otherwise controls us. Patience no longer connotes disempowerment," Roberts says. "Perhaps now patience is power."

Spending time looking at great works of art is precisely that—a powerful form of time unmoored from the demands of the immediate present, whose interstitial moments we tend to fill by turning to our smartphones to alleviate micro-boredom. As the critic Holland Cotter writes, "From a digital distance, you see an image. In person, in a gallery, you feel that image breathing." This state of reverie is the opposite of the efficiency and instant review common to our digital age. It is a state of pleasant, almost dreamlike calm, which is why when we describe it to others, we often say we felt "lost" in reverie. What we have lost is the hurried, anxious sense of time passing quickly. It is why great poetry, music, and art are sometimes described as evoking a state of reverie; they leave the viewer and listener with a sense that time has been ever so briefly suspended.

Yet our behavior in museums is beginning to resemble our behavior online, and many museums are happy to encourage the convergence. Ask a dozen people why they take photos of artwork or record live concerts with their smartphones, and most will tell you they do it to remember the experience. Some museumgoers embrace this new reality. The website Culture Themes designated January 22, 2014, the first "Museum-Selfie Day," encouraging patrons of the arts to pose with their favorite works and post them online (it is now celebrated on the third Wednesday of every January). Rapper Jay-Z posted a self-consciously surreal image of himself lounging on a couch in front of an image of Andy Warhol lounging on a couch at the Warhol Museum in Pittsburgh. And many museums, including the Metropolitan Museum of Art in New York, have lifted their restrictions on photo-taking by patrons. "I say hooray," writes WNYC art critic Deborah Solomon. "When we photograph, e-mail, tweet and Instagram paintings, we capitalize on technological innovation . . . Much can be gained. Nothing is lost."

But technology isn't augmenting our memory; in fact, it is blunting it. Research from Fairfield University found that patrons in a museum who took pictures of the art remembered less about it than those who did not take photos. Lead researcher Linda Henckel calls this the "photo-impairment effect" and cautioned, "The camera's 'eye' is not the 'mind's eye.'" "People remembered fewer objects overall and remembered fewer details about the objects they had photographed compared with objects they had observed," she writes. Henckel's original study has been replicated twice by other researchers, most recently in 2021.

Most of us assume that taking a picture will give us something to look back on to remember a particular piece of art—a kind of digital postcard that we create. A student at Williams College who had spent a semester abroad told me she took dozens of pictures at every museum she visited and often goes back and scrolls through the pictures to remind herself of her travels. But she is an exception; researchers have found that the vast, disorganized state of most people's digital photos in fact discourages reviewing and reliving moments. Despite the ubiquity of photo-sharing online, researchers have also found that families today spend *less* time together sharing their photos than they did when images were physical prints displayed in photo albums; few families gather regularly around someone's phone to scroll through thousands of images. Pictures offer exceptional "retrieval cues" for memory, but only if we take the time to look at them; increasingly, we don't.

New ways of seeing and storing also transform how we attribute meaning to works of art. Debates over the consequences of reproduction in art are long-standing, as are extravagant claims by those who invent ways of reproducing it. Louis-Jacques-Mandé Daguerre, whose 1837 images, or daguerreotypes, mark the beginning of the era of photography, said his creation was "not merely an instrument which serves to draw nature" but one that "gives her the power to reproduce herself."

Oliver Wendell Holmes called the photo the "mirror with a memory," and in 1859 he predicted that the "image would become more important than the object itself and would in fact make the object disposable." But praise for the photograph was not universal. "A revengeful God has given ear to the prayers of this multitude. Daguerre was his Messiah," said the poet Charles Baudelaire in an essay written in 1859. "Our squalid society rushed, Narcissus to a man, to gaze at its trivial image on a scrap of metal." As a result, Baudelaire worried, "artistic genius" was being impoverished.

Contemporary critiques of photography have at times echoed

Baudelaire's fear. In her elegant extended essay *On Photography,* Susan Sontag argued that images—particularly photographs—carry the risk of undermining true things and genuine experiences, as well as the danger of upending our understanding of art. "Knowing a great deal about what is in the world (art, catastrophe, the beauties of nature) through photographic images," Sontag notes, "people are frequently disappointed, surprised, unmoved when they see the real thing." This is not a new problem, of course. It plagued the art world when the printing process allowed the mass reproduction of great works of art, and its effects can still be seen whenever one overhears a museumgoer express disappointment that the Van Gogh he sees hanging on the wall is nowhere near as vibrant as the one on his coffee mug.

Other critics have worried about how reproduction transforms our understanding of authenticity and originality. In his 1936 essay "The Work of Art in the Age of Mechanical Reproduction," Walter Benjamin argued that technological change, particularly mechanical reproduction, fosters a new perspective which he called the "progressive reaction." This reaction is "characterized by the direct, intimate fusion of visual and emotional enjoyment with the orientation of the expert." Today, an increasing number of us consume culture through mediating technologies—the camera, the recording device, the computer—and these technologies are increasingly capable of filtering culture so that it suits our personal preferences. As a result, we are more willing to become critics.

While our media for viewing culture encourage us to be critics, they do not require much critical judgment or even focused attention. As Benjamin suggested, "the public is an examiner, but an absent-minded one." Benjamin feared that this avid but absent-minded criticism would lead to a lowering of culture and a public increasingly vulgar and simple-minded in its ability to understand art. "The conventional is uncritically enjoyed, and the truly new is criticized with aversion."

This brings us to another tendency fostered by the mediation of art: an impatience for what art demands. The more convenient our entertainments, the weaker our resolve to meet the challenges posed by difficult or inconvenient expressions of culture. Music and images are now delivered directly to us, and we consume them in the comfort of our own homes. You can see reproductions of major works of art by perusing the Internet; but to what effect? As Benjamin argued, "one of the foremost tasks of art has always been the creation of a demand which could be fully satisfied only later."

This is the difference between the canvas and the screen. "The painting invites the spectator to contemplation; before it the spectator can abandon himself to his associations," Benjamin wrote. "Before the movie frame he cannot do so. No sooner has his eye grasped the scene than it has already changed." The qualities of the canvas—uniqueness, permanence—are the opposite of the screen, which fosters "transitoriness and reproducibility." And the canvas cannot be consumed in one's home, at will. It requires that we venture forth into the world that lies beyond convenience.

Benjamin feared that our impatience would eventually destroy the "aura" of art and eliminate the humility we ought to bring to our contemplation of it. But we haven't destroyed art's aura so much as we have transferred it to something else. Aura now resides in the technological devices with which we reproduce art and image. We talk about our technologies in a way, and grant to them the power over our imagination, that used to be reserved for art and religion, and each device brings with it its own series of individualized rituals. Reproducibility in the age of digitization allows nearly any work of art—paintings, sculpture, literature, music—to be transformed into *information*. And with the advent of AI, this digital information about art can be transformed into novel approximations of art, all generated by machines, not humans. Is the pleasure and meaning we attach to it transformed as well?

The reception of the Google Art Project, launched with great fanfare in 2011, suggests one answer. Offering Google Street View–level tours of many major museums across the world, including the Metropolitan Museum of Art in New York and the Uffizi in Florence, Italy, the project urges us to "Explore museums from around the world, discover and view hundreds of artworks at incredible zoom levels." The project also encourages users to "build your own personalized gallery," add comments about paintings, and "share" them with friends. Like digital music devices' "shuffle" mode, the Google Art Project removes the museum curator's eye and expertise and replaces it with our own—aided, of course, by the behind-the-scenes curation Google itself has already performed in choosing which pieces of art to digitize in the first place. With Google Art Project, you can see only what you like.

Much of the praise for Google's Art Project has focused on how it makes art more accessible, and in the sense that it brought higher-resolution reproductions of art to the masses, it is a success. But embedded in the project's pixelation is another message. Threaded through Google's descriptions of the Art Project are subtle reminders that *this* way of experiencing art is better than the alternatives. Google's "incredible zoom levels" and "gigapixel photo capturing technology" will enable "the viewer to study details of the brushwork and patina beyond that possible with the naked eye." Art critic Jed Perl said the project made him feel more like a dermatologist than an art appreciator. Users might reasonably assume that looking at art through Google's eye is superior to standing in front of the same piece of art in a museum. It is certainly more convenient.

Virtually wandering through the Art Project, Perl noted, "Museum-going is turned into a computer game. The museumgoer is the robot." He takes issue with Google's claim that the Art Project gives access to the world's greatest museums: "A reproduction is a reproduction, even if it is in the highest imaginable resolution and you can move around it with the flick of a fingertip." The Art Project, he argues, produces "the illusion of democratic experience." It is also now much more like a computer game. Visit the Google Arts & Culture page, select a painting and then

"Art Remix," and Google's AI will generate a random image incorporating the style and some of the objects in the original painting, which it will then let you save as "My Artwork" in your Google account.

The encroachment of technology into museums has happened swiftly; it was only in 2011 that the Metropolitan Museum of Art began allowing visitors to use their cellphones to explore the collection and take pictures, for example. But as more people become habituated to having their viewing pleasure met at home, on demand and mediated by technology, institutions that display art are attempting to compete with the screen for our attention.

In cities around the world, the Van Gogh Immersive Experience invites visitors to "step into a painting" by viewing wall-sized projections of images of Van Gogh's sunflowers or donning VR headsets to walk through *Starry Night*. In 2011, the New Museum in New York hosted "Carsten Holler: Experience," an "art world amusement park," as one reviewer described it, that included upside-down goggles, a sensory-deprivation tank, and a 102-foot indoor slide (as well as the signing of a thorough personal injury liability waiver). Glenn Lowry, the director of the Museum of Modern Art in New York, has argued that museums should "shift away from passive experiences to interactive or participatory experiences, from art that is hanging on the wall to art that invites people to become part of it." The Cleveland Museum of Art reimagined itself for the digital age by unveiling galleries where visitors can use facial recognition software to match their faces to items from the museum's collections or create movie-trailer or comic-book versions of the museum's large medieval tapestry of the myth of Perseus.

Museums now have sophisticated social media strategies, describe how their work will translate on multiple platforms, and boast of having a "digital first" mindset, as one curator described her institution's approach to the *New York Times*. "You want the way people live their lives to happen in the museum," said Carrie Rebora Barratt, the Met's deputy director for collections and administration.

Do we? A large portion of our daily lives has already been colonized by technology as we constantly look down at our smartphones and computers. Shouldn't museums, by contrast, be bastions of "look up" experiences, places where we set aside the way we usually live our lives and expose ourselves to something different—perhaps even challenging or uncomfortable? We know museums are good for us. One study by Stephen Kaplan at the University of Michigan found that museums serve as "restorative environments." Another study by Daniel Fujiwara at the London School of Economics and Political Science discovered that museum visits have positive impacts on people's self-reported happiness and health.

In a much-debated opinion piece in the *New York Times*, writer Judith Dobrzynski argued that museums are making a mistake by emphasizing participatory art experiences rather than focusing on cultivating appreciation of art for its own sake. "Looking at great art actually is an experience on its own—or should be," she wrote. "People may be losing that ability, given the current environment, but should museums hasten its demise? I don't think so."

What Dobrzynski is describing is frustration with the way mediation further conflates the pleasures of art with entertainment. Art demands something from us. Entertainment does not; we seek out entertainment to give something *to* us. Critics have commented on this misunderstanding for generations. "Cultivated philistines are in the habit of requiring that a work of art 'give' them something," philosopher Theodor Adorno complained in 1951. Today we want art to give us the same thing our technologies do: instant seamless access to our preferred experiences.

But art also should demand something from us: a willingness to set aside our own preferences and submit to another person's vision. The capitulation of the museum to digital technology suggests that in an image-based culture, art will only be valuable insofar as it can be marketed as entertainment. If we don't pause to consider the consequences of this choice, we will become a society with a million Instagrammed pictures but without much memory, a society that expects immediate replication but one that does not sustain the difficult labor of transmitting culture from one generation to the next.

––––

In the image, the young couple stands in the foreground, with water and the remains of a beautiful sunset behind them. They look like they have just paused on their way home from a day at the beach—she is in a bikini and cut-off shorts, her long hair still damp; he is bare-chested. He is holding their flip-flops in his left hand while his right hand cradles her face as he leans down to kiss her. She stands on tiptoe to receive his kiss. Captured by a photographer on the beach in Santos, Brazil, it is a tender scene—save one element that also makes it a thoroughly modern one: in the woman's right hand, raised and angled to capture the precise moment of their kiss, is a cellphone, with which she is taking a picture.

In 2014, the most Googled question in the world was "What is love?" We searched for the answer to this question five times more than we searched for "What is science?" In a sign of our continued enthusiasm for mediated leisure, the most Googled question in 2022 was "What to watch?"

In years past we asked Google for advice on "How to kiss" more than we did for any other activity, including "How to survive." In a short span of time, we have accepted the interjection of technology into our most intimate moments—not only in search of love but also to satisfy our lust. Writing about his students' avid use of dating and hookup apps, philosophy professor Richard Kearney noted the paradox inherent in the fact that "ostensible immediacy of sexual contact was in fact mediated digitally." Many of his students' sexual interactions are "vicarious, by proxy, and often voyeuristic." He argues that we might be entering an age of "excarnation" where we "obsess about our bodies in increasingly disembodied ways," distancing ourselves from our own and others' bodies in everyday acts of "carnal alienation."

But is it alienation? The people who engage in mediated carnality—

largely a younger generation raised with the Internet and smartphones and social media—don't experience it that way. A study in the *Journal of Sex Research* found that 67 percent of male college students consider pornography "an acceptable way to express one's sexuality." Express— and consume it—they do, at an order of magnitude greater than previous generations did. As writer Rob Henderson noted in an essay about Gen Z, OnlyFans, a site that features "real-life sex workers, currently boasts an incredible one billion visits a month." Compare that to *Playboy* magazine, which at its peak in the 1970s had 5 million readers. New technologically mediated experiences appear every week. Henderson describes a new app, Replika, which functions as an "AI girlfriend chatbot" and already has 10 million users.

On the screen, lust is transformed into the reliable repetitions of vicarious pleasure. We can present ourselves as we wish to be seen— photoshopped, filtered, free of physical and emotional blemishes. But we also sacrifice something in the digital rendering. There is no scent of stale perfume on Match.com, no taste of a lover's skin in the algorithms deployed by Tinder.

Of course, pornography has long thrived by satisfying lust virtually, to the satisfaction of millions of human beings. And anyone, not just porn actors, can create pornography-for-profit on sites such as OnlyFans. The difference is that today the frequency and ease with which we can vicariously mediate and assuage our lust is changing the way we treat one another in the non-virtual world. If, as we saw in chapter 2, the motivational enhancement effect of communicating in mediated forms encourages lying, what does it encourage in intimate settings? Writing in *New York* magazine about pornography's impact on men, including himself, Davy Rothbart noticed that many of the men he interviewed "had a tendency to describe the act of watching porn as though it were a real sex act they had participated in—making their emotional investment in porn all the more concrete."

One therapist suggested that heavy porn users suffered from a kind of "sexual attention deficit disorder" when confronted with the different tempo and complexities of sex with a real partner rather than a pixelated depiction of one. "There's a failure to distinguish between porn reality and reality reality," one woman told Rothbart of the men she had encountered; they approached their relationships with real women with expectations of having the "PSE," or "porn-star experience," she said.

Writing in *GQ* about her male peers' insistence on mimicking sex acts they have seen in porn films, a twenty-something woman noted, "It hardly seems fair to call that sex. It's more like masturbation with a fellow 3-D person." She notes, correctly, that "this kind of scene was once what you streamed when no human lady was available" and concludes on a pessimistic note: "Porn used to be the poor man's substitute for sex; now the latter has to be gussied up . . . to be even half as enticing as porn." It's not a surprise that the first software application developed by independent programmers for augmented reality goggles and other AR devices is almost always a point-of-view porn app (the popular website PornHub features a category devoted entirely to "VR porn"). In Barcelona, Toronto, Moscow, Turin, and other cities, "sex doll brothels" allow customers to indulge themselves not with human prostitutes, but with technologically sophisticated sex dolls they can rent by the hour at rates far lower than a human prostitute costs.

Moralists have always fretted about the impact of pornography, particularly on the young, and for every anecdote about alienation you can find others who praise pornography for its beneficial effects on their sex lives. Porn has always been part of the human experience; indeed, when scientists at the University of Montreal launched a research study on male porn use, they faced an immediate obstacle. "We started our research seeking men in their twenties who had never consumed pornography," one of the professors said. "We couldn't find any."

There is something machinelike about the way sex is performed in porn, and it is that very predictability and repetitiveness that is intrinsic to its appeal. Although the scale at which we practice it today is new (many estimates note that porn sites get more traffic than Amazon, Twitter, and Netflix combined, which tells you something about the hierarchy of human pleasures) porn is peculiarly suited to our times, with its emphasis on efficiency and streamlined, machinelike performance in all realms of life. As cognitive scientist Donald Norman reminds us, "The machine-centered viewpoint compares people to machines and finds us wanting, incapable of precise, repetitive, accurate actions." What is porn if not humans acting like efficient sexual machines?

Many of our pleasures developed by accident or as by-products of evolutionary urges. Our desire to look at naked people having sex is a by-product of our evolutionary urge to *be* a naked person having sex. Porn is only one example of this urge. The technologies we create to facilitate those pleasures can also transform them; for example, social networking software is a by-product of our interest in being connected to others and to feel part of a social group, but it has thoroughly transformed friendship from a private bond into a publicly performed ritual. And the Internet has transformed the experience of searching for a mate via online dating, both for good and for ill.

Sex is the proving ground and, at times, the Waterloo for the impulse to connect to others. But in embracing these mediating technologies and software, we are outsourcing far more than merely our sex lives; we are outsourcing intimacy. We are a society that supports a professional cuddling industry—where cuddle-for-hire businesses with names like Cuddle Comfort send another human being to you for some physical reassurance.

Today, when sexting is mundane foreplay and every right-swipe on Tinder a potential sexual conquest, our technologies offer us peak sexual efficiency. Whether these technological surrogates can deliver sexual satisfaction, however, remains to be seen. In Japan, a country with some of the most active technology users in the world, a survey by the Japan Family Planning Association of young people aged sixteen to twenty-four found that nearly half of the women and more than one quarter of the men were "not interested in or despise sexual contact." In an interview with the *Guardian*, one of Japan's self-appointed sex therapists told the story of a client, a thirty-year-old male virgin, who could only become sexually aroused if he watched female robots in a Power Rangers–like video game. Roland Kelts, who writes about Japanese youth, argues that the future of Japanese romance is a world of technology-driven relationships in "incredibly sophisticated virtual worlds." It is monumentally simpler to experience technologically mediated sexual pleasure than it is to find it with another human being, in real time, in person. It would be a shame if we used our technological tools to avoid the latter because the former was so much more convenient.

———

Sex isn't the only pleasure we are sacrificing on the altar of efficiency. "What if you never had to worry about food again?" Soylent, a food replacement drink developed by a Silicon Valley technology entrepreneur, offers the tantalizing promise of "maximum nutrition with minimum effort." Order Soylent online, have it delivered to your front door, and you never need waste time planning for, shopping for, or preparing meals again. The company's website urges you to "Free Your Body" by treating eating as just another solvable engineering problem. As with sex, we can now make our relationship with food as efficient as possible and as infused with the spirit of Silicon Valley; the company notes that people are already "hacking" and "customizing" Soylent's "open-source formula."

"Unlike other foods, which prioritize taste and texture, Soylent was engineered to maximize nutrition, to nourish the body in the most efficient way possible," an early promotional video boasted. It featured images of a young energetic woman bustling around her minimalist office, pausing only to take restorative sips of the glass of Soylent located conveniently next to her computer; later, we see more fresh-faced young people working off their daily Soylent intake by energetically kickboxing.

"Soylent gives you the freedom to live life the way you want to live," the company claims.

What it doesn't give is much pleasure. After consuming Soylent for a week when it was first introduced, one reviewer called it a "punishingly boring, joyless product" marked by a "stultifying utilitarianism." Its bland greige color and gritty aftertones produced unpleasant side effects: Soylent's online message boards included an active "Soylent and Flatulence" discussion thread, a terrifying narrative of "burbling stomachs," "rapid gastric emptying," and "volatile sulfur compounds" that offered an alternative to the happy exercise and workplace images promoted in the company's marketing materials. Craigslist featured many people trying to offload their unfinished Soylent packs, with little luck. Soylent has worked to improve the taste of its product; a subreddit devoted to Soylent drinkers prompted praise for the Creamy Chocolate flavor in particular, although Amazon's summary of thousands of reviews still found that "some customers have reported stomach issues and nausea. Customers also differ on taste, and value."

Although Soylent has received a great deal of press attention, with its founder expounding often on his hope for a world where maltodextrin replaces Mom's apple pie and where we embrace "a separation between our meals for utility and function, and our meals for experience and socialization," it is unlikely to replace the pleasures of preparing and eating food for most of us any time soon. But Soylent represents something about our age; it is the logical conclusion of an era defined by what one critic called "Wi-Fi cuisine" and, more broadly, a sign of our complicated relationship to the pleasure of food in the twenty-first century. Ours is an era when pleasure is more likely to be devised by the engineer rather than the voluptuary, one in which efficiency is often more valued than enjoyment.

Food is a cultural signifier in every era, a signal of class position, wealth, individual self-control, and values. I once devised a kind of culinary Rorschach called the Velveeta Test. Ask someone if they've ever eaten or cooked with the heavily processes "cheesefood" and their reaction will tell you a great deal about their background and sensibilities. Today digital culture mediates our experience of food in many ways—offering us a great deal of information about what we consume, access to millions of recipes, and the instant gratification of online ordering of takeout food through websites like GrubHub and Seamless. All this information has not made us healthier; we cook fewer of our meals at home, eat more processed and prepared foods, and have the health problems and obesity epidemic to show for it.

At the same time, we can participate in a tantalizing virtual world of cooking and eating. Countless cooking shows, online video tutorials, and other food porn are available constantly on television and the Internet. We don't even seem to notice or mind that we will never taste the food whose preparations we spend so much time watching. When we do eat, we post images of our latest meal on Instagram, efficiently documenting and humble-bragging about our carefully curated gluttony. Such gluttony has spawned an industry of its own—mukbang videos featuring people consuming enormous amounts of food in one sitting. The practice, which originated in South Korea (the word means "eating broadcast" in Korean) is now a global phenomenon thanks to YouTube, and millions of people every day enjoy watching and listening to strangers consume enormous buckets of fried chicken and platter after platter of noodles. Instagram and TikTok feature countless "What I Eat in a Day" videos that allow users to track the eating habits of strangers.

Chefs are also using technology to cater to diners. When Spanish chef Paco Roncero's Ibiza-based restaurant Sublimotion opened in 2014, he described it as a place where "culinary vanguard and technological innovation unite to create a complete and up to now unseen emotional experience." The restaurant, one of the most expensive in the world (and booked solid more than six months in advance) serves only 12 diners per evening at a communal table whose surface is also a screen, in a room where images are constantly projected on all four walls. The meal includes music, aroma, and temperature fluctuations that are meant to "incite the guests' most forgotten feelings," among them "humor, pleasure, fear, reflection, and nostalgia." Amid virtual images of the North Pole, guests "taste a cold snack carved out by themselves from their own iceberg"; later, they are transported to "baroque Versailles, where the subtlety and elegance of a rose will melt in their mouths." One wonders where the fear factor emerges. Do we see the iceberg melting because of global warming, or aristocrats from Versailles being trundled off to the guillotine? In the last few years, the restaurant has embraced the use of VR headsets for its guests for an even more immersive experience; the average cost is around $1,600 per person.

Like art, sex, and food, the pleasure of playing games is also becoming increasingly more mediated. Toy companies have given traditional board games like Monopoly digital makeovers in versions such as "Monopoly Live," which features an infrared tower in the center of the board that monitors play, speeds up the game by demanding property auctions, and issues instructions to players. Meanwhile, technology companies coopt games such as Scrabble—which becomes Words with Friends on your smartphone—and call it "social gaming." Rather than sit around a table, face-to-face with others, social gaming encourages you to use your devices to play multiple games against several people at a time, none of whom you need know or ever actually see. As critic Rob Horning noted, "The networked mediation of games—in other words, playing them on your phone or through Facebook—undermines the function of games in organizing face-to-face social time." It also turns games into yet another means of data gathering. As one online game designer said, "Games can produce enormous volumes of data because it's really simple to gather every little interaction the player has in the game and report it back to a central server."

Even live sports events that used to be synonymous with physical presence now have competition from the virtual world. At TIAA Bank Field (formerly EverBank Field) in Jacksonville, Florida, the

National Football League's Jaguars compete for fans' attention with a 7,000-square-foot fantasy football lounge installed in the stadium that plays host to fans focused not on the live game but on their fantasy football teams on their screens. "We have to have a very compelling reason for fans to come to the game," the Jaguars' owner told the *New York Times*. The video games, multiple lounge chairs, and WiFi are an effort to "marry live football with the digital experience." The windows that look down from the fantasy football lounge onto the field are an anachronistic nod to the ritual of gathering to watch live sport.

Or consider skiing, which now offers technologies such as goggles made by Smith and Recon Instruments that let you read incoming text messages or real-time statistics on your altitude and speed on its heads-up display. If your helmet is embedded with a Bluetooth connection, which many now are, you can even chat with friends or stream music while you ski. Many lift tickets now include embedded radio frequency identification tags, gondolas have WiFi, and numerous apps offer snow forecasts and suggested runs on popular mountains. The entire experience from the lift ride up to the run downhill can be mediated.

Mediation has also altered the experience of other outdoor recreational pleasures, such as deer hunting and birding. Although the population of white-tailed deer in the U.S. has never been higher and successfully hunting one never easier, hunting supply stores are packed with sophisticated electronics, all designed, as one hunter lamented, "to eliminate every last shred of chance from the pursuit." Technology has also caused controversy among avid birders, many of whom deplore the use of digital birding guides that broadcast recordings of birdsong via smartphones to lure birds into the open. According to one news report, the American Birding Association had to revise its Code of Birding Ethics to deal with smartphone use; the code now states that birders should "limit the use of recordings and other audio methods of attracting birds." Jeffrey Gordon, then president of the American Birding Association, told the *Wall Street Journal*, "When we're getting out, we're trying to become more attentive to what's around us, and playback [broadcasting birdsong on a phone]—or any kind of overreliance on gadgetry—can quickly start to erode the experience."

Many people use these technologies because they believe they enhance their experience. The birder who can now identify exactly which warbler he heard by summoning its call on his iPhone is a happier birder than he was without this ability; the skier who can ski to the sounds of her own personal playlist feels more connected to her world while on vacation. But these new ways of mediating pleasurable experiences also alter the experience itself, not least by tethering users to the everyday world of technology rather than freeing them from it.

What is lost when this happens isn't easily measurable or even always immediately noticeable. Yet as technology encroaches on our pleasurable hobbies, we might find those pleasures significantly altered. Just as publicizing our private feelings and relationships is now rewarded on social media, so might our hobbies become so geared to documentation and public performance that we lose the singular experience of enjoying them in the moment.

———

In *Anarchy, State, and Utopia*, philosopher Robert Nozick posed a challenge to the hedonism of other philosophical traditions by asking a simple question: If we could create a machine that would offer us the illusion of a life of constant pleasure while also erasing from our memory any inkling that we were hooked up to such a machine, would we choose to plug in? The assumption has always been that most people will choose "no." "We want to *do* certain things, and not just have the experience of doing them," Nozick argued. "We want to *be* a certain way, to be a certain sort of person." He likened plugging into the machine as "a kind of suicide."

I'm not so sure.

We already spend a lot of time consuming secondhand experiences presented as entertainment in the form of movies, television, and video-games. We have accelerated this consumption while also turning more of our direct experiences—with sex, art, food, game-playing and hobbies—into something immediately consumable by others. We can immerse ourselves in online games of great creativity and appeal and experience genuine feelings of accomplishment, even earning the respect of anonymous others with whom we play. We do this because we believe it enhances our experience of pleasure.

But technologies that mediate our pleasurable experiences also increase our self-consciousness about them, as the phrase "pics or it didn't happen" suggests. This captures something genuine—and genuinely disturbing—about our relationship to pleasure. Our world resembles less the Experience Machine than it does Nozick's two other hypothetical philosophical contraptions: the Transformation Machine, "which transforms us into whatever sort of person we'd like to be (compatible with our staying us)" and the Result Machine, "which produces in the world any result you would produce." Both sound like the promises of contemporary technologies.

Our technologies actively encourage us to view our world as something in need of transformation by the latest app or gadget so that we can enjoy the results of a personalized, convenient experience. It's not that these technologies live our lives for us, as Nozick feared. It's that we are embracing a *way* of living in which there are increasingly few arenas where we don't live our lives *through* these technologies and conform to the behaviors the technologies are designed to encourage.

———

One day I was standing on the outdoor terrace of the Kennedy Center in Washington, DC, waiting to go inside to watch a play, when the remnants of an earlier thunderstorm produced a fantastic rainbow. I watched as most of the other people milling around noticed the rainbow and then immediately reached for their smartphones and started taking pictures—a man standing nearby said to his friend, "I'm sending it to him now! I'm going to say I'm somewhere over the rainbow!"

For the next several minutes, many of the people I watched spent twice as much time looking at the rainbow through screens pointed skyward than at the rainbow. The image of the thing received more attention than the thing itself. I'm sure most of the people taking pictures were doing so because they wanted to share the image (I appreciated the cleverness of the over-the-rainbow quip) but how can you share an experience that you've barely paused to have? Were they even having an experience or merely documenting a scene wherein an experience might happen?

More and more of us are living in what Ian Kerr and others have called the evidentiary society—"a world where the recording of an event is at least as valuable as its meaning." In fact, we live in a world where, increasingly, we participate in experiences for the *purpose* of broadcasting them.

In one sense this is nothing new. Enthusiasts of the daguerreotype in the nineteenth century overwhelmingly took pictures of a single subject: themselves. By 1849, more than one hundred thousand daguerreotype portraits were made in Paris alone. This transformed not just how we viewed ourselves but how we understood our role in social groups. As the inventor of the Polaroid camera, Edward Land, observed in 1974, "A new kind of relationship between people in groups is brought into being... when the members of the group are photographing and being photographed and sharing the photographs." There is no doubt that the range of our visual experience has expanded remarkably since the advent of the photograph, the moving image, and digital technology.

But a few salient things are different. The "sharing" idealized by Land now takes place over digital platforms that require us to conform to their standards and also take ownership of the images we so eagerly "share." Our memories of pleasurable experiences are more ephemeral for us (digital bits in the Cloud) and more useful to others (technology companies, governments) than at any time in history. Pleasures that used to be private are now public, and we seem to have a compulsion to turn even the most mundane acts into public performance. Unboxing .com, a site devoted to watching other people take new products out of their boxes (overwhelmingly high-end electronics or videogame consoles), promises "vicarious thrills from opening new gear."

This is a world where we've willingly exchanged the experience of the present moment for the guarantee of a future record of it. In the twentieth century, the rise of the camera prompted one critic to call this "the contamination of the pleasurable present, by the photographic urge." Today the urge to digitally document every experience has eliminated the pleasure of even participating in an unmediated present, as the people capturing images of rainbows on rooftops suggests.

We have always mediated our experiences of pleasure, which in turn alters the experience. Nineteenth-century attendees of the opera who made use of binoculars had a different experience of the performance than those who did not, just as audience members who spend a concert filming with their phones are "creating new contexts for experience," as theorist Peter-Paul Verbeek notes. This doesn't mean we've always successfully *improved* the experience. The twentieth-century critic Dwight Macdonald thought it would be "good discipline for Americans, just to look at things once in a while without touching them, using them, converting them into means to achieve power, profit, or some other practical end. The artist's vision, not the hunter's."

We are heading in the opposite direction. When a "user-experience researcher" at Facebook was interviewed a few years ago, he enthusiastically searched public Facebook posts for "feeding 2 am." Immediately a long list of posts appeared of women breastfeeding their infants and scrolling Facebook on their phones with a free hand, which he showed to the journalist interviewing him. The Facebook researcher, not surprisingly, heralded this as a positive trend. Sharing private moments for public consumption would make everyone feel more connected, he noted—while generating valuable data for Facebook, of course.

Should every experience be mediated? Technology companies treat our intimate lives and human pleasures as territory to be conquered, ore in the data mine. In their pursuit of digital *lebensraum* they promise to enhance our experience of pleasure while extending our memories of it. But something is lost when we choose to pursue pleasure through the mediating platforms and machines offered by these companies: the privacy of our experiences and our memories of them.

Today pleasure is often enjoyed in the harsh light of technology-enabled "transparency"—a sharp contrast to the hazy reaches of memory. It is not a coincidence that much of science fiction is preoccupied with the terrifying consequences of reading other people's minds and mining other people's memories. Pleasure requires the presence of shadows and ambiguities. It thrives in private. The human drama in which we are all both actors and audience needs a stage with curtains.

Our mediation of pleasure poses the risk of creating a future in which we have convinced ourselves that the virtual is not merely an acceptable substitute but a superior replacement, where "the ersatz is so commonly accepted that the reality is almost forgotten," as Trappist monk Thomas Merton wrote in *The Monastic Journey*. Indeed, this is many technologists' hope.

In a profile in 2007 in *The New Yorker,* Microsoft's Gordon Bell described a future where homes no longer needed windows. "It won't matter where they are—screens on the walls will display whatever we want to look at," he predicted. On its newest ship, the *Quantum of the Seas,* Royal Caribbean cruise lines features "virtual balconies" on interior cabins that lack windows. The virtual balconies feature a "full-definition 80-inch screen" with audio piped in from outside to mimic the experience of a real view. Of the customers who have tried the virtual balconies, "We were surprised in early focus groups . . . to learn they valued the experience to such a degree that they would rank a Virtual Balcony stateroom not only above an inside stateroom, but even above a stateroom with a window," said Ronnie Farzad, Manager of Entertainment Technology at

Royal Caribbean International. Guests preferred the reliable and convenient virtual view to the real one.

We know that virtual things can often evoke the same feelings and reactions as real things. A study conducted in Spain found that people reacted positively to "green" images of waterfalls and soaring eagles used by an energy company as part of its environmental marketing efforts. "The visual simulations were meeting a human desire to experience nature and reap its psychological benefits (pleasure, stress reduction, and so on)," writes Sue Thomas, who studies such instances of "techno-biophilia." If we can make a simulation as pleasurable as the real thing, why worry about encouraging the real thing? To do so is to fetishize the "real" world compared to the digital one, some might argue. By this logic, the world's art museums could be replaced with Jumbotron projections of paintings scanned by Google's Art Project.

The real can't be controlled in the same way as the virtual, however.

Programmed by others, virtualizations create ample opportunities to manipulate people—the energy company eager to appear eco-conscious, for example, or the tourist eager to forget he can't afford a stateroom with a window on his cruise. Unless we place thoughtful limits on where and when the virtual is suitable, we will create a world where we live what scholar Michael Benedikt described as "a life not really lived anywhere but arranged for the viewing."

In the fall of 1929, writer Aldous Huxley visited the Escorial, a complex of buildings built in the sixteenth century, not far from Madrid, that had served as the historical residence and burial place of the kings of Spain. There he saw El Greco's painting *Dream of Philip II*. This elaborate work, which depicts the Spanish king surrounded by images of heaven, hell, purgatory, and prayer, prompted Huxley to conclude that the people of the past were more firmly rooted in the realities of physical pleasure and pain than in his own age. El Greco and his contemporaries recognized a "primary visceral consciousness" in nearly every aspect of their lives, Huxley argued, so much so that one could fairly say the "heart and the liver, the spleen and the veins did all a man's feeling for him." Even the "loftiest experiences" were expressed physically, as the Escorial itself demonstrated. The building's architect designed it to resemble a gridiron as a nod to the grill on which Saint Lawrence, the building's patron saint, was martyred.

El Greco's painting also prompted Huxley to think about another pleasure he had relished during his travels in Spain: the "luxury" of ignorance. "The pleasures of ignorance are as great, in their way, as the pleasures of knowledge," he wrote. Although he found it satisfying to "place the things that surround one in the categories of an ordered and comprehensible system," he thought it was also good to have to muddle around in the dark—whether the darkness of a baroque artist's vision or the darkness of an unfamiliar place. Travel helped Huxley achieve that sensibility, but we can all experience that "vague bewilderment" by pausing before we mediate every pleasure we pursue.

There has always been and likely always will be a percentage of people who prefer armchair travel to the real thing, reproductions of paintings to the inconvenience of going to a museum, the safety and predictability of pornography to sex with a real person, and the cooking show to the cooked meal. But in an age when nearly everything is reproducible as data, it's worth remembering that information about pleasure is not the same thing as the experience of it. As Huxley reminds us, understanding of this kind requires "a direct, unmediated contact with the new, the mystery, moment by moment, of our existence."

CHAPTER 7

∗ ∗ ∗

Place, Space, and Serendipity

I n his evocative descriptions of McSorley's Old Ale House in the East Village in New York City in the 1940s, writer Joseph Mitchell paid homage to the idea of place. In Mitchell's depiction, the physical space of the saloon was sacrosanct, developed over years of use and, although haphazardly designed, eminently suitable for McSorley's customers. The chairs, like the patrons, were often battered and rickety, and the sawdust and grime notorious. Reading Mitchell's stories, you can almost smell the smoke and raw onions that permeated the atmosphere.

And the dust. The dust in McSorley's was legendary. It formed a thick layer on shelves and on the wishbones that dangled from the gas chandelier, wishbones supposedly placed there by soldiers going off to fight in World War I. But a few years ago the New York City Health Department insisted on its removal, citing health risks. The owner did so "reluctantly," according to the *New York Times*. "It's kind of—how would you put it? It's something you didn't want to touch. It's the last thing I wanted to touch or see touched," he said. He eventually removed it and, like any good tender of a monument, saved the dust in a container to take home with him. McSorley's tavern is a reliquary to place. It is also the kind of place that's on the verge of extinction.

Civil society has long been rooted in physical places—sidewalks, neighborhoods, cafés, plazas, taverns. In the late nineteenth century, when my great-grandfather immigrated to the United States from what was then called Bohemia, he worked different jobs until he could scrape together enough money to open a tavern in Lorain, Ohio. Setting down roots in his adopted homeland meant creating a physical space where locals could gather for food and conversation, and where he could earn just enough profit from his weekly fish fries to stay in business.

Such *places* are being replaced by *spaces*. The distinction isn't negligible. As geographer Yi-Fu Tuan has noted, "Space is transformed into place as it acquires definition and meaning." A space becomes a place when it has been "enclosed and humanized." This is why we have something called cyber*space*, but not cyber*place*, and why the dominant social network in the pre-Facebook era was called MySpace, not MyPlace. The writer James Joyce coined the word "iSpace" in *Finnegans Wake* (1939) to play with the idea that space could be punctured by time—an ideographically prescient use—but also an acknowledgment that place is bounded, while space is without limits.

Of course, the limitlessness of cyberspace is a large part of its appeal. For centuries engineers and inventors have tried to help us transcend place—or, at least, to make its practical realities less important to our everyday experience. If the telephone allowed anyone access into the once private domain of the home, the invention of the digital answering machine heralded a new era of place-shifting; you could be virtually "at home" within your message while being physically miles away. Today, the mobile phone effectively ensures that place matters very little; place seems to be an obstacle that technology has quite painlessly overcome.

Smartphones not only allow place-shifting; they are part of the way we understand our own place in the world. Our phones allow us to remain constantly connected but also tell us where we are, where we are going, and, thanks to GPS, how to get there. Twitter, Facebook, and other social networking sites allow us to geotag our updates, so that friends and followers will know precisely where we are as well. Unlike McSorley's, which oriented its patrons in a specific place and neighborhood, today we rely on our technologies and software to remind us of who we are by constantly calibrating our followers, friends, and likes. Where we are doesn't really matter unless we're posting a vacation selfie to Instagram (#tulumsunset #blessed). We rarely pause to note the irony that the same technology that liberates us from place also allows ubiquitous location tracking. Today you can go anywhere, but you can also be found anywhere.

The informal and often inefficient process of learning a place—finding one's way around a new neighborhood or city—has been replaced by algorithms that offer on-demand information about places while also privileging algorithmic judgment over individual discovery, all while tracking us constantly. The seemingly endless array of choices returned to you when you Google "best coffee shop in Seattle" masks the fact that Google is redacting or burying the options that don't conform to the platform's logic or business model—just ask any local shop that refuses to pay for ads on Yelp or Google.

Such is the price of convenience and information. But these new spaces—online, always accessible, brimming with novelty—offer us better opportunities for serendipitous interaction than the old places, or so we are told. Consider an interview Eric Schmidt gave to the *Wall Street Journal* when he was still CEO of Google: "We know roughly who you are, roughly what you care about, roughly who your friends are," he said. Why do Google and Apple want to know where you are? So that one day soon, when you're walking home from work, they can remind you to get milk or urge you to stop into a nearby store that carries your favorite brand of soap. "That serendipity [of experience] can be calculated now," Schmidt said enthusiastically. "We can actually produce it electronically."

But is "electronic serendipity" desirable? Such technological efficiency is as likely to kill serendipity as create it. For example, many of today's elevators group passengers based on destination to maximize efficiency and speed, which means the unexpected bumped-into-George-from-accounting moments, the serendipitous moments, happen less frequently than they used to. Today you are likely to spend the brief moments of your elevator ascent to work surrounded by the same colleagues who share your cubicle warren. A small change, to be sure, but the accumulation of such engineered changes to public places influences how we interact.

Technology has not merely encroached on place; it now tries to remake place in its own image. This effort to engineer space and manufacture serendipity, what technology critic Nicholas Carr called "the industrialization of the ineffable," is a hallmark of our times. The industrialization of the ineffable is perhaps most evident in the continued effort to merge the virtual with the real or to overlay the virtual on the real (such as the brief craze for the game Pokemon Go). At scale, this effort creates "smart cities" such as Songdo, South Korea, designed around technologies and information-gathering rather than around people.

If mobile phone technology eliminated the need for individuals to be in certain places at certain times to communicate, the future might well make place itself irrelevant. Using virtual reality headsets such as Oculus Rift, which is owned by Meta, and Apple's Vision Pro, we may soon be able to "seamlessly blend digital content with your physical space." VR promises a world where you can go anywhere—or at least a sophisticated simulacrum of anywhere—without ever having to leave your home. As we saw in chapter 6, such mediated pleasures appeal to an ever larger number of people.

What will this do to public spaces? We had a glimpse of our VR future in the fall of 2016, when Facebook founder Mark Zuckerberg gathered a large audience to announce the company's quarter-billion-dollar investment in its VR program. In a photo taken at the conference, a smiling

Zuckerberg strides down the aisle of the packed auditorium. Everyone seated was wearing Oculus Rift headsets and was no doubt excited to be among the first to test this new technology, which is now in widespread use, particularly by gamers.

And yet the contrast between Zuckerberg's upbeat stride and headset-free face and the passive, lumpen techno-masses was startling. As Zuckerberg hailed the power of "presence" fostered by VR technology, the people in the auditorium willfully and literally blinded themselves to the presence of everyone around them. They chose to block out the physical world to enter the virtual. Granted, this was precisely the reason they were there—to see what the new technology could do— but Zuckerberg's pitch does not allay concerns that the device is likely to have a narcotic effect on its users while undermining our sense of physical place. "You have the space where you can do anything you want," Zuckerberg said of Oculus Rift. "You can play a game, you can do work . . . You're free to explore." But as his use of the word "space" rather than "place" suggests, these virtual worlds are not humanized places that have developed organically over time, such as the café or tavern, but technology-dominated spaces in which we are invited to become spectator-participants in virtual worlds created by others.

For technology companies like Facebook, which renamed itself Meta to signal its commitment to this future, that means the Metaverse—a shared, immersive, VR space where humans are no longer limited by the things they can do in the physical universe. The portmanteau "meta- verse" comes from "meta," which means beyond, and "universe." Per- haps this is what we've wanted all along. In daily life we filter our physical experiences through virtual media so often that the divide already feels semipermeable. At the same time, the power that physical place used to exercise in our lives—the way it grounded us in specific communities and determined our friendships and careers, for better or worse—has waned. "*Where* one is has less and less to do with what one knows and experi- ences," notes communications scholar Joshua Meyrowitz.

But we lose something when place becomes engineered space, or when we cede physical reality to a pleasurably engineered form of virtual reality "presence." Place used to define us not only physically—as a Southerner or a New Yorker, as an immigrant or an explorer—but also emotionally. To leave the place where you were born was to disconnect from far more than geography. It meant taking on the exhilarating challenge of forming a new identity. Today, when we think of being disconnected, we think of losing Internet; and our identities—tracked, ranked, measured, and parsed with more precision than at any time in history— follow us from the moment we first appear on a social media platform, which for many young people today happens right after they are born. Identities that used to be firmly linked to a particular place on the map (a city or town, a region) have given way to online profiles that offer the world the curated digital presence we most want others to see. The place you are from matters less than the way you present yourself in the space available to you online.

We are in the process of trading the spatial and social cues that once defined a particular place—a public square, for example, or a local meeting spot—for a more seamless and less physically bounded experience of space engineered by technology companies. The promise is a more efficient delivery of "engineered serendipity," but the reality may end up being a more predictable homogeneity.

———

Once, at an academic conference about place, I was on a panel with sociologist Ray Oldenburg, who has written compellingly about the value of "third places"—cafés, local pubs, and other "great, good places" that form the backbone of traditional communities. He emphasized that real community requires face-to-face interaction and interdependence, something third places were excellent at providing but that virtual worlds have not yet and probably never will perfect. Other participants at the conference noted that although our embrace of vicarious experience and mediating technologies has long been a source of tension in American culture (Thoreau fretted about the demoralizing influence of the telegraph), in the past people didn't have the option of spending time living in virtual worlds. Now that we do, it is rapidly becoming the norm.

This raises questions about the role place plays in human behavior, as well as situational ethics. Do we act differently when we are physically close to others? Does being in the same physical place, face-to-face, change our response to others? As we saw in chapter 2, our mediated experiences are qualitatively different from in-person interactions. Are we more likely to behave in certain ways if we are bound to a particular physical space? Civil society has long been rooted in particular places—places that foster sociability among strangers. They create opportunities for us to run into people we know and to meet new people in a familiar context. Often, they serve as proving grounds for protest and political action. It is not a coincidence that large-scale civic engagement often begins in the physical town square, or in public meeting places where people of different backgrounds come together. In physical places we are forced to confront, compromise, and get along with those around us in ways that we can avoid when we are online.

Long before the invention of mobile technology, French philosopher Simone Weil called uprootedness the disease of the modern age. Weil was concerned about the lack of community participation and place-based ties among modern people of her age. Today we have embraced a technology-enabled uprootedness—rebranded as "connection," or "mobility"—and made it the standard for work and leisure. You can be anywhere in physical space and yet still be close to home and work thanks to your phone or, soon, the VR visor on (or the future chip implanted in) your face. But as we race into this mobile, placeless future, it is worth remembering that we are leaving behind older notions of place that were crucial to the formation of civic life. The new ways of discovery are compelling, but the old ones are dying without even a brief eulogy—and without an accounting of what their disappearance heralds for what it means to be human.

Science fiction writer William Gibson once said, "If you believe, as I do, that all cultural change is essentially technology-driven, you pay attention to Japan." If you want to understand the meaning of place in a technologically advanced age, you also pay attention to Japan, because in addition to its embrace of advanced technology, it is a country that still rigorously monitors the boundaries of formal and informal public space.

On a trip to Okinawa with a small group of people from a range of countries, ages, backgrounds, and opinions, I was pleased to discover that we all agreed on the community-building powers of karaoke. Karaoke originated in the late-1960s in Kobe. The club singer who created karaoke, Daisuke Inoue, described it as an invention that "teaches people to bear the awful singing of ordinary citizens, and enjoy it anyway," Karaoke encapsulates many longstanding, unspoken Japanese rituals about behavior in social space; it imposes a particular etiquette on its participants, who tend to follow its dictates even when enjoying what should be a leisure activity. Or, to put it another way, Japanese karaoke has a lot of rules.

Not wanting to offend our Japanese hosts by flouting these rules, we decided to engage in an American-style karaoke night with just our small group before joining the Japanese a few days later for traditional karaoke. Our American-style karaoke evening involved a lot of raucous singing and promiscuous use of tambourines and heckling; there may or may not have been several sake-fueled performances of "Bohemian Rhapsody." In other words, there were no rules.

A few days later we experienced Japanese karaoke, which celebrated what karaoke really is: a ritualized form of embarrassment. We went to a private karaoke club, where our Japanese hosts sat quietly waiting for us. Someone calmly tended bar nearby, and the feeling was that of a sedate cocktail party. When it was time to perform, each person took a turn, while the others sat quietly and listened. Most of the songs our Japanese hosts performed were traditional Okinawan folk songs, and some of the participants had clearly rehearsed in advance. They took pride in their singing (no ironic renditions of "Dancing Queen" here). It was much more like a recital, albeit one where Japanese beer was served, than a free-for-all.

The two starkly different experiences got me thinking about how places influence our behavior. We pick up on cues, both subtle and straightforward, whenever we enter a place. Our first karaoke night occurred in a loud, Western-style restaurant that catered to tourists and soldiers from the nearby military base; the second was in a private space, tucked away in a neighborhood, catering to the Japanese. Both places sent signals to us from the moment we walked in the door—signals about how loudly to speak and how formally to address the people who greeted us, for example, as well as cues about how we were expected to behave throughout the evening.

"In growing up people learn literally thousands of spatial cues, all of which have their own meaning in their own context. These cues *release* responses already established in much the same way as Pavlov's bells started his dogs salivating," wrote anthropologist Edward T. Hall in *The Silent Language*. "Literally thousands of experiences teach us unconsciously that space communicates."

Hall was the founder of proxemics, the science of how we understand our physical place in the world and our relationship to others. Central to the study of proxemics is the idea that where we are in space influences how we feel about one another and thus how we will behave. It's why we are unnerved when someone intrudes on our "personal space," and why modern air travelers sometimes experience "air rage" after spending hours penned in overcrowded jets. Proxemics has also revealed significant cultural differences in how people understand personal and public space—an individual's personal space might, in a different country, be another person's social space.

Our general awareness of the rules of social space has been deteriorating as technology encroaches on public places. Proxemics teaches that people want to understand how to navigate social space with their fellow human beings, but this can no longer be taken for granted. Our near-constant use of mediating technologies, especially phones, means we now follow the rules of virtual space, with its demands for immediacy and its rewards for behaviors that keep us focused on the virtual world. Our dedication to the virtual world has come at the expense of the physical world.

We turn to our virtual worlds for things that we used to seek in the physical world. We are as much or more likely to seek advice about everyday problems from strangers online than from a familiar face in our neighborhood, for example. A study by the Pew Research Center found, "only 43 percent of Americans know all or most of their neighbors by name. Twenty-nine percent know only some, and 28 percent know none." A follow-up survey by Pew found further that even those who know their neighbors don't spend much time with them; "social events among neighbors are relatively rare," the study found. One of the culprits of this decline in neighborhood interactions? A preference for online relationships. "Users of social networking services are 26 percent less likely to use their neighbors as a source of companionship." Today, it's likely people are more familiar with a YouTube or TikTok star than they are the local "public characters" that Jane Jacobs once described as integral members of the public landscape—the people who acted as familiar, reliable figures, available to answer questions and help, particularly in cities.

There is also this paradox: at a time when we are more "connected" than ever before, we are also, as a country, experiencing higher rates of social isolation. Research from the General Social Survey found that between 1985 and 2004, the number of people who reported having no one with whom they could discuss "important matters" tripled, for example. By 2023, the problem had grown so severe that the U.S. Surgeon General, Dr. Vivek Murthy, took the unusual step of issuing an advisory, "Our Epidemic of Loneliness and Isolation," that noted how, even before the COVID-19 pandemic, Americans were experiencing danger-ous levels of social isolation. The report compared the health effects of loneliness to smoking fifteen cigarettes a day.

As many have argued, technology use is a major culprit. As National Public Radio reported, "across age groups, people are spending less time with each other in person than two decades ago." This trend was most pronounced among Americans aged fifteen to twenty-four, who had "70 percent less social interaction with their friends," in large part due to social media. As Murthy told NPR, "What we need to protect against, though, are the elements of technology, and social media in particular, that seek to maximize the amount of time that our children are spending online at the expense of their in-person interactions."

The first recommendation in the advisory was to "strengthen social infrastructure" such as libraries, parks, and other public spaces to encourage people to gather in-person. This makes sense. Virtual spaces have their appeal, but unlike civic spaces they lack what Ray Oldenburg has called a natural "leveling influence"—that is, virtual spaces by their nature insist on identifying, ranking, and tracking everyone in them. By contrast, third places allow people to know one another in ways that are neither transactional nor instrumental. "The great bulk of human asso-ciation finds individuals related to one another for some objective pur-pose," Oldenburg notes. In contrast to schools or workplaces, third places are devoted to what sociologist Georg Simmel called "pure sociability"—people getting together for no reason other than the pleasure of each oth-er's company. Unburdened by expectations of purpose, pure sociability encourages "the most democratic experience people can have and allows them to be more fully themselves," Oldenburg noted.

Yet, online spaces are replacing those third places. Spaces governed by technology companies insist by their very design that participation in the space requires likes or other endorsements from followers as well as strangers. As a result, social media platforms replace pure sociability with quantified popularity.

Many of our new technological arbiters of physical space embrace such ranking as central to the experience of place. New apps and digital mapping services, for example, are not merely guiding us through real physical places but also attempting to influence the way we encounter new places by altering what is or is not displayed on their maps and by encouraging us to perform certain actions. ("Rate your recent meal at Applebees!")

The Google Lens app allows you to point your phone at anything and call up information, reviews, and even links to purchase items. Lens "ranks those images based on their similarity and relevance to the objects in the original picture," which is convenient for summoning immediate information. However, using the Lens transforms the public place you're standing in, perhaps one designed to encourage sociability, into a virtual space that is designed by Google's engineers to encourage you to keep using Google, which profits from your use.

"We lie in bed and listen to a broadcast from Cairo, and so on. There is no distance. We are intimate with people we have never seen and, unhappily, they are intimate with us," poet Wallace Stevens observed in *The Necessary Angel*. What Stevens was articulating even before the Internet era was the sense of loss and confusion that comes when distance is eliminated and intimacy with others becomes unmoored from any sense of place. The experience changes our understanding of our own place in the world. "Moral psychology tells us that ethical thinking and our sense of value are rooted in specificity, not universality—that is to say, in the lived experience of place, with specific natural and social characteristics, landscapes, and cultures," political scientist Bruce Jennings argued in *Minding Nature*. If this is true—and history suggests that it is—when we trade place for cyberspace, we risk altering not only our individual experiences but also our social and communal bonds.

In 1969, journalist William H. Whyte began studying the ways ordinary people used public places. The goal of his Street Life Project was deceptively modest: to see how people behaved in the public spaces designed by architects and city planners for their use. What did they do when confronted with a fountain? Why did they choose to sit here rather than there? How did physical place influence their behavior?

Although Whyte is known for his bestselling study of 1950s-era conformity *The Organization Man*, he was, first and foremost, a street watcher— someone who used the ordinary opportunities of pedestrian life to look critically at the way people behaved. Like his protégé Jane Jacobs, Whyte believed that sidewalks, front porches, and plazas mattered because human values were implicated in the choices of their design. More importantly, those choices influenced the daily lives of people.

Whyte was particularly intrigued by the plaza of the Seagram Building in midtown Manhattan, a minimalist expanse of granite designed by Mies van der Rohe and completed in 1957. In *The Social Life of Small Urban Spaces*, the film that grew out of the Street Life Project, Whyte used the word "choreography" to describe what he saw unfolding on the plaza. "We tracked people in scores of crossing patterns with a digital timer and never do they collide," he says in the film. "A tiny hand signal. A brief *ritard*. A tenth of a second. The timing is absolutely superlative. Think of the computers, the radar it would take, to make their equivalent."

I thought about those computers and radar when I revisited some of Whyte's plazas and squares. The "traveling conversations" Whyte described still occur, but they take place between the person in the plaza and the absent presence on the other end of that person's cellphone. The plaza's patterns are less an elegant ballet than a series of uncoordinated and often awkward movements as pedestrians immersed in technology swerve around and occasionally run into each other. In the early days of the Walkman, when the portable cassette player became a popular way to enjoy a private soundtrack in public space, the isolating impact of the technology was often noted. "With the advent of the Sony Walkman came the end of meeting people . . . It's like a drug: you put the Walkman on and you blot out the rest of the world," said Susan Blond, then-vice president of CBS Records. Science fiction writer William Gibson was correct when he said the Walkman "has done more to change human perception that any virtual reality gadget." By the time the iPod debuted in 2001 and Apple's wireless earbuds, AirPods, came to market in 2016, we had accepted that it was normal for people to choose to block out those around them.

In Whyte's film, his 1970s-era subjects were engaged in two public activities now hurtling toward extinction: smoking and reading newspapers. In one shot, Whyte pans across a typical group of plaza ledge-sitters in New York City; it contained five people reading and one couple playing backgammon. But something else was noticeable in Whyte's world: the number of people doing absolutely nothing. "Life swirls about and they let it all pass by," Whyte said. "They just stand there."

On a beautiful May morning, on the plaza of the main branch of the New York Public Library, I saw only one man challenging the city's outdoor smoking ban; three people on the plaza were reading. No one was just standing there. Perched on steps or sitting at tables, most plaza users were happily talking or texting on cell phones. A similar scene greeted me in Farragut Square in Washington, DC. One woman, earbuds intact and eyes cast downward, texted while walking briskly across the square until, halting abruptly, she realized she was about to step into the busy street. After several hours spent sitting on a bench, watching people with the same hunchback texting pose bustle past me, I was seized by a perverse desire to test the inattentional blindness of these innocent passersby, a weakness to which Whyte would never have succumbed. I saw two mild-mannered, texting businessmen approaching. I leaned forward and stuck out my tongue to see if they would notice. They did not.

What do some distracted businessmen have to do with the extinction of certain experiences in public space? A great deal, as it turns out. In 2010, Professor Keith Hampton of the Annenberg School of Communication at the University of Pennsylvania and his students observed WiFi users in public spaces in Philadelphia, New York City, San Francisco, and Toronto. What they report suggests that those who argue that mobile technologies are improving the social life of public spaces are engaging in an elaborate exercise in wishful thinking.

Hampton found that WiFi and phone users in public space "were considerably less likely to participate in serendipitous social exchanges of any type." Nearly 80 percent of the users he observed were alone and ignored polite overtures from strangers, prompting Hampton to concede the blindingly obvious, that "a high density of wi-fi use thus appears to reduce public sociability."

Nevertheless, like many techno-enthusiasts, Hampton wanted to offer a more Panglossian take on his own findings. He gushed to *Smithsonian* that people with their heads buried in their laptops "are not alone in the true sense," because although they are ignoring the people around them, they reported to him that they *felt* engaged while checking Facebook. "We found that the types of things that they are doing online often look a lot like political engagement," Hampton said, "like sharing information and having discussions about important matters." This might well be true, but should we really call people who are scrolling through their newsfeeds active participants in the public sphere?

I think not. Although we are still in the early stages of this transformation of public space, it is not unreasonable to worry that citizens who prefer the private worlds of their screens to the public activities of social space might, en masse, have a negative impact on social life. More than a decade since Hampton made his observations, the saturation of public space by technology has only increased, and our behavior worsened.

When our engagement with virtual communities interferes with our ability to interact with others in public space, we risk contributing to an already growing intolerance of the people we physically coexist with—on the bus, waiting in line, in the grocery store. We don't see the people in front of us, such as the old woman who needs a seat but whom we don't notice because we are buried in a phone. Such mundane indignities have a cumulative effect on the quality of public space and public life.

A feedback loop comes into effect as well. As journalist John Free-man has noted, "sitting in the modern coffee shop, you don't hear the murmur or rise of conversation but the continuous insect-like patter of typing. The disuse of real-world commons drives people back into the vir-tual world, causing a feedback cycle that leads to an ever-deepening iso-lation and neglect of the tangible commons." The coffee shops and other third places described by Oldenburg have been colonized by technology.

Professor Hampton and his clipboard-wielding graduate students also revisited some of William Whyte's old haunts in New York City to assess how mobile technology has changed the public square. When Hampton revisited Bryant Square Park, one of Whyte's original obser-vation spots, he found that there were far fewer self-isolating cellphone users than one would think given the many complaints and trend pieces about cell-yellers and oblivious texters in public space. Embracing a counterintuitive approach popular among techno-enthusiasts—the things we thought were bad are actually good!—Hampton concludes that cellphone use is neither a blight on the commons nor a serious challenge to our behavior in public space. Why? Because he didn't see as many people on the phone as he expected to, and most of those peo-ple were women, of whom there were far more out and about than in Whyte's era.

Of course, this misses the point that critics of mobile technology are making, which is that counting up the number of cellphone users (who were, it should be noted, adults during a workday, not teenagers who are far more likely to be in thrall to their phones) tells you some things about how public space has changed but doesn't engage the more impor-tant questions: Does it matter that in small ways, every day, our behavior demonstrates that we value our online connections more than we value the interactions we might have with people in the commons? Does it matter that in the space of a generation, the norm has shifted so that it is now common for parents and caregivers to talk on their phones while pushing a child in a stroller rather than to talk to that child? As sociologist Richard Sennett asks, "If people are not speaking to each other on the street, how are they to know who they are as a group?"

The transformation of public space by mobile technology is not an easily quantifiable phenomenon. Nevertheless, our unmooring from physical space has had a gradual but noticeable impact on civic life. As technology critic Sherry Turkle has noted, "Communities are constituted by physical proximity, shared concerns, real consequences, and common responsibilities." Although she understands the feelings of connection and support that people receive from online communities, "I think when we decided to call these online connections 'communities' and 'relationships,' we chose the words we had available to us and we confused ourselves."

Ray Oldenburg agrees that genuine community requires face-to-face interaction, the kind that engagement with mobile technology undermines. "I would insist that real community is local [and in person]," he told a journalist. "Most of what we communicate is nonverbal . . . You can't fully understand people if you're never face-to-face." Peter Block, co-author of *The Abundant Community*, agreed, noting that, whatever its many pleasures and conveniences, "Facebook can't substitute for the safety and security that comes from living in a community where your neighbors know your kids' names." The appeal of online pseudo-communities is understandable. They require only limited commitment while still providing a sense of belonging, and participants can opt out and disappear at any time, something not always possible in real communities. However, they are neither a substitute for nor an improvement on traditional community.

Nor should we assume that tuning out strangers in public space is a cost-free behavior. Gillian Sandstrom, a researcher at the University of Essex, studies how even the seemingly innocuous interactions with strangers that we have in a day contribute to our sense of well-being. When those experiences disappear we don't always notice right away, but the cumulative effect is real.

"I've spent many years studying the people who are the furthest out of our social networks," she says, "and they really do add a richness to our life that we miss when we're not there."

In the 1970s, when William Whyte filmed *The Social Life of Small Urban Spaces*, he identified a category of person in public space called "the undesirable." To illustrate the behavior of an "undesirable" in his natural habitat, Whyte filmed a man walking across a plaza, holding what appears to be a transistor radio about three inches in front of his face. He looks perfectly happy, but his focus on the radio puts him on a collision course with other pedestrians. What made him undesirable, in Whyte's view, was the fact that he was utterly unaware of his surroundings. If you placed him in on a sidewalk today, he would look like most people in public space; he looks like someone walking while texting.

We compromise experience in public space by using technology to remove ourselves temporarily from it. We've known this for some time, of course, and people who violated the rules of social space were with us long before the first iPhones issued their siren's call. Twentieth-century sociologists such as Erving Goffman saw every encounter in public space as its own little social system, replete with symbols and behaviors. Over time we cultivate a "very pretty capacity for dissociated vigilance" in public space, meaning we don't necessarily engage with everyone around us, but we are aware and vigilant about the requirement to do so. What does this dissociated vigilance look like now that we've introduced technologies that remove us mentally but not physically from sidewalks, parks, gardens, or plazas?

Here is one clue: Observe what happens when strangers bump into each other on the street. I performed my own experiment on a busy sidewalk in Washington, DC, during morning rush hour. After spying a businessman walking with a purposeful commuter's stride, I deliberately bumped into him, then gave him my most winning smile and said,

"I'm *so* sorry! Please excuse me." He looked a little annoyed but quickly responded, "No problem," and walked on. I repeated the same experiment, this time with a businessman walking and talking on his cellphone. I received a rather different reaction. "Look the hell where you're going!" he yelled, before returning to his phone conversation.

My experience is anecdotal, but researchers who study public behavior note that, traditionally, when both parties are following the unspoken rules of civility, strangers who collide accidentally should both apologize. "By defining the situation as one in which both parties must abase themselves," one sociologist noted, "society enables each to keep his self-respect."

Technology has upended this social bargain. Researchers at Nagaoka University and the University of Tokyo conducted an experiment to test what happens when the usual flow of sidewalk traffic, with its intuitive lane formation and mutual anticipation, is disrupted by distracted walkers. They set up the experiment as follows: "Two groups of 27 people (one team wearing yellow beanies, the other wearing red) walked head-on. In each experiment, one of the groups included three people looking at smartphones," and the distracted walkers were either at the front, middle, or back of the groups. Cameras tracked the routes and speeds of each group.

What they found was that if even one walker was distracted by his phone, it ruined the flow of pedestrian traffic for everyone behind him; mutual anticipation disappears because the person on the phone is not reciprocating. The researchers found that "the phone-distracted pedestrians placed at the front of a crowd slowed everyone behind them. The distracted leaders couldn't negotiate that subtle yet complex nonverbal interaction with their counterpart at the head of the approaching group."

These small acts of mutual reciprocity are really acts of civic deference. "The individual may desire, earn, and deserve deference," Goffman observed, "but by and large he is not allowed to give it to himself, being forced to seek it from others." Goffman was writing at a time when one could assume that deference would come from others in public space. Today, we can seek affirmation and validation from millions of people in an instant on our phones; as a result, there's less incentive to seek it from strangers in public space. This poses new challenges to our use of public space. "If the individual could give himself the deference he desired there might be a tendency for society to disintegrate into islands inhabited by solitary, cultish men, each in continuous worship at his own shrine," Goffman warned.

Traditional rules of conduct governing how we behave in social space are, as Goffman noted, "recommended not because it is pleasant, cheap, or effective, but because it is suitable or just." Today, with pleasant, (relatively) cheap, and effective technology that makes immediate distraction available during even brief moments of downtime, we have forgotten the requirement to enforce the suitable and just—the pursuit of which isn't always enjoyable but is necessary for civility. As Richard Sennett has noted, civility is in fact a form of thoughtfulness. It has as its aim "the shielding of others from being burdened with oneself." Incivility, as Sennett notes, "is burdening others with oneself . . . those 'friends' who need others to enter into the daily traumas of their own lives, who evince little interest in others save as ears into which confessions are poured."

This is an apt description of contemporary public life. We no longer wear civil masks so that we might engage in interactions with others while sparing them the many boring details of our lives. Rather, we invade others' space with our documentation of our daily lives; gyms have had to enact new rules about members filming themselves and others in public spaces, for example, and even hospitals frequently must remind patients and visitors not to film or take pictures of others.

As the technologies we use to remain in contact with others become less obvious, ritual codes of behavior become even more challenging to maintain. We cease to offer others what sociologists call public gestures of association.

These individual choices have an impact because they influence even the people who aren't wearing earbuds or are buried in their phones. As one critic noted, the people who engage in this behavior effectively penalize those who do not: "They reinforce the idea that networked products and not particular shared spaces provide common ground, positing a world where people don't really interact with strangers in public." Eventually, if enough people have earbuds in or their phones out, "physical proximity will no longer confer a social expectation of shared experience." This fosters an atomized public square, "full of people ignoring one another, doing their best to be nowhere."

"In the street people astound and interest me more than any sculpture or painting," artist Alberto Giacometti once said. "Every second the people stream together and go apart, then they approach each other to get closer to one another. They unceasingly form and re-form living compositions in unbelievable complexity." He claimed that it was "the totality of this life I want to reproduce in everything I do." Giacometti's sculpture *Piazza, 1947–1948*, visualized that feeling; the work depicts four men walking across a plaza while a single female figure stands alone near the center. The figures themselves are somewhat surreal—elongated versions of the human form with exaggerated proportions. Each of the figures is facing in a slightly different direction, as if captured mid-movement, on their way to their individual destinations. But the sculpture captures something of the haste and isolation of urban life, as well as the possibility of a kind of serendipitous interaction that city life provides. Those moments of acknowledgment among strangers in public space, as simple as a nod, a split second of eye contact, or a brief shuffle to the side to allow another to get by, are each also moments of potential connection.

In the early years of the Internet, many of its enthusiasts hoped it would eventually mimic what Ian Leslie described as "the greatest serendipity machine ever invented: the city." Today, however, as Leslie acknowledges, "some of our most serendipitous places are under threat from the Internet." That includes the city and its public spaces. Engineers now turn their skills to manufacturing so-called "smart" cities such as Songdo in Korea and PlanIT in Portugal, whose sidewalks and streets are embedded with sensors monitoring everything from traffic to pollution to noise levels, and where the people who live in them are treated as an engineering problem to be solved rather than the city's most vital resource. In smart cities, the intelligence rests in the machines and software that power the city, not the people who live in it.

And yet, in many cases, planners failed to engineer the serendipity they had promised. "The funny thing about these cities programmed for efficiency, you find a lot of conversations about how to design serendipity back into them to make them more interesting," Usman Haque, founder of Pachube, a company that manages real-time data, told *Salon* a few years ago. French chemist Louis Pasteur is credited with observing that chance favors the prepared mind, but in our over-engineered age, chance isn't supposed to favor anyone because nothing is supposed to be left to it.

Critics who worry that the quirky and unexpected aspects of public space are slowly being leached away by our slavish devotion to technology are told to lighten up and embrace the algorithmic possibilities. "People who think the Web is killing off serendipity are not using it correctly," says techno-enthusiast writer Steven Johnson. Other critics, such as Anthony Daniels, suggest it's futile to try to restore old notions of serendipity in our wired age. "You cannot have the joys of serendipity and those of the convenience of immediate access to everything," he argues. "Furthermore, it seems you cannot choose between them as technology advances . . . To refuse to use the new technology in the hope of preserving old pleasures will not work because to do so would be no more authentic or honest than Marie Antoinette playing shepherdess."

We don't need to reject the new technology to recognize that technology companies spoon-feeding us algorithmically recommended places, like Amazon and Spotify do with recommendations for books or music, is not the same thing as serendipity but a sophisticated feat of engineering. It's a testament to our uncritical embrace of technology that we can't be bothered to notice the difference. We shouldn't become nostalgic for some long-forgotten past where community life was always supposedly thriving and providing people with life-enhancing outlets for sociability. Communities are never perfect (if you doubt this, read about the history of utopian communities in the U.S.) and not all communal spaces encourage benign behavior (Hitler's failed putsch occurred in a convivial Munich beer hall, after all).

But we are social creatures. We need public spaces where our social impulses can flourish. Writing about virtue ethics and community, author Mark Vernon observes, "We discover who we are by discovering who others are, those to whom we are connected by way of family, affection, community, and society ... but we also need [others] because the communities to which we belong are also the repositories for the skills that we need to live well." We've gained many new skills thanks to new technologies, but the old repository of skills that once rested in third places and vibrant public spaces has deteriorated. We need to revive it.

The places where we choose to spend our time influence who we are; they can encourage or discourage freedom of mind and sociability, or make us feel uncomfortable, watched, and controlled. British researchers who studied pub culture in the UK before World War II noted how the pub is "the only kind of public building used by large numbers of ordinary people where their thoughts and actions are *not* being in some way arranged for them; in the other kinds of public buildings they are the audiences, watchers of political, religious, dramatic, cinematic, instructional, or athletic spectacles." Today, technologists hope to expand the realms in which engineering is dominant in our lives; as MIT scientist Ben Waber told the *New York Times*, we are "still in the very early stages of engineering serendipity," but he envisions a "sensor-strewn office that reconfigures itself each morning courtesy of algorithms that plug any nagging structural holes," for example. Restaurants and other public spaces could use sensors and monitors to track both employees and customers as they move about the space. We are losing freedom from technical control in both our public and private spaces, and we need it more than ever given how engineered our lives have become.

Whether these are third places devoted to sociality, or public places that encourage interaction, we have allowed our use of technology—and the absent presence it encourages—to overtake these crucial civic environments. By eliminating certain kinds of places, we eliminate the opportunity for certain experiences: conversations with strangers in public space, places that encourage fellowship and civic engagement without being dominated by technology use, a public square open to all and free from surveillance and the demands of commerce. "The environment in which we live out our lives is not a cafeteria containing an endless variety of passively arrayed settings and experiences," Ray Oldenburg notes. "It is an active, dictatorial force that adds experiences or subtracts them according to the way it has been shaped." When third places and public spaces disappear, opportunities for serendipity also disappear—replaced by fully wired and often corporatized spaces like Starbucks, with its predictable, homogenized appearance, where patrons spend their time engaged with the online world rather than with each other. Poet Walt Whitman wrote, "Every cubic inch of space is a miracle." Today, every inch of public space is a WiFi hotspot.

Sense of place is like *terroir* in wine. It requires cultivation; its alchemic properties are not reducible to a simple formula or even a sophisticated algorithm. Today, we seem more concerned with the maintenance of our online image than the maintenance of the integrity of the public square, and as a result we have reengineered our public spaces (and, in some cases, entire cities such as one that a group of wealthy Silicon Valley figures including Laurene Powell Jobs, Marc Andreessen, and Reid Hoffman hope to build sixty miles outside of San Francisco) to embrace the values of the digital world. What's lost is not as quantifiable as what's gained. We can count the number of laptop and cellphone users in public space and the speed of our wireless connections, but we can't quantify the loss of eye contact between strangers or the kind of public social interactions—informal but dependable, untracked, and undatabased—that used to exist but are now rapidly disappearing from the landscape.

We are amid a period of great confusion over place; instant communities formed online can be powerful and inspiring, but they often fail to solve the problems of social isolation that plague many contemporary Americans. "It is by knowing where you stand that you grow able to judge where you are," novelist Eudora Welty wrote. "Place absorbs our earliest notice and attention; it bestows on us our original awareness; and our critical powers spring up from the study of it and the growth of experience inside it." And where those critical powers develop matters; younger generations of Americans spend much more time in limitless space online than grounded in the physical places where they were born. It matters less if you're from rural Oklahoma or the swampy environs of southern Florida if you spend most of your time seeing, hearing, and speaking to people through a screen, online.

But these experiences of place are necessary not just in youth, when we tend to give more value to and have stronger connections to place, but throughout our lives. "Sense of place gives equilibrium; extended, it is sense of direction too," Welty wrote. The places we now spend the most time are online spaces—and the engineer's hand is heavy in their design. Judging by the ubiquity of complaints about loneliness, incivility, and the frenetic pace of our lives these days, these new spaces might offer ready access to fascinating virtual worlds, but they haven't helped us achieve equilibrium.

Conclusion

* * *

The Metaverse may be virtual, but the impact will be real.

—META ADVERTISEMENT, 2023

Humane is an experience company that creates the technologies
and platforms for the intelligence age . . . Humane believes in a
future of technology that feels familiar, natural, and human.

—IMRAN CHAUDHRI, TED TALK, VANCOUVER, 2023

When software engineer and venture capitalist Marc Andreessen was asked about the possibility of a future where people's inability to distinguish between reality and unreality might harm humanity, he called this concern "Reality Privilege." "A small percent of people live in a real-world environment that is rich, even overflowing, with glorious substance, beautiful settings, plentiful stimulation, and many fascinating people to talk to, and to work with, and to date," he said. "Everyone else, the vast majority of humanity, lacks Reality Privilege—their online world is, or will be, immeasurably richer and more fulfilling than most of the physical and social environment around them in the quote-unquote real world."

He noted the likelihood of naysayers: "The Reality Privileged, of course, call this conclusion dystopian," but "reality has had five thousand years to get good, and is clearly still woefully lacking for most people; I don't think we should wait another five thousand years to see if it eventually closes the gap." Instead, he argued, the reality deprived should be happy to spend their time in "online worlds that make life and work and love wonderful for everyone, no matter what level of reality deprivation they find themselves in."

As Andreessen acknowledges, this does indeed sound like dystopian science fiction, as in Ernest Cline's 2011 book *Ready Player One*, which was set in a near future where most people "live" online in a vast virtual-world game called OASIS while existing in poverty and environmental degradation in the physical world; it also resembles themes explored in more recent dystopian entertainment such as the television show *Severance*. Unlike Andreessen's story, *Ready Player One* at least had a moral to it.

In 2018, researchers restaged Robert Nozick's Experience Machine thought experiment, which we read about in chapter 6, to see if, forty years later, Nozick's findings—that people would reject the Experience Machine because it offered pleasurable experiences that were not "in contact with reality"—still held. They discovered that if you replaced Nozick's invasive machine with an Experience Pill that promised a lifetime of pleasurable experiences with no side-effects, people were more likely to say they would take it. The researchers hypothesized (correctly, as it turned out) that "the less invasive an intervention is—the less it severs contact with reality—the more people will be prepared to accept it."

Andreessen's vision and the new Experience Pill experiment are examples of two paths ahead for humanity's relationship with technology: total immersion, à la Andreessen's 24/7 virtual reality, for most of the population whose real lives aren't satisfying; or an Experience Pill world of sensors and ubiquitous computing and augmented reality technologies that track, measure, surveil, and nudge us in public and private space during most of our waking hours but don't entirely remove the "human in the loop," as computer scientists like to say.

In a way, this is merely an update of an argument technologists have been having for decades about whether humanity is the problem or the solution to the world's challenges, and whether our technologies should serve as extensions of humans or replacements for them. The well-known exchange between engineers Douglas Engelbart and Marvin Minsky at the Massachusetts Institute of Technology in the 1950s summed up the difference starkly. Minsky, a pioneer of AI, purportedly declared, "We're going to make machines intelligent. We are going to make them conscious!" Engelbart, a proponent of Intelligent Augmentation rather than AI, responded, "You're going to do all that for the machines? What are you going to do for the people?"

Both paths claim to make life better for their users. Both bring moral hazards.

Defending reality is not a privilege; it's crucial to ensuring a flourishing human future. A vision of the future where large portions of the population are relegated to virtual existences *is* dystopian because it is one in which human choice is severely curtailed. It's notable that Andreessen says nothing about what might happen to the physical bodies of those who will supposedly be living, laughing, and loving all day online. But we already know from contemporary experience that the more time we spend in sedentary interaction with our screens, the higher the national obesity rate and increase in related physical ailments. Likewise, an epidemic of mental health problems such as anxiety and depression, particularly among younger people, has occurred in tandem with increased time spent on social media platforms and other mediated experiences. A world modified by an Experience Pill world might seem less pervasive than an all-VR world, but they both pose threats to our mental and physical health.

Both worlds are unfree. The builders of the platforms in which we spend all this time, whether it is Meta/Facebook in the "Metaverse" or various corporations outfitting futuristic cities like NEOM in Saudi Arabia, control the design of these spaces and limit our choices via surveillance, nudges, and other techniques. As we saw in chapter 5, sophisticated technologies that can sense our physiological and emotional state are already here; it is only a matter of scale for these technologies to make more "smart" cities and "smart" workplaces. Such a world seeks to control or displace human experience through mediating technologies, predictive algorithms, and surveillance, all in the name of limiting irrational behavior and risk and increasing convenience and efficiency.

There is another path available to us if we choose to take it. This book has described a range of human experiences that are at risk of becoming or have already gone extinct, in part because we are choosing to mediate so much of our lives with technology and accepting its systemic imposition on areas of life that used to be free from it. Some of these experiences might seem mundane, such as the decline of handwriting or the rarity of finding someone in public space who is not immersed in a smartphone. Others are now so common as to go unnoticed, such as our waning ability to experience human pleasure without mediation, or our discomfort with face-to-face interactions.

One of the challenges in documenting the disappearance of qualitative things in a world that elevates the quantitative is the rapid pace of change. By the time we reckon with the loss caused by one way of doing things, a new thing has already come along. The social media platforms that began as a tool for sharing vacation photos or reconnecting with old friends have morphed into something far more algorithmically driven, for example, with more sophisticated ways of nudging you toward what it knows you really want to see and more granular predictions of your likely future behavior. Culture critic Jess Joho claims TikTok's algorithms were so precise that the platform knew she was bisexual before she did. It was as if TikTok was "reading your soul like some sort of divine digital oracle, prying open layers of your being never before known to your own conscious mind," she said of her algorithmically enabled awakening. Other awakenings spawned by technology platforms have been less satisfying, and some downright menacing; indeed, platforms like TikTok and others have contributed to political polarization, to the spread of hateful ideologies and beliefs, and even incited violence.

These kinds of experiences will become more common as more powerful AI tools come to market; these technologies will also have a further distorting effect on our ability to distinguish reality from unreality, the virtual from the real, and genuine experiences of connection from manufactured instances of discovery.

Attempts to graft more authentic experiences onto these digital platforms thus far have been unsuccessful—and further proof of a century of warnings by technology critics from Jacques Ellul to Marshall McLuhan to Neil Postman about the dominance of technological ways of seeing the world once they are in place. For a moment in 2022, for example, the BeReal app successfully marketed itself as the anti-Instagram, a social media platform that encouraged qualitative over quantitative interaction and claimed to restore authenticity to a social media landscape that preferred the perfectly filtered, staged, and inauthentic image. Users of BeReal were expected to snap one photo a day and post it without filters, to share with friends.

Authenticity itself proved to be novel; BeReal users at first might have been willing to perform authenticity on demand, but they soon tired of it. And much of the authenticity proved to be neither "real" nor "spontaneous." As one user told Mashable, "There was a lot of social pressure to be posting things that were not real." Another agreed, noting, "I realized it wasn't the 'live in the moment' version of social media, but just another way to superficially document your life with your friends . . . People don't use it to document their real lives, they just wait until they are doing something interesting." Those that did use the app as it was intended quickly grew bored of their own and others' posts. "I mean, how many times can I take a photo of me at my desk doing boring work?" one user asked. The app experienced a steep drop-off in users.

Too many social media users were primed to respond to the incentive structure built into large platforms like Instagram and TikTok, which encourage a supposedly value-neutral metric of "engagement" rather than authenticity. We prefer to ignore the fact that the pursuit of such engagement habituates users in behaviors that are far from neutral. By design, these platforms seek to maximize the time we spend on them, which in turn deepens the habits of mind we form while using them. As we have seen, some of those habits—anger, anxiety, mistrust, and reactionary responses to everyday challenges—are contributing to the fracturing of society.

In our daily lives, we're replacing the time we used to spend with others with time online and other mediated pursuits. According to the U.S. Census Bureau American Time Use Survey, beginning in 2014, the time we reported spending with friends started to decline, and by 2019, we spent only four hours per week with friends, a drop of 37 percent from 2014.

These are quantifiable losses. But there are unquantifiable ones as well. The quality of our experiences matters, and by limiting the time we spend face-to-face with others, technology alters our understanding of the things we have in common, including things as mundane as having to wait in line together, or having to engage in the social pleasantries that make public space a healthy rather than hostile place.

The easier it is to use technology to tune out others around you, the more those interpersonal skills deteriorate. A focus group convened by the *New York Times* to explore questions of trust in public life found that many participants, unprompted, spoke of the values eroded by our collective immersion in virtual worlds. "Both Democrats and Republicans talked mostly about values—showing more respect to other people, communicating better, listening better—and about spending less time isolating in social media," the focus group reported. One participant told the group's convener that she traced a decline of trust to "2008, with iPhones," as this was when "people started to prefer to have their face turned toward a machine rather than a person."

Technology is supposed to extend the power of our senses, not replace them with sensors and algorithms that claim to be better at divining our needs and wants than our own bodies and minds. And yet our growing acceptance of these tools as effective replacements for our senses is reshaping our relationships. This is now a fact that is celebrated. Food delivery company Seamless tells customers it will "satisfy your craving for zero human contact," for example, and the "contactless" interactions that arose of necessity during the pandemic have remained because we appear to prefer a photograph of our takeout order dropped on our doorstep to any chance of an interaction with the anonymous human being who delivered it.

The young who have grown up using these technologies and platforms express a clear preference for them. "Online feels more peaceful and calming," fourteen-year-old Nate told the *New York Times*. "You don't have to talk with anybody in person or do anything in person. You're just sitting on your bed or chair, watching or doing something." Eleven-year-old Andrew agreed. "When I'm online, I can mute myself, and they can't really see me. I can't just mute myself in real life." When we choose to conform to the demands of the machine and replace human interactions with mediated experiences, we risk becoming more machinelike ourselves; it is the subtle but important difference between putting something you like *on* Instagram and doing something specifically *for* Instagram because you want to be liked.

A decade ago, a book about how technology is changing us would offer solutions for a more balanced relationship with our devices, such as take a digital Sabbath, avoid multitasking, and put those phones away at the dinner table! These are no longer enough. We need to be more like the Amish in our approach to technology, cultivating a robust skepticism about each new device and app, even if most of us will not be as strict as the Amish in rejecting them. The Amish ask the right questions before embracing something new: How will this impact our community? Is it good for families? Does it support or undermine our values? When they decide against adopting something new, the community supports the decision as a group.

This approach can work in a secular setting. Parents concerned about the impact of smartphones on their children have formed groups like "Wait Until 8th" that allow families to join and sign a pledge that they will not give their children smartphones before the eighth grade. Parents have also successfully pressured schools to limit or ban smartphone use during the school day.

More broadly, consumers should hold technology companies accountable for what their products do to their users. Stop buying into the PR message of Silicon Valley, which masks its mercenary self-interest in gauzy claims about connecting people to one another. Like alcohol, tobacco, firearms, and gambling, our platforms and devices should be subject to regulations that take an honest look at their effects.

This is particularly important when it comes to their impact on children, and we are amid a period of novel legislation and policymaking in this arena. Several states are considering or have passed legislation demanding stricter enforcement of age requirements for social media use, for example, and similar bills have been introduced in Congress.

According to Common Sense Media, seven out of ten American children have a smartphone by the age of twelve and spend approximately eight hours every day online. The risk for children is not only in the opportunity cost of the time spent online—according to the Reboot Foundation, the average teenage TikTok user "spends more than two hours daily on the app, with 23 percent on it for more than four hours"—but that the more they use it, the more trustworthy they believe the information they consume is. And there is this: "When asked to choose between suspending their social media use for one year or giving up their right to vote for a year, teen users overwhelmingly—64 percent—said they would give up their voting rights."

Technology isn't neutral. It is ambivalent. As historian Lewis Mumford noted in his book *Technics and Civilization*, "It is both an instrument of liberation and one of repression." To liberate ourselves from its unhealthy influence, we need to reintroduce friction into the seamless lives technology has made possible. We need to engage in more face-to-face interactions, practice greater awareness of others in public space, and cultivate more smartphone-free spaces in public life. We need to gain a better understanding of how we use our time and consider the opportunity costs of spending so much of it online. We need to curb our impulse for instant gratification. We need to revive virtues and practices that we know lead to healthier communities.

People are already doing this. Kate Gladstone of Albany, New York, who has run a handwriting coaching business for decades, now finds that nearly all of her clients are aged eighteen to thirty-five—the first generation who came of age without being taught handwriting and are now eager to learn.

Artists are finding novel ways to get us to think about how we live with technology by making plain the physical reality of what we're doing when we are in virtual space. Dutch artist Erik Kessels created a project called "24 Hours in Photos" that prints out and piles up in gallery spaces a fraction of the millions of photos people upload to photo-sharing sites in a single day, creating the claustrophobic and disorienting feeling of being trapped in an episode of *Hoarders*. "I visualize the feeling of drowning in representations of other people's experiences," he told the *New York Times*.

Drowning is not a good feeling, but it captures what a lot of us feel when we consider how we use technology—and how it uses us. We have already made many choices that risk rendering crucial human experiences extinct, but that doesn't mean we can't find better ways to live with technology. You shouldn't need an app to understand how to be real. And you shouldn't feel compelled to perform your reality every moment of every day. Nor should we want to live in a world where more and more people cannot distinguish between the real and the unreal.

When she was a technology reporter for the *New York Times,* Nellie Bowles wrote a piece about how human contact was becoming a "luxury good." She was describing an emerging reality wherein the poor are given technological alternatives or mediated contact while the rich still seek out and can afford in-person experiences.

She talked to a consultant to luxury companies who noted, "What we are seeing is the luxurification of human engagement."

This was not merely a matter of preferring a human concierge at your hotel to a computer screen or a real live waiter at a restaurant to scanning a QR code. It has an impact on people's lives at some of their most vulnerable moments, as we saw in chapter 2 with the growing use of mediation tools in medicine. Bowles described a hospital in Fremont, California, where "a tablet [computer] on a motorized stand recently rolled into a hospital room, and a doctor on a video feed told a patient, Ernest Quintana, 78, that he was dying." Nursing homes are embracing the use of companion robots for the elderly, reasoning that some attention, even if does not come from a fellow human being, is better than none.

The moral ambivalence many of us feel about these kinds of mediated or robot-replacement interactions is a feeling we should attend to. And yet we are moving in the opposite direction. Even after loved ones are gone, their family can use technology to experience a more efficient grieving process. The Empathy technology company offers a suite of services to streamline the handling of death, including a feature, "Finding Words," that automates the process of writing a loved one's obituary. Or, if they have the resources, they can hire a company that will use AI technology to sift through any recordings they might have of the dead person's voice and bring it back to life, as the documentarians who released a film about the late chef Anthony Bourdain did, using "his" AI-generated voice. "We've crossed into replacing the dead," philosopher Patrick Stokes told the *New York Times*.

This has broader cultural implications. We live lives of relentless self-documentation, but this has failed to produce an increase in self-awareness or a deepening of cultural memory. In fact, we now outsource our individual and collective memory to technology. Google Photos can create sophisticated montages from people's vast collections of images.

New York Times technology columnist Farhad Manjoo expressed excitement over this "dawning of a new age of personalized robot historian" that will "curate memories and construct narratives about our most intimate human experiences." He predicts a future where "the robots will know everything about us—and they will tell our stories," shaping not only our reality but also the formation of memory in significant ways. The story of your life, curated by Google, might not be the story you want to tell.

Soon, even assuming we can win the battle against the deterioration of digital material known as bit rot, the only tangible memories that people who lived their lives online will leave behind will be owned by companies like Meta—a reminder that recording an experience is a much easier task than preserving it. Children growing up today won't experience their memories as physical things in the way that earlier generations did. No photo albums or VHS cassettes; no letters. They will leave behind a more ephemeral inheritance—a digital mausoleum in the form of defunct Instagram posts and dormant TikTok accounts.

Is there a place for memory in such a world? When the artifacts that preserve memory, from photographs to letters to print books, migrate to the digital ether, we gain new powers for searching and making connections (and, with AI-enabled techniques, new powers of creation). But we also lose something. We lose control over those artifacts if they are on platforms owned by large corporations like Meta or Google; we lose the tactile experience of holding in our hands something touched by an ancestor or made by another human being for us; we lose those many physical prompts of memory. We lose a sense of our fragility and limits and, as a result, an understanding of what it means to be an embodied human being.

Of course, technology enthusiasts want us to think about pushing beyond existing human limits, even unto death. Entrepreneurs such as Peter Thiel and transhumanists such as Ray Kurzweil hope to cheat death—or at least radically delay it. Thiel funds a nonprofit called the Methuselah Foundation, whose goal is "to make 90 the new 50 by

2030." As Thiel says, "Death will eventually be reduced from a mystery to a solvable problem." For enough money, the Alcor Life Extension Foundation will keep your dead body on ice in the hope that one day technology might allow for its reanimation (and, one assumes, a means to download one's consciousness). "A fulfilling life doesn't have to end," is the company's motto.

But life is finite—even if acknowledging our human limits is not a popular pastime in a culture eager to understand technology as a story of endless gains for mankind. Accounting for what we have lost is also the beginning of the process of reclaiming it. Despite what Silicon Valley marketing messages insist, history is not always a steady march toward progress, and not every new thing is an improvement on the old.

If we are to reclaim human virtues and save our most deeply rooted human experiences from extinction, we must be willing to place limits on the more extreme transformative projects proposed by our techno-enthusiasts, not as a means of stifling innovation but as a commitment to our shared humanity. Only then can we live freely as the embodied, quirky, contradictory, resilient, creative human beings we are.

Acknowledgments

＊ ＊ ＊

I am fortunate to work for an organization, the American Enterprise Institute, that offers its scholars a great deal of support as well as freedom in our research and writing. I am grateful to AEI's president, Robert Doar, and my wonderful colleagues for their insights and intellectual generosity, particularly my colleagues in the Social, Cultural, and Constitutional Studies program.

I owe special thanks to Yuval Levin for his encouragement over the years, and to my other fellow *New Atlantis* founders, Eric Cohen, Adam Keiper, and Eric Brown. Much of what is in this book began twenty years ago as a conversation with them about the impact of technology on human behavior, and I remain grateful for their encouragement and friendship.

I am lucky to spend several days a week talking, laughing, and arguing with my colleagues at *Commentary* magazine. The ongoing conversations and friendship of John Podhoretz, Abe Greenwald, Matthew Continetti, Seth Mandel, and my former colleague Noah Rothman have brought me immeasurable pleasure over the years.

I am also grateful for the superb scholars at the Institute for Advanced Studies in Culture at the University of Virginia, who read and commented on early drafts of the book and who have been a tirelessly supportive intellectual community, as have the fellows and staff at the Ethics & Public Policy Center and New America. I owe special thanks to Andrés Martinez and Tori Bosch for the many lively exchanges about technology we've had over the years.

A writer can have no better advocate than Elyse Cheney, whose wise counsel and energetic support of her writers is remarkable to behold. I am incredibly thankful to be one of them.

I am also grateful to have had the opportunity to work with an editor as insightful and creative as Brendan Curry; I have learned from his keen editorial judgment and benefited from his patience and consistent encouragement. Caroline Adams gave the book an incredibly thoughtful edit as well as managing the many parts of book production with elan and good humor.

I am thankful to have such a wonderful and supportive family. Thanks are due Louis and Pam Stolba, Cathy and Isabelle Remick, and Cynthia, Brian, Quade and Quinlan Wilhelm.

Many friends have provided support, laughter, and encouragement, especially Marnie Kenney, Sarah Despres, Naomi Riley, Stephanie Cohen, Christine Whelan, and Jennifer Place.

My DC Aikido dojo family reminds me every day of the importance of awareness and discipline, but also the joys of challenging oneself to try new things. I am especially grateful for the friendship and support (and *ukemi*) of Ryan, John, Noah, Caleb, Alex, Jochem, Mo, Al, Albert, and Mounir.

Notes

* * *

INTRODUCTION

1 **Different people speak different languages**: On storytelling and language as human enterprises, see Stephen Crites, "The Narrative Quality of Experience," *Journal of the American Academy of Religion* 39, no. 3 (September 1971): 291–311.

2 **In 2018, Matthew Wright**: Stephanie K. Baer, "An Armed Man Spouting a Bizarre Right-Wing Conspiracy Theory Was Arrested After a Standoff at the Hoover Dam," BuzzFeed News, June 17, 2018.

3 **"has been like I watched a movie"**: "Interview of Douglas Austin Jensen," January 8, 2021, p. 5, in *United States of America vs. Douglas Austin Jensen*, Case 1:21-cr-00006-TJK, Document 69-1, filed April 8, 2022.

3 **Mike Sparks struggled**: Peter Manseau, "His pastors tried to steer him away from social media rage. He stormed the Capitol anyway," *Washington Post*, February 19, 2021. See also Peter Manseau (@plmanseau), Twitter, February 6, 2021.

3 **One family physician writes**: Gavin Francis, "Scrolling," *New York Review of Books* 68, no. 14 (September 23, 2021): 60.

3 **historian Daniel Boorstin**: Daniel J. Boorstin, *The Image: A Guide to Pseudo-Events in America* (New York: Vintage, 1992), 11.

5 **The philosopher Theodor Adorno**: Theodor Adorno, *The Culture Industry: Selected Essays on Mass Culture* (Abingdon, UK: Routledge Press, 2001), ch. 6, "How to Look at Television."

6 **"revolutionizing digital communications"**: Sensorium website, accessed May 15, 2023.

CHAPTER 1: YOU HAD TO BE THERE

10 **"withering of experience"**: Theodor Adorno, *Minima Moralia* (New York: Verso, 2002), 40.

10 **As mathematician Isaac Milner wrote**: Mary Milner, *The Life of Isaac Milner* (London: John W. Parker, 1842), 120.

11 **Joseph Weizenbaum noted**: Joseph Weizenbaum, *Computer Power and Human Reason: From Judgment to Calculation* (New York: W. H. Freeman, 1976), 25–27.

12 **"The forecast on many"**: Jason Samenow, "The Drawbacks of the Automated Weather App and the Need for Human Touch," *Washington Post*, February 4, 2014.

12 **"As Facebook becomes a more integral"**: Tom Simonite, "Facebook's Telescope on Human Behavior," *MIT Technology Review*, April 13, 2012.

13 **"It does us no good to make fantastic progress"**: Thomas Merton, *Conjectures of a Guilty Bystander* (New York: Crown, 2009), 67.

13 **the fastest year-over-year increase in Americans' smartphone use**: "How Many Americans Have Smartphones, 2010–2021," Oberlo statistics.

13 **One popular genre of YouTube videos**: Sam Anderson, "Watching People Watching People Watching," *New York Times Magazine*, November 27, 2011, 60.

14 **"véjà du"**: Ayesha Khanna and Parag Khanna, "Welcome to the Hybrid Age," *Slate*, June 13, 2012.

14 **Google now offers a "field-trip simulation system"**: Natasha Singer, "Helping Students Explore the World, with Virtual Reality from Google," *New York Times*, September 29, 2015, B4.

14 **In 2010, in South Korea**: Andrew Salmon, "Couple: Internet Gaming Addiction Led to Baby's Death," CNN, April 2, 2010.

15 **a Japanese man "married"**: Kyung Lah, "Tokyo Man Marries Video Game Character," *CNN*, December 17, 2009.

15 **the *New York Times* described a subculture**: Ben Dooley and Hisako Ueno, "In Dolls and Cartoons, Devoted Fans in Japan See Marriage Material," *New York Times*, April 25, 2022, B1.

15 **Walter Benjamin**: Walter Benjamin, "Experience and Poverty," *Selected Writings*, vol. 2, 1931–1934 (Cambridge, MA: Harvard University Press, 1999), 732, 735.

17 **Robert Michael Pyle**: Robert Michael Pyle, *The Thunder Tree: Lessons from an Urban Wildland* (Boston: Houghton Mifflin, 1993).

18 **B. Joseph Pine II and James H. Gilmore**: B. Joseph Pine II and James H. Gilmore, "How to Profit from Experience," *Wall Street Journal*, August 4, 1997.

18 **Apple ad**: Two-page advertisement in *New York Times*, June 16, 2013.

18 **Social psychology research finds**: Christopher Bergland, "Want More In-the-Moment Happiness? Buy Experiences, Not Stuff," *Psychology Today*, March 12, 2020.

19 **An advertisement from Omni Hotels**: Advertisement in *The New Yorker*, April 26, 2016.

19 **Target collaborates with SoulCycle**: Megan Garber, "Sweat: The Hottest Accessory," *Atlantic*, January 14, 2016.

19 **"It's not just the product that you end up drinking"**: Austin Carr, "The Secret Sauce in Square's Starbucks Partnership: Discovery, QR Codes," *Fast Company*, November 7, 2012.

19 **Huggies diaper marketing campaign**: "Case Study: How Huggies uses social media to engage consumers as a challenger brand in Hong Kong diapers 'battlefield,'" *Campaign Asia*, September 19, 2011.

19 **"It becomes more useful to have preferences"**: Rob Horning, "Presumed Conspicuous," *New Inquiry*, May 2, 2012.

20 **"A better photographer, built in"**: Apple advertisement, back cover of *New York Times Magazine*, December 15, 2013.

21 **rather lose their sense of smell**: Chris Gayomali, "Study: 53% of Youngsters Would Choose Technology Over Sense of Smell," *Time*, May 27, 2011.

21 **"requires the embrace of chance and rupture"**: Richard Sennett, "Humanism," *Hedgehog Review*, Summer 2011, 24.

21 **"The Internet and virtual realities easily satisfy"**: Monica Kim, "The Good and the Bad of Escaping to Virtual Reality," *Atlantic,* February 18, 2015. Although still an enthusiast, Bailenson has moderated his views since 2015. See Jeremy Bailenson, *Experience on Demand: What Virtual Reality Is, How It Works, and What It Can Do* (New York: W. W. Norton, 2018).

21 **Palmer Luckey, founder of Oculus VR**: Alexandra Wolfe, "Palmer Luckey: Making Virtual Reality a Reality," *Wall Street Journal,* August 7, 2015.

22 **"Science is no substitute for virtue"**: Bertrand Russell, *Icarus, or The Future of Science* (Boston: E. P. Dutton, 1924), 57–58.

22 **"Those who mourn the loss of the offline"**: Nathan Jurgenson, "The IRL Fetish," *New Inquiry,* June 28, 2012.

23 **"exited their vehicles and started snapping selfies"**: "Los Angeles motorists stranded on freeway because of suicidal man threatening to jump off an overpass snap selfies with the would-be jumper in the background," *Daily Mail,* April 11, 2014.

23 **"The narcissist is not hungry for experiences"**: Richard Sennett, *The Fall of Public Man* (New York: W. W. Norton, 1992), 325.

23 **"experience is the overcoming of perils"**: Yi-Fu Tuan, *Space and Place: The Perspective of Experience* (Minneapolis: University of Minnesota Press, 2001), 9.

24 **Delphic Oracle's guidance**: First published in Christine Rosen, "Virtual Friendship and the New Narcissism," *New Atlantis,* Summer 2007.

24 **memories are now of experiences that occurred online**: On the role of the Internet on memory formation, see Daniel M. Wegner and Adrian F. Ward, "How Google Is Changing Your Brain," *Scientific American* 309, no. 6 (December 2013): 58–61.

24 **In 2016, at Comet Ping Pong**: Adam Goldman, "The Comet Ping Pong Gunman Answers Our Reporters' Questions," *New York Times,* December 9, 2016, A16.

24 **American philosopher of technology Lewis Mumford**: Lewis Mumford, *Technics and Civilization* (Chicago: University of Chicago Press, 2010), 3.

CHAPTER 2: FACING ONE ANOTHER

27 **He was self-testing a theory**: Charles Darwin, *The Expression of the Emotions in Man and Animals* (New York: Penguin, 2009), 47.

28 **Darwin was especially keen on studying the face**: Darwin, *The Expression of the Emotions,* 301, 179, 172.

29 **"I was following a tour guide"**: David Zax, "Wifarer's Indoor GPS and the Never-Lost Generation," *Fast Company,* June 7, 2012.

30 **"And repayeth them that hate him"**: Exodus 33:11, Deuteronomy 7:10.

30 **"the science of human character"**: John Stuart Mill, "Of Ethology, or the Science of the Formation of Character," in *The Collected Works of John Stuart Mill,* vol. 8, edited by John M. Robson (Toronto: University of Toronto Press, 1974).

32 **"Humans are a primate"**: Jonathan H. Turner, *Face to Face: Toward a Sociological Theory of Interpersonal Behavior* (Palo Alto, CA: Stanford University Press, 2002), 28.

32 **less than 1 percent of it, by some estimates**: Ned Kock, "The Psychobiological Model: Towards a New Theory of Computer-Mediated Communication Based on Darwinian Evolution," *Organization Science* 15, no. 3 (May–June 2004): 331.

32 **Intense eye contact increases one's heart rate**: A. Rodney Wellens, "Heart-Rate Changes in Responses to Shifts in Interpersonal Gaze from Liked and Disliked Others," *Perceptual and Motor Skills* 64, no. 2 (1987): 595–98.

32 **everything about our "biological apparatus"**: Kock, "The Psychobiological Model," 330–31.

33 **"We must have *automatic* appraising mechanisms"**: Paul Ekman, *Emotions Revealed* (New York: St. Martin's Press, 2003), 14, 21.

33 **"Our faces can perform"**: Author interview with Paul Ekman, Being Human Conference, San Francisco, CA, March 25, 2012.

34 **"accurately predict someone's emotional state"**: Kate Crawford, *Atlas of AI: Power, Politics, and the Planetary Costs of Artificial Intelligence* (New Haven: Yale University Press, 2021), 171.

34 **"the specific dangers of Ekman's theories"**: Maria Gendron and Lisa Feldman Barrett, "Facing the Past: A History of the Face in Psychological Research on Emotion Perception," in J. M. Fernandez-Dols and J. A. Russell, eds., *The Science of Facial Expression* (Oxford: Oxford University Press, 2017), 30.

34 **"motivational enhancement effect"**: Michael Woodworth and Jeff Hancock, "The Motivational Enhancement Effect: Implications for Our Chosen Modes of Communication in the 21st Century," *Proceedings of the 38th Annual Hawaii International Conference on System Sciences*, January 6, 2005.

34 **"underestimated the relative advantage"**: M. Mahdi Roghanizad and Vanessa K. Bohns, "Should I Ask Over Zoom, Phone, Email, or In-Person? Communication Channel and Predicted Versus Actual Compliance," *Social Psychology and Personality Science* 13, no. 7 (2022): 1163–72.

35 **"There is something the mind is picking up"**: Tara Parker-Pope, "Who's Trustworthy? A Robot Can Help Teach Us," *New York Times*, September 11, 2012, D5.

35 **Researchers at the University of Toronto**: Maciek Lipinski-Harten and Romin W. Tafarodi, "A Comparison of Conversational Quality in Online and Face-to-Face First Encounters," *Journal of Language and Social Psychology* 31, no. 3 (2012): 331–41.

35 **"lovers quarrel, make it up again"**: Michel de Montaigne, *The Complete Essays* translated by M. A. Screech (New York: Penguin, 1991), 507.

35 **"the silent language"**: Edward T. Hall, *The Silent Language* (New York: Anchor, 1973).

35 **"implicit communication"**: Albert Mehrabian, *Silent Messages: Implicit Communication of Emotions and Attitudes* (Belmont, CA: Wadsworth, 1980).

36 **"The more attuned to others you become"**: Barbara L. Fredrickson, "Your Phone vs. Your Heart," *New York Times*, March 24, 2013, SR14. See also Barbara L. Fredrickson and Thomas Joiner, "Reflections on Positive Emotions and Upward Spirals," *Perspectives on Psychological Science* 13, no. 2 (2018): 194–99.

36 **Marina Abramović**: Holland Cotter, "700-Hour Silent Opera Reaches Finale at MoMA," *New York Times*, May 31, 2010, C1. See also Arthur Danto, "Sitting with Marina," *New York Times*, May 23, 2010.

37 **"The gestures which we sometimes call empty"**: Erving Goffman, *Interaction Ritual: Essays on Face to Face Behavior* (New York: Pantheon, 1982), 91.

37 **When people meet, Goffman argued**: Erving Goffman, *Relations in Public: Microstudies of the Public Order* (New York: Harper and Row, 1972), 239; Goffman, *Interaction Ritual*, 12.

38 **"to be looked at as through air"**: Eric D. Wesselmann, Florencia D. Cardoso, Samantha Slater, and Kipling D. Williams, "To Be Looked at as Through Air: Civil Attention Matters," *Psychological Science* 23 (2012).

38 **Brooklyn roofing contractor**: George Packer, "The View from a Roofer's Recession," *New Yorker*, April 9, 2009.

38 **"whereby one treats the other"**: Goffman, *Interaction Ritual*, 145.

39 **Clinique**: Elizabeth Holmes, "Leave Me Alone, I'm Shopping," *Wall Street Journal*, June 28, 2012.

40 **"Entered Apple store"**: Ginger Gibson, tweet, reposted on Mediabistro's subsite Fishbowl, accessed April 10, 2012, but no longer available.

40 **"A lot of our passengers are frequent fliers"**: Jack Nicas and Daniel Michaels, "The Self-Service Airport," *Wall Street Journal*, August 28, 2012.

41 **"Maybe it's just us"**: Elizabeth Garone, "You Gotta Believe: Comparing Santa Video Chats," *Wall Street Journal*, December 8, 2011.

41 **When the coronavirus began**: This section originally appeared in Christine Rosen, "Technosolutionism Isn't the Fix," *Hedgehog Review*, Fall 2020.

41 **"why Zoom is terrible"**: Kate Murphy, "Why Zoom Is Terrible," *New York Times*, May 4, 2020, A23.

42 **Psychologists Gabriel Radvansky and Jeffrey Zacks**: Gabriel A. Radvansky and Jeffrey M. Zacks, "Event Boundaries in Memory and Cognition," *Current Opinion in Behavioral Sciences* 17 (October 2017): 133–40.

42 **"I think what it is, sometimes we are the first"**: Norimitsu Onishi, "A Last Smile and a Wave for Bay Area Commuters," *New York Times*, March 25, 2013, A16.

43 **RP-VITA, a medical robot**: Neal Ungerleider, "Autonomous robots coming to U.S. hospitals," *Fast Company*, January 24, 2013.

43 **computer-on-wheels, named Louise**: Ranit Mishori, "Hospitals Look at Ways to Reduce Readmissions," *Herald-Tribune*, December 26, 2011.

43 **Grace, a humanoid robot**: Sabrina Jonas, "Meet Grace, the humanoid robot offering companionship in a Montreal nursing home," CBC News, October 22, 2022.

43 **Wellpoint, the second-largest health insurer**: Anna Wilde Mathews, "Doctors Move to Webcams," *Wall Street Journal*, December 21, 2012, B1.

43 **"your personal mental health ally"**: Woebothealth.com.

44 **"There are volumes one can say medically"**: Denise Grady, "What's in a Face at 50?," *New York Times*, July 31, 2011, SR4.

44 **"This artful production"**: Charles Isherwood, "Booth for Two, Dialogue Optional," *New York Times*, June 9, 2011, C1.

44 **the Pew Internet and American Life Project found**: Amanda Lenhart, "Teens, Smartphones, and Texting," Pew Research Center, March 19, 2012.

45 **Updated research in 2018**: Monica Anderson and JingJing Jiang, "Teens' Social Media Habits and Experiences," Pew Research Center, November 28, 2018.

45 **study published in *Developmental Psychology***: R. Pea, C. Nass, et al., "Media Use, Face-to-Face Communication, Media Multitasking, and Social Well-being among 8–12-year-old girls," *Developmental Psychology* 48, no. 2 (March 2012): 327–36.

45 **Professor Nass admitted**: Rachel Emma Silverman, "Study: Face Time Benefits Preteens," *Wall Street Journal*, January 31, 2012; Mark Milian, "Study: Multitasking Hinders Youth Social Skills," *CNN*, January 25, 2012.

46 **Jean Twenge and others**: Jean Twenge, "Teens Have Less Face Time with Their Friends, and Are Lonelier Than Ever," *Conversation*, March 20, 2019.

46 **"Tech skills are great"**: Author interview with Gary Small, September 28, 2011.

46 **SmileScan**: Mark Gawne, "The modulation and ordering of affect," *Fibreculture Journal* 21 (2012): 98, 108–10.

47 **"Gamers need to be informed"**: Jeremy Bailenson, "Your Kinect Is Watching You," *Slate*, March 7, 2012.

47 **"social acts with consequences"**: Marianne LaFrance, *Lip Service: Smiles in Life, Death, Trust, Lies, Work, Memory, Sex, and Politics* (New York: W. W. Norton, 2011), ix.

48 **"It is plausible that the intensity"**: Arvid Kappas and Nicole C. Kramer, eds., *Face-to-Face Communication over the Internet: Emotions in a Web of Culture, Language, and Technology* (Cambridge: Cambridge University Press, 2011), 8.

49 **"Despite the positive impact of emerging communication technologies"**: Kyungjoon Lee, John S. Brownstein, et al., "Does Collocation Inform the Impact of Collaboration?," *PLOS One* 5, no. 12 (December 2010).

49 **"These weren't concealed movements"**: "Police: Rail Commuters on Phones Didn't Notice Gun," ABC7 News, October 8, 2013.

50 **"WorldStar that!"**: Ali Winston, "Man Charged in Subway Attack on 78-Year-Old Woman That Was Caught on Video," *New York Times*, March 25, 2019, A21.

51 **In a 1968 study**: Aronson, *The Social Animal*, 46–47, 51.

51 **A more recent study of the bystander effect**: Susan Pinker, "Bystanders Who Intervene in an Attack," *Wall Street Journal*, July 20–21, 2019, C4.

53 **"What makes performances false"**: Goffman, *Relations in Public*, 273.

53 **"Attention is the rarest"**: Simone Weil, letter to Joe Bousquet, April 13, 1942, in Simone Petrement, *Simone Weil: A Life*, translated by Raymond Rosenthal (New York: Pantheon, 1976).

CHAPTER 3: HAND TO MOUSE

55 **A *Washington Post* journalist had trouble**: Lisa Rein, "Washington's Signature-Writing Machines Rumble into the Digital Age," *Washington Post*, April 11, 2014.

56 **"The Autopen has long been a tool"**: Damilic website.

56 **During the George W. Bush administration**: Brian Resnick and *National Journal*, "When a Robot Signs a Bill," *Atlantic*, January 3, 2013.

56 **"often reluctant to admit its use"**: Gregory Korte, "White House Aides Use Autopen to Sign Highway Bill While Obama Is Overseas," *USA Today*, November 20, 2015.

56 **Vice President Mike Pence invoked the autopen**: Steven Nelson, "Mike Pence Calls Biden a 'Trojan Horse for a Radical Agenda,'" *New York Post*, July 17, 2020; Darren Rovell, "Autographed Trump Hats and Books Sold on His Website Were Signed by Machine," *ABC News*, November 18, 2016.

56 **Fans of singer Bob Dylan**: Alexander Larman, "Bob Dylan's Curious Book-Signing Controversy," *Spectator*, December 2, 2022.

57 **Calligraphist Bernard Maisner**: Gena Feith, "With Pen in Hand, He Battles On," *Wall Street Journal*, September 4, 2012.

57 **But handwriting is disappearing**: Emily Freeman, "Cursive Joins the Ranks of Latin and Sanskrit," *Wall Street Journal*, November 22, 2013. The Common Core State Standards do not require handwriting instruction after grade 1, and don't require cursive handwriting at all; after grade 1 states can choose to continue handwriting instruction or eliminate it altogether. See Saperstein Associates, "Handwriting in the 21st Century? A Summary of Research Presented at the Handwriting in the 21st Century Educational Summit," Winter 2012; Valerie Bauerlein, "The New Script for Teaching Handwriting Is No Script at All," *Wall Street Journal*, January 31, 2013, A1.

58 **A newspaper in Toronto recorded the lament of a pastry instructor**: Louise Brown, "Why Johnny Can't Sign His Name," *Toronto Star*, June 23, 2012.

58 **China Youth Daily Social Survey Center**: Ben Schott, "Tibiwangzi," *New York Times*, September 8, 2010.

59 **"an option, and often an unattractive"**: Philip Hensher, *The Missing Ink: The Lost Art of Handwriting* (New York: Farrar, Straus and Giroux, 2013), 6.

59 **Theorists of embodied cognition**: Maurice Merleau-Ponty, *Phenomenology of Perception*, translated by Donald Landes (New York: Routledge, 2013). George Lakoff and Mark Johnson, *Metaphors We Live By* (Chicago: University of Chicago Press, 2003).

59 **"Many of our physicians don't write legibly"**: "'Handwriting Challenged' Doctors to Take Penmanship Class at Cedars-Sinai Medical Center," *Science News*, April 27, 2000.

60 **Neuroscientist Karin James**: Karin H. James and Laura Engelhardt, "The effects of handwriting experience on functional brain development in pre-literate children," *Trends in Neuroscience Education* 1, no. 2 (December 2012): 32–42.

60 **psychologist Virginia Berninger**: Virginia Berninger, Katherine Vaughan, Robert Abbott, and Sylvia Abbott, "Treatment of Handwriting Problems in Beginning Writers: Transfer from Handwriting to Composition," *Journal of Educational Psychology* 89, no. 4 (December 1997): 652–56.

61 **Berninger updated her work**: Perri Klass, "Writing to Learn," *New York Times*, June 21, 2016, D6; Virginia Berninger, Robert Abbott, Clayton R. Cook, and William Nagy, "Relationships of Attention and Executive Functions to Oral Language, Reading, and Writing Skills and Systems in Middle Childhood and Early Adolescence," *Journal of Learning Disabilities* 50, no. 4 (July–August 2017): 434–39; Zachary Alstad, Elizabeth Sanders, Robert D. Abbott, et al., "Modes of Alphabet Letter Production During Middle Childhood and Adolescence: Interrelationships with Each Other and with Other Writing Skills," *Journal of Writing Research* 6, no. 3 (February 2015): 199–231.

61 **Psychologists Pam Mueller and Daniel Oppenheimer**: On distraction of laptop users, see Faria Sana, Tina Weston, and Nicholas Sepeda, "Laptop Multitasking Hinders Classroom Learning for both Users and Nearby Peers," *Computers and Education* 62 (March 2013): 24–31; Pam A. Mueller and Daniel Oppenheimer, "The Pen Is Mightier Than the Keyboard: Advantages of Longhand over Laptop Note Taking," *Psychological Science* 25, no. 6 (June 2014): 1159–68. A study in *Frontiers in Psychology* built on Mueller and Oppenheimer's study and measured electroencephalography activity in subjects using keyboards or drawing images by hand. They found that writing by hand stimulated regions of the brain associated with optimal learning. Audrey L. H. van der Meer and F. R. van der Weel, "Only Three Fingers Write, but the Whole Brain Works: A High-Density EEG Study Showing Advantages of Drawing over Typing for Learning," *Frontiers in Psychology* 8 (2017): 706.

62 **"The digitization of writing entails"**: Anne Mangen, "The Disappearing Trace and the Abstraction of Inscription in Digital Writing," in *Exploring Technology for Writing and Writing Instruction*, edited by Kristine E. Pytash and Richard E. Ferdig (IGI Global, 2013), 100–13.

62 **feathers from a goose or swan's**: Ann Wroe, "Handwriting: An Elegy," *1843 Magazine*, October 8, 2012.

62 **"I believe that the labor has virtue"**: Mary Gordon, "Putting Pen to Paper, but Not Just Any Pen to Any Paper," *Writers on Writing: Collected Essays from the New York Times* (New York: Times Books, 2002), 79.

63 **"a record of time spent fitting new thoughts together"**: Deborah Madison, "The Case for Handwriting," *Daily Zester*, August 4, 2010.

63 **a family-run bento box business**: Martin Fackler, "In High-Tech Japan, the Fax Machines Roll On," *New York Times*, February 14, 2013, A1.

64 **"The technology is shaping me"**: Mohsin Hamid and Paul Antonio speaking on handwriting, "The Forum," BBC World Service, February 3, 2015. See Hensher, *Missing Ink*, 244.

64 **As calligraphist Paul Antonio notes**: "The Forum," BBC World Service.

64 **"The sheer extent to which we are using our hand"**: Manfred Spitzer, "To Swipe or Not to Swipe? The Question in Present-Day Education," *Trends in Neuroscience and Education* 2 (August 2013): 95–99.

65 **"I was trying to make a double curved line"**: "Architect Frank Gehry Finds CAD a Boon to Art and Business," CADigest, February 23, 2004. The most popular CAD software, Auto-CAD, now has plenty of competition from programs such as Revit.

65 **"The computer has ceased to be a technology"**: Stan Allen, "The Future That Is Now," *Places*, March 2012.

66 **CAD's automation of the creative process**: Quotations from Nicholas Carr, *The Glass Cage: Automation and Us* (New York: W. W. Norton, 2014), 142, 144–46.

66 **"Architecture cannot divorce itself"**: Michael Graves, "Architecture and the Lost Art of Drawing," *New York Times*, September 2, 2012, SR5.

67 **"By focusing exclusively on computer-generated illustration"**: James Wines, "Why Architects Should Never Stop Drawing by Hand," *Architizer*, accessed March 2, 2023.

67 **"Drawing shapes, shadows and lines"**: Laura Landro, "The Man of a Thousand Face-Lifts," *Wall Street Journal*, August 17, 2012.

67 **"Painting fulfills a need"**: Ray Bradbury quoted on Brainpickings.org, accessed August 22, 2012.

67 **"Audacity is the only ticket"**: Winston S. Churchill, *Painting as a Pastime* (New York: Cornerstone Library, 1965).

69 **"When we focus on making a physical object"**: Suzanne Ramljak, "Richard Sennett on Making," *American Craft* (October–November 2009). See also Richard Sennett, *The Craftsman* (New Haven: Yale University Press, 2009).

69 **Lee Miller, a bootmaker**: Rachel Emma Silverman, "The Yankee King of Cowboy Boots," *Wall Street Journal*, January 14, 2012.

69 **"We are knowing as well as sensing creatures"**: Julian Baggini, "Joy in the Task," *Aeon*, January 9, 2013.

70 **the American Time Use survey**: "American Time Use Survey Summary," Bureau of Labor Statistics, June 23, 2022.

70 **"Mastering tools and working with one's hands"**: Louis Uchitelle, "A Nation That's Losing Its Toolbox," *New York Times*, July 22, 2012, BU1; blog post from Close Grain, April 1, 2013, accessed June 4, 2015.

70 **"Making something that starts virtual"**: Chris Anderson, *Makers: The New Industrial Revolution* (New York: Crown Business, 2012), ch. 2; Evgeny Morozov, "Making It," *New Yorker*, January 13, 2014.

71 **Patricia Kuhl of the Institute for Learning and Brain Sciences**: Patricia Kuhl, "The Linguistic Genius of Babies," TEDx Rainier, October 2010.

72 **"The purpose of a for-profit"**: Ian Bogost, "Educational Hucksterism," blog post, January 5, 2013.

72 **"requires one mind engaging with another"**: Pamela Hieronymi, "Don't Confuse Technology with College Teaching," *Chronicle of Higher Education*, August 13, 2012.

73 **"Reality, by comparison, is uninteresting"**: Matt Richtel, "Technology Changing How Students Learn, Teachers Say," *New York Times*, November 1, 2012, A18.

73 **An unwelcome form of reality-testing**: An earlier version of this section originally appeared as "Technosolutionism Isn't the Fix," *Hedgehog Review*, Fall 2020.

73 **"The grade from students, teachers"**: Tawnell D. Hobbs and Lee Hawkins, "The Results Are in for Remote Learning: It Didn't Work," *Wall Street Journal*, June 5, 2020.

74 **"It may be wise"**: Ursula Franklin, *The Real World of Technology* (Toronto: House of Anansi Press, 2004), 51.

74 **"The science is clear"** ... **"Whether children play enough"**: Tom Bartlett, "The Case for Play," *Chronicle Review*, February 20, 2011.

75 **"Although play is often thought frivolous"**: A. Diamond, W. S. Barnett, J. Thomas,

and S. Munro, "Preschool Program Improves Cognitive Control," *Science* 318, no. 5855 (November 30, 2007): 1387–88.

75 **"a major method of becoming reconciled"**: Brian Sutton-Smith, *The Ambiguity of Play* (Cambridge, MA: Harvard University Press, 1997). There are also real physical consequences to a world where screens replace physical play, and not just in the upward trend of our global obesity epidemic. "Children who spend more time in front of television and computer screens and less in outdoor physical activity have narrower blood vessels in their eyes," according to a 2011 study cited in a *New York Times* article. "For adults, this form of constriction of the blood vessels is associated with an increased risk of cardiovascular disease." Another study found that "a child's corticospinal tract—which reaches the fingertips and impacts fine motor skills—is not fully developed until age 10." The corticospinal tract is the arrangement of nerve cells that carries motor commands from the brain to the spinal cord. See Nicholas Bakalar, "Television Time and Children's Eyes," *New York Times*, April 26, 2011 (original study published in the journal *Arteriosclerosis, Thrombosis and Vascular Biology*); and G. Conti, "Handwriting Characteristics and the Prediction of Illegibility in Third and Fifth Grade Students," paper presented at "Handwriting in the 21st Century? An Educational Summit," Washington, DC, January 23, 2012.

75 **"When we deny young children play"**: Erika Christakis and Nicholas Christakis, "Want to Get Your Kids into College? Let Them Play," CNN.com, December 29, 2010.

75 **Michel de Montaigne**: Michel de Montaigne, *The Complete Essays*, translated by M. A. Screech (New York: Penguin, 1993), 1269.

76 **"internalize aspects of [our tools]"**: Joseph Weizenbaum, *Computer Power and Human Reason: From Judgment to Calculation* (New York: W. H. Freeman, 1976), 22.

76 **"The body is our first and most natural"**: Marcel Mauss, "Techniques of the Body," *Economy and Society* 2, no. 1 (1973): 70–88.

76 **"could kill a chicken, and dress it"**: Wallace Stegner, *Angle of Repose* (New York: Vintage, 2014), 437–38.

77 **"For our flesh surrounds us"**: "Ignorance," in Philip Larkin, *The Complete Poems*, edited by Archie Burnett (New York: Farrar, Straus and Giroux, 2012), 67.

CHAPTER 4: HOW WE WAIT

80 **"It's our number-one guest complaint"**: About.com, Disney World forum, accessed February 13, 2018. See also "Fixing FastPass: How Disney's Virtual Queue Was Born, Broken, and Could Work Again," Theme Park Tourist, March 6, 2020.

81 **"an immersive fifteen minutes"**: Stephanie Rosenbloom, "Manifest Fantasy," *New York Times*, December 23, 2012, TR1.

82 **"We do not ride on the railroad"**: Henry David Thoreau, *Walden* (New York: Thomas Y. Crowell, 1910), 120.

82 **"Our ability to mute"**: Frank Partnoy, "Beyond the Blink," *New York Times*, July 8, 2012, SR5.

83 **"Perhaps there is only one cardinal sin"**: W. H. Auden, *The Dyer's Hand and Other Essays* (New York: Vintage, 1989), 162.

84 **Americans spend a combined 37 billion hours**: Alex Stone, "Why Waiting Is Torture," *New York Times*, August 19, 2012, SR12.

84 **researcher Jacob Hornik**: Jacob Hornik and Dan Zakay, "Psychological Time: The Case of Time and Consumer Behavior," *Time and Society* 5, no. 3 (October 1996): 385–97.

84 **retail consultants Envirosell**: Ray A. Smith, "Find the Best Checkout Line," *Wall Street Journal*, December 8, 2011.

85 **Richard Larson, a professor at MIT**: Richard C. Larson, "Perspectives on Queues: Social Justice and the Psychology of Queuing," *Operations Research* 35, no. 6 (November–December 1987): 897.

85 **"Consumers in a queue make downward comparisons"**: Rongrong Zhou and Dilip Soman, "Looking Back: Exploring the Psychology of Queuing and the Effect of the Number of People Behind," *Journal of Consumer Research* 29 (March 2003): 518–19.

86 **"If Universal didn't offer a VIP option"**: Brooks Barnes, "A VIP Ticket to Ride," *New York Times*, June 10, 2013, B1.

86 **extensive "abuse of this system"**: Scott Martindale, "Disney Overhauling Disabled-Access Program to Curb Abuse," *Orange County Register*, September 24, 2013.

87 **"the number of people who admit they feel"**: Ashley Halsey III and Bonnie S. Berkowitz, "Number of Drivers Who Say They Feel Road Rage Has Doubled, Poll Finds," *Washington Post*, September 1, 2013.

87 **"nearly 80 percent of drivers expressed"**: American Automobile Association, "Aggressive Driving."

88 **"42 people a month on average"**: Grace Hauck, "Road Rage Shootings Are Increasing. There Were More than 500 Last Year, Report Finds," *USA Today*, March 20, 2023.

88 **"Everyone is anonymous to us"**: Jenni Bergal, "Cops Scramble to Deal with Deadly Road Rage During Pandemic," Stateline.org, July 13, 2021.

89 **"the form of ecstasy"**: Milan Kundera and Linda Asher, "The Ecstasy of Speed," *Queen's Quarterly* 108, no. 3 (Fall 2001): 382.

89 **"What may take 30 to 60 seconds"**: Austin Carr, "Google's Project Glass: Inside the Problem Solving and Prototyping," *Fast Company*, June 5, 2012. See also Steve Lohr, "For Impatient Web Users, an Eye Blink Is Just Too Long to Wait," *New York Times*, March 1, 2012, A1.

90 **A granular study of online video use**: S. Shunmuga Krishnan and Ramesh K. Sitaraman, "Video Stream Quality Impacts User Behavior: Inferring Causality Using Quasi-Experimental Designs," *IEAA/ACM Transactions on Networking* 21, no. 6 (December 2013): 2001–14.

90 **"a minor form of despair"**: Ambrose Bierce, *The Devil's Dictionary* (1906; Seattle: Sirius, 2023).

90 **"In the age of the smartphone"**: Nick Bilton, "Thanks? Don't Bother," *New York Times*, March 11, 2013, B1.

91 **"I have decreasing amounts of tolerance"**: Bilton, "Thanks? Don't Bother."

91 **"We're sacrificing attention and care"**: Evan Selinger, "We're Turning Digital Natives into Etiquette Sociopaths," *Wired*, March 26, 2013.

91 **Isaac Asimov's 1975 story**: Isaac Asimov, "The Life and Times of Multivac," *New York Times*, January 5, 1975, SM4.

91 **According to the National Center for Substance Abuse**: The National Center for Addiction and Substance Abuse at Columbia University, "The Importance of Family Dinners VII," September 2011.

91 **link between family dining rituals and childhood obesity**: Amber J. Hammons and Barbara H. Fiese, "Is Frequency of Shared Family Meals Related to the Nutritional Health of Children and Adolescents?," *Pediatrics* 127, no. 6 (June 2011): 1565–74.

92 **"I feel that the nightmare of *1984*"**: Aldous Huxley to George Orwell, October 21, 1949, accessed at lettersofnote.com.

92 **"Shepherds do it, cops do it"**: Marshall McLuhan, *Understanding Media: The Exten-*

sions of Man (Cambridge, MA: MIT Press, 1996), 78. The website Atlas Obscura features a museum devoted to *komboloi* in Nafplion, Greece.

92 **"structure ambiguous social situations"**: Peter Stromberg, Mark Nichter, and Mimi Nichter, "Taking Play Seriously: Low-Level Smoking Among College Students," *Culture, Medicine and Psychiatry* 31, no. 1 (March 2007): 1–24.

93 **"the 'microflow' activities"**: Mihaly Csikszentmihalyi, *Flow: The Psychology of Optimal Experience* (New York: Harper Perennial, 2008), 52.

93 **According to the Pew Internet and American Life Project**: Pew Research Center, "Mobile Fact Sheet," April 7, 2021.

93 **An extensive survey of phone users**: Amanda Lenhart, "Cell Phones and American Adults," Pew Internet and American Life Project, Pew Research Center, September 2, 2010.

93 **"Stimulation is the indispensable requisite"**: William James, *The Principles of Psychology*, vol. 1 (New York: Henry Holt, 1918), 626.

94 **"There's Latin graffiti about boredom"**: Peter Toohey, "The Thrill of Boredom," *New York Times*, August 7, 2011, SR4.

94 **"for all their scales and graphs"**: Margaret Talbot, "What Does Boredom Do to Us—and for Us?," *New Yorker*, August 20, 2020.

94 **"boredom on the installment plan"**: Benjamin Kunkel, "Lingering," *n+1*, May 31, 2009.

95 **"We're very used to being passively entertained"**: Linda Rodriguez McRobbie, "The History of Boredom," *Smithsonian*, November 20, 2012.

95 **"What information consumes is rather obvious"**: Herbert Simon, "Designing Organizations for an Information-Rich World," in *Computers, Communications, and the Public Interest*, edited by Martin Greenberger (Baltimore: Johns Hopkins University Press, 1971).

95 **"For a living organism"**: Sigmund Freud, *Beyond the Pleasure Principle* (London: International Psychoanalytical Press, 1922), 31.

95 **Some researchers who study schizophrenia**: Martin Harrow, Gary J. Tucker, and Paul Shield, "Stimulus Overinclusion in Schizophrenic Disorders," *Archives of General Psychiatry* 27, no. 1 (1972): 40–45.

96 **what philosopher Blaise Pascal described**: Blaise Pascal, *Pensées* (New York: Penguin, 1995).

96 **"Attention is our most important tool"**: Csikszentmihalyi, *Flow*, 33.

96 **A fascinating study of machine gambling**: Natasha Dow Schüll, *Addiction by Design: Machine Gambling in Las Vegas* (Princeton, NJ: Princeton University Press, 2014).

97 **psychologist Jerome L. Singer**: Jerome L. Singer, *The Inner World of Daydreaming* (New York: Harper and Row, 1975).

97 **As one student of Singer's noted**: Rebecca L. McMillan, Scott Barry Kaufman, and Jerome L. Singer, "Ode to Positive Constructive Daydreaming," *Frontiers in Psychology* 4 (September 2013).

97 **"self-awareness, creative incubation"**: Scott Barry Kaufman, "Mind Wandering: A New Personal Intelligence Perspective," *Scientific American*, September 25, 2013.

97 **"I've been daydreaming more"**: Hope Mills, "The History of Humans Is the History of Technology: The Millions Interviews Robin Sloan," *The Millions*, November 8, 2012.

98 **"In the space between anxiety and boredom"**: Po Bronson and Ashley Merryman, "The Creativity Crisis," *Newsweek*, July 10, 2010. See also Scott Barry Kaufman, "Why Daydreamers Are More Creative," *Psychology Today*, February 28, 2011.

98 **"The world of real things is very inefficient"**: Max Levchin, DLD13 keynote, January 21, 2013.

99 **"For this one day we'll give to idleness"**: William Wordsworth, "To My Sister," in *Selected Poems* (New York: Penguin Classics, 2005), 25.

100 **"Very few people want to enter monasteries"**: Brother Benet Tvedten, *The View from a Monastery* (New York: Riverhead, 2000), 50.

101 **"interior freedom"**: Thomas Merton, *Thoughts in Solitude* (New York: Farrar, Straus and Giroux, 1999), xi, 89.

103 **"You can just imagine"**: Claire Cain Miller, "New Apps Know the Answer before You Ask the Question," *New York Times*, July 30, 2013, A1.

104 **"vacationers displayed greater pre-trip happiness"**: Jeroen Nawijn, Miquelle A. Marchand, Ruut Veenhoven, and Ad J. Vingerhoets, "Vacationers Happier, but Most Not Happier after a Holiday," *Applied Research in Quality of Life* 5, no. 1 (March 2010): 35–47.

105 **Slow Messenger**: Jennifer Leonard, "Hurry Up and Wait," GOOD, January 7, 2010.

105 **"imagination response"**: Antonio Damasio, *Descartes' Error: Emotion, Reason, and the Human Brain* (New York: Picador, 1994), ch. 1.

106 **report in the *Journal of Biosocial Science***: John Komlos, Patricia Smith, and Barry Bogin, "Obesity and the Rate of Time Preference: Is There a Connection?" *Journal of Biosocial Science* 36, no. 2 (March 2004): 209–19.

106 **"Even after controlling for well-known determinants"**: Charles Courtemanche, Garth Heutel, and Patrick McAlvanah, "Impatience, Incentives, and Obesity," *Economic Journal* 125, no. 582 (February 2015): 1–31.

106 **Other researchers have found**: See, for example, David Laibson, "Impatience and Savings," National Bureau of Economic Research, *Reporter*, Fall 2005; and Alessandro Grecucci et al., "Time Devours Things: How Impulsivity and Time Affect Temporal Decisions in Pathological Gamblers," *PLOS One*, October 8, 2014.

107 **"patient people are indeed more cooperative"**: Oliver S. Curry, Michael E. Price, and Jade G. Price, "Patience Is a Virtue: Cooperative People Have Lower Discount Rates," *Personality and Individual Differences* 44, no. 3 (February 2008): 780.

109 **"Every man rushes elsewhere"**: Michel de Montaigne, *The Complete Essays*, translated by Donald Frame (Stanford: Stanford University Press, 1958), 799.

CHAPTER 5: THE SIXTH SENSE

112 **"Single people who use emojis"**: Laura Stampler, "People Who Use Emojis Have More Sex," *Time*, February 4, 2015; Amanda N. Gessleman, Vivian P. Ta, and Justin R. Garcia, "Worth a thousand interpersonal words: Emoji as affective signals for relationship-oriented digital communication," *PLOS One*, August 15, 2019.

112 **"32 percent of Gen Z'ers"**: "The Future of Creativity: 2022 U.S. Emoji Trend Report Reveals Insights on Emoji Use," Adobe blog, September 13, 2022.

113 **"These days a text"**: Caitlin Macy, "The Age of Emotional Overstatement," *Wall Street Journal*, June 11, 2022.

114 **"naked little spasms of the self"**: Erving Goffman, *Interaction Ritual: Essays on Face to Face Behavior* (New York: Pantheon, 1982), 269–70.

115 **"know more than we can tell"**: Michael Polanyi, *The Tacit Dimension* (Chicago: University of Chicago Press, 2009), 4.

115 **Damasio draws a useful distinction**: Antonio Damasio, *The Feeling of What Happens: Body and Emotion in the Making of Consciousness* (New York: Harcourt, 1999), 36; Antonio Damasio and Gil B. Carvalho, "The Nature of Feelings: Evolutionary and Neurobiological Origins," *Nature Reviews Neuroscience* 14 (February 2013): 143–52.

115 **"Life is the art of being well deceived"**: William Hazlitt, *The Round Table* (London: Sampson Low, Son, and Marston, 1869), 102.

116 **"science" of "guestology"**: Bruce Jones, "Understanding Your Customers Using Guestology," Disney Institute, August 21, 2012; Virginia Chamlee, "Here's What it Takes to be a Full-Time Disney Princess," Buzzfeed, January 19, 2018.

116 **Disney employees engaged in "surface acting"**: Anne Reyers and Jonathan Matusitz, "Emotional Regulation at Walt Disney World: An Impression Management View," *Journal of Workplace Behavioral Health* 27, no. 3 (2012): 139–59.

116 **psychologists Stanley Schachter and Jerome L. Singer**: Stanley Schachter and Jerome L. Singer, "Cognitive, Social, and Physiological Determinants of Emotional State," *Psychological Review* 69 (1962): 379–99.

117 **"Human interaction is a learned skill"**: Elizabeth Cohen, "Does Life Online Give You Popcorn Brain?," CNN, June 23, 2011. See also Eyal Ophir, Clifford Nass, and Anthony Wagner, "Cognitive Control in Media Multitaskers," *Proceedings of the National Academy of Sciences* 106, no. 37 (2009): 1–5.

118 **"social reprimands such as nonverbal communication"**: Ashley A. Anderson, Dominique Brossard, et al., "The 'Nasty Effect': Online Incivility and Risk Perceptions of Emerging Technologies," *Journal of Computer-Mediated Communication* 19, no. 3 (April 2014): 373–87.

118 **boasted "with satisfaction"**: Dan Levin, "Slur, Surfacing an Old Video, Alters Young Lives and a Town," *New York Times*, December 27, 2020, A1.

118 **One university professor discovered**: Jonathan Mahler, "Who Spewed That Abuse? Anonymous Yik Yak Isn't Telling," *New York Times*, March 9, 2015, A1.

118 **"Ourself behind ourself concealed"**: Emily Dickinson, "One Need Not be a Chamber—to be Haunted," in *The Poems of Emily Dickinson, Variorum Edition*, edited by R. W. Franklin (Cambridge, MA: Harvard University Press, 1998), 431.

119 **"If things are happening too fast"**: Mary Helen Immordino-Yang, Andrea McColl, Hanna Damasio, and Antonio Damasio, "Neural Correlates of Admiration and Compassion," *Proceedings of the National Academy of Sciences* 106, no. 19 (May 12, 2009): 8021–26.

119 **"rampant nature of envy"**: Hanna Krasnova, Helena Wenninger, Thomas Widjaja, and Peter Buxmann, "Envy on Facebook: A Hidden Threat to Users' Life Satisfaction?," *Wirtschaftsinformatik Proceedings 2013*, paper 92.

119 **"For the first time, we have a microscope"**: Tom Simonite, "What Facebook Knows," *Technology Review*, June 13, 2012.

120 **"Anger and hate is the easiest way"**: Jeremy B. Merrill and Will Oremus, "Five Points for Anger, One for a 'Like': How Facebook's Formula Fostered Rage and Misinformation," *Washington Post*, October 26, 2021.

120 **Engineers at the dating website OKCupid**: Christian Rudder, "We Experiment on Human Beings!," OKTrends, July 28, 2014.

120 **Some OKCupid users were horrified**: OKCupid's privacy policy states, "Of course, we also process your chats with other users as well as the content you publish to operate and secure the services, and to keep our community safe," although most users probably don't read it.

120 **"We Experiment on Human Beings!"**: OKCupid originally posted about this on its blog, but has since deleted the post. See Laura Stampler, "Facebook Isn't the Only Website Running Experiments on Human Beings," *Time*, July 28, 2014.

120 **"It's an instinctive preference"**: Caeli Wolfson Widger, "Don't Pick Up," *New York Times Magazine*, October 6, 2013, 58.

121 **"When we see a stroke aimed"**: Adam Smith quoted in Roy Porter, *Flesh in the Age of Reason* (New York: W. W. Norton, 2003), 337–38.

121 **"College kids today are about 40 percent lower"**: Sarah H. Konrath, Edward H. O'Brien, and Courtney Hsing, "Changes in Dispositional Empathy in American

College Students Over Time," *Personality and Social Psychology Review* 15, no. 2 (May 2011): 180–98; see also "Empathy: College Students Don't Have as Much as They Used To," EurekAlert, May 28, 2010.

122 **A 2022 study of college students**: Janelle S. Peifer and Gita Taasoobshirazi, "College Students' Reduced Cognitive Empathy and Increased Anxiety and Depression before and during the Covid-19 Pandemic," *International Journal of Environmental Research and Public Health* 19, no. 18 (September 2022): 11330.

122 **"more likely to be followed in real life"**: Amy L. Gonzales and Jeffrey T. Hancock, "Identity Shift in Computer-Mediated Environments," *Media Psychology* 11, no. 2 (2008): 167–85.

122 **"The research is getting clearer"**: Nick Bilton, "Linking Violent Games to Erosion of Empathy," *New York Times*, June 16, 2014, B6. See also Bruce D. Bartholow, Brad J. Bushman, and Marc A. Sestir, "Chronic violent video game exposure and desensitization to violence: Behavioral and event-related brain potential data," *Journal of Experimental Social Psychology* 42, no. 4 (July 2006): 532–39.

122 **"become muted by violent images"**: Jeanne Funk Brockmyer, "Playing Violent Video Games and Desensitization to Violence," *Child Adolescent Psychiatric Clinics of North America* 24, no. 1 (January 2015): 65–77; see also Jeanne Funk Brockmyer, "Desensitization and Violent Video Games: Mechanisms and Evidence," *Child Adolescent Psychiatric Clinics of North America* 31, no. 1 (January 2022): 121–32.

123 **Consider nursing**: Richard Pérez-Peña, "Memorizing, Accessing," *New York Times Education Life*, January 22, 2012, 27; Debra Wood, "Social Media: Cautionary Tales for Nurses," Nursezone.com, August 16, 2012.

123 **Sim Man . . . Nursing Anne**: Michelle Aebersold and Dana Tschannen, "Simulation in Nursing Practice: The Impact on Patient Care," *Online Journal of Issues in Nursing* 18, no. 2 (May 2013): 6. Nursing Anne is viewable on Laerdal's website.

124 **"I get worried when I hear about nursing programs"**: Pérez-Peña, "Memorizing, Assessing," 27.

124 **"My boss outsources patience to me"**: Arlie Russell Hochschild, "The Outsourced Life," *New York Times*, May 6, 2012, SR1.

125 **"emotional spell-check"**: Paola Antonelli, "Talk to Me: Design and Communication Between People and Objects" (New York: Museum of Modern Art, 2011).

125 **"YouTube is our global campfire"**: A description of the Brite 2015 conference can be found at davidrogers.digital/blog. The video is no longer available online.

125 **"We worked with our partners at Google"**: Mary Beech, "Empathy made me a better leader and marketer. Here's what it could do for your brand," Think with Google, April 2018.

125 **"elegant instruments of their mutual estrangement"**: E. J. Mishan, *Economic Myths and the Mythologies of Economics* (Abingdon, UK: Routledge Revivals, 2011), 180.

126 **Like-a-Hug**: John Metcalfe, "A Jacket That Hugs You for Getting Facebook Likes," *Atlantic*, October 4, 2012.

126 **A study conducted by the University of Maryland's**: Jacqui Cheng, "Students face withdrawal, distress when cut off from the Internet," *Ars Technica*, April 6, 2011.

126 **Credit Suisse Youth Barometer report**: Credit Suisse, "Smartphone Fever," bulletin, May 2012.

126 **"There is no need to be lonesome"**: Luke Fernandez and Susan J. Matt, "Americans Were Lonely Long before Technology," *Slate*, June 19, 2019; excerpt from Luke Fernandez and Susan J. Matt, *Bored, Lonely, Angry, Stupid: Changing Feelings About Technology from the Telegraph to Twitter* (Cambridge, MA: Harvard University Press, 2019).

128 **"digital sixth sense"**: Don Clark, "Electronics Develop a Sixth Sense," *Wall Street Journal*, January 7, 2013.

128 **"Ubiquitous computing"**: Egon L. van den Broek, "Ubiquitous Emotion-Aware Computing," *Personal and Ubiquitous Computing* 17 (2013): 53–67.

128 **"The ability to continuously and universally measure"**: Alex Pentland, *Honest Signals: How They Shape Our World* (Cambridge, MA: MIT Press, 2008). See also Alex Pentland, *Social Physics: How Good Ideas Spread—the Lessons from a New Science* (New York: Penguin, 2014), 58–59, 219.

129 **"While some might see it as an invasion of privacy"**: Nick Bilton, "Devices That Know How We Really Feel," *New York Times*, May 5, 2014, B6.

129 **"measure actual behavior in an objective way"**: Rachel Emma Silverman, "Tracking Sensors Invade the Workplace," *Wall Street Journal*, March 7, 2013.

130 **"Every few minutes, it snapped a screenshot"**: Adam Satariano, "How My Boss Monitors Me While I Work from Home," *New York Times*, May 7, 2020, B1.

130 **"organizations are expected to introduce"**: Roshni Raveendhran and Nathanael J. Fast, "Humans judge, algorithms nudge: The psychology of behavior tracking acceptance," *Organizational Behavior and Human Decision Processes* 164 (2021): 11–26.

130 **"reality mining"**: Kate Greene, "What Your Phone Knows about You," *Technology Review*, December 20, 2007.

131 **"We've moved beyond just"**: Chip Cutter and Rachel Feintzeig, "Smile! Your Boss Is Tracking Your Happiness," *Wall Street Journal*, March 7–8, 2020, B1.

131 **"sensible" society where "everything is arranged"**: Alex Pentland, "Society's Nervous System: Building Effective Government, Energy, and Public Health Systems," *Pervasive and Mobile Computing*, Annual Special Issue (October 2011): 10.

131 **"We like to say a phone has eyes"**: Wade Roush, "Inside Google's Age of Augmented Humanity," xconomy.com, February 28, 2011.

132 **the Moodies app**: Bianca Bosker, "Beyond Verbal's New App Tells You How Cheating Politicians Really Feel," *Huffpost*, June 4, 2013.

133 **"We are measuring more than ever"**: Gary Shapiro, "What Happens When Your Friend's Smartphone Can Tell That You're Lying," *Washington Post*, October 31, 2014.

133 **"In each present experience you were only aware"**: Alan M. Watts, *The Wisdom of Insecurity: A Message for an Age of Anxiety* (New York: Vintage, 2011), 81, 107–9.

133 **"It is not enough to 'use technology'"**: B. F. Skinner, *Beyond Freedom and Dignity* (New York: Knopf, 1971), 4–5.

134 **"mass interpersonal persuasion"**: BJ Fogg, "Mass Interpersonal Persuasion: An Early View of a New Phenomemon," in *Persuasive*, edited by Harri Oinas-Kukkonen et al. (Berlin: Springer, 2008), 23–34.

134 **"enchanting perceptual distortions"**: Natasha Dow Schüll, *Addiction by Design: Machine Gambling in Las Vegas* (Princeton, NJ: Princeton University Press, 2012), 96, 108.

135 **"The proposed processing scheme enables"**: Egon L. van den Broek, Marleen H. Schut, Kees Tuinebreijer, and Joyce H. D. M. Westerink, "Communication and Persuasion Technology: Psychophysiology of Emotions and User-Profiling," *Persuasive 06: Proceedings of the First International Conference on Persuasive Technology for Human Well-Being*, May 2006, 154–57.

135 **"electronic environments that are sensitive"**: van den Broek et al., "Communication and Persuasion Technology."

135 **the rise of "persuasion profiling"**: Maurits Kaptein and Dean Eckles, "Selecting Effective Means to Any End: Futures and Ethics of Persuasion Profiling," in *Persuasive 2010: Persuasive Technology* edited by T. Ploug et al. (Berlin: Springer, 2010), 82–93.

136 **"Ask yourself whether your technology persuades"**: Daniel Berdichevsky and Erik Neuenschwander, "Toward an Ethics of Persuasive Technology," *Technology Information Communications of the ACM* 42, no. 5 (May 1, 1999): 51.

136 **"The issue of whether the techniques"**: Bran Knowles, Benjamin Wohl, Paul Coulton, and Mark Lochrie, "'Convince Us': An Argument for the Morality of Persuasion," Lancaster University eprint.

136 **"Everything can be taken from a human being"**: Victor Frankl, *Man's Search for Meaning* (Boston: Beacon, 2006), 66.

137 **"auto-manage" your relationships**: PPLKPR description from iTunes app store; promotional video at pplkpr.com.

137 **One young man told *Fast Company***: Sophie Weiner, "This App Wants to Help You Get Rid of People Who Stress You Out," *Fast Company*, January 26, 2015. See also Sarah Buhr, "The pplkpr App Wants to Tell You Which Friends Are Better to Hang With," *Techcrunch*, January 19, 2015.

138 **"A single sentence will suffice"**: Albert Camus, *The Fall*, translated by Justin O'Brien (New York: Vintage, 1991), 6.

138 **"relates to, arises from, or influences emotion"**: Rosalind W. Picard, "Affective Computing," MIT Media Laboratory Perceptual Computing Section Technical Report No. 321 (1995); see also Rosalind Picard, *Affective Computing* (Cambridge, MA: MIT Press, 1997).

138 **"I think that, ten years down the line"**: Raffi Khatchadourian, "We Know How You Feel," *New Yorker*, January 19, 2015.

140 **"It has nothing to do with"**: Joseph Weizenbaum, *Computer Power and Human Reason: From Judgment to Calculation* (New York: W. H. Freeman, 1976), 270.

CHAPTER 6: MEDIATED PLEASURES

141 **Sarai Sierra**: J. David Goodman, "Mystery Deepens as Staten Island Woman's Body Is Returned from Turkey," *New York Times*, February 8, 2013, A22; Sebnem Arsu and J. David Goodman, "Man Says He Killed Tourist after She Rejected Kiss," *New York Times*, March 19, 2013, A24.

143 **"It's becoming a safety issue"**: Geetika Rudra, "Lake Tahoe Hikers Taking Too Many Dangerous Bear Selfies," *ABC News*, October 26, 2014.

143 **A survey conducted by Ford Motor Company**: Ford Newsroom, "Ford Launches Icon50 to Celebrate Mustang Influence on Pop Culture, Rekindle Americans' Sense of Adventure," press release, October 1, 2014.

146 **"Unnaturally strong explosions"**: Robert M. Sapolsky, *Why Zebras Don't Get Ulcers*, 3rd ed. (New York: Holt, 2004), 351.

147 **"Whereas travel is about the unexpected"**: Ilan Stavans and Joshua Ellison, "Reclaiming Travel," *New York Times*, July 8, 2012.

148 **Adventurer David Roberts views**: David Roberts, "When GPS Leads to SOS," *New York Times*, August 14, 2012, A19. See also David Roberts, "Exploits, Now Not So Daring," *New York Times*, September 16, 2011, A29.

148 **"In the best travel, disconnection is a necessity"**: Paul Theroux, *The Tao of Travel: Enlightenments from Lives on the Road* (New York: Houghton Mifflin Harcourt, 2011), 5, 145–46.

148 **survey by Royal Caribbean cruise lines**: Michael Gadd, "How a Family Uses Social Media During a Week's Holiday," *Daily Mail*, October 13, 2014.

148 **"Cyberspace intercourse vitiates"**: Dervla Murphy, "First, Buy Your Pack Animal," *Guardian*, January 2, 2009.

149 **Journalist Paul Salopek**: Paul Salopek, "A Stroll Around the World," *New York*

Times, November 24, 2013, SR1. Follow Salopek's journey at "Out of Eden Walk," *National Geographic* website.

149 **"Every map is someone's way"**: Oliver Burkeman, "How Google and Apple's Digital Mapping Is Mapping Us," *Guardian*, August 28, 2012.

150 **"It was a beautiful moment"**: Emily Brennan, "Caterina Fake, of Flickr and Findery, on Creating Wonder," *New York Times*, December 8, 2013, TR3; Brian Patrick Eha, "Caterina Fake's Findery Aims to Be an Adventure Machine," *Entrepreneur*, April 3, 2013.

151 **"photograph-trophies"**: Susan Sontag, *On Photography* (New York: Picador, 1977), 9.

151 **"We realized the bigger opportunity"**: Nick Bilton, "A Camera of Daredevils Gains Appeal," *New York Times*, October 22, 2012, B1.

152 **"stage" where "you want the tools"**: Farhad Manjoo, "Instagram Goes Beyond Its Gauzy Filters," *New York Times*, June 5, 2014, B1.

152 **"experiences [of dining out]"**: T. M. Brown, "How Instagram Is Eating Dining," *Fast Company*, August 14, 2017.

152 **"He showed the vacation to his camera"**: Wendell Berry, "The Vacation," in *New Collected Poems* (Berkeley: Counterpoint, 2012).

152 **"reality disappointment"**: Alexandra Molotkow, "New Feelings: Reality Disappointment," *Real Life*, November 8, 2021.

153 **"It was so vast and so familiar"**: Ari N. Schulman, "GPS and the End of the Road," *New Atlantis*, Spring 2011.

153 **"I wondered if we were trying to reproduce"**: Simon Bainbridge, "Photo Opportunities," *British Journal of Photography* 157 (October 2010): 19–26.

153 **"over the vast features of Rameses"**: Oliver Wendell Holmes, "The Stereoscope and the Stereograph," *Atlantic* (June 1859).

153 **in places like Heidelberg, Germany**: Bernd Stiegler, *A History of Armchair Travel*, translated by Peter Filkins (Chicago: University of Chicago Press, 2010), 110.

153 **"Virtual armchair travel has never been easier"**: Kevin Sintumuang, "A Digital Odyssey," *Wall Street Journal*, July 2, 2011.

154 **"Ten things you've never been able to do"**: "10 Things You've Never Been Able to Do on a Cruise Ship Before," Royal Caribbean Cruises, press release, August 25, 2014.

154 **"Think of the long trip home"**: Elizabeth Bishop, "Questions of Travel," in *Elizabeth Bishop: Poems, Prose, and Letters* (New York: Library of America, 2008), 74.

155 **"And the beholder, is he through"**: Paul Klee, *Creative Confession and Other Writings* (London: Tate Gallery Act Editions, 2014), 10.

155 **average person visiting a museum today spends**: Stephanie Rosenbloom, "A Museum of Your Own," *New York Times*, October 12, 2014, TR1.

155 **"good art possesses a kind of super-truth"**: Aldous Huxley, *Collected Essays* (New York: Harper & Brothers, 1958), 97.

155 **"time batteries" and "stockpiles"**: Jennifer L. Roberts, "The Power of Patience," *Harvard Magazine*, November–December 2013: 40–43.

156 **"The painting now travels to the spectator"**: John Berger, *Ways of Seeing* (London: BBC/Penguin, 1972), 19–20.

156 **"The only way to understand painting"**: Jean Renoir, *Renoir: My Father* (New York: New York Review of Books, 2001), 58.

156 **"Most works of art yield their secrets"**: Philippe de Montebello and Martin Gayford, *Rendez-Vous with Art* (New York: Thames and Hudson, 2014).

156 **"Just because you have *looked* at something"**: Roberts, "The Power of Patience," 43.

156 **"From a digital distance, you see an image"**: Holland Cotter, "Just Being. There," *New York Times*, March 19, 2015, F1.

157 **"Museum-Selfie Day"**: "Happy Museum-Selfie Day," artinfo.com, blog post, January 22, 2014; Gideon Bradshaw, "Jay Z Takes an Iconic Selfie at the Warhol Museum," *Pittsburgh Magazine*, January 23, 2014.

157 **"I say hooray"**: Deborah Solomon, "Hey 'Starry Night,' Say 'Cheese!,'" *New York Times*, September 29, 2013, SR5.

157 **"photo-impairment effect"**: Linda A. Henkel, "Point-and-Shoot Memories: The Influence of Taking Photos on Memory for a Museum Tour," *Psychological Science* 25, no. 2 (2014): 396–402. See also Julia S. Soares and Benjamin C. Storm, "Does Taking Multiple Photos Lead to a Photo-Taking-Impairment Effect?," *Psychonomic Bulletin and Review* 29 (July 2022): 2211–18.

158 **Pictures offer exceptional "retrieval cues"**: Simon Bowen and Daniela Petrelli, "Remembering today tomorrow: Exploring the human-centered design of digital mementos," *International Journal of Human-Computer Studies* 69, no. 5 (May 2011): 324–37.

158 **New ways of seeing and storing**: The passages that follow draw on Christine Rosen, "The Image Culture," *New Atlantis* (Fall 2005), and Christine Rosen, "The Age of Egocasting," *New Atlantis* (Fall 2004–Winter 2005).

158 **"not merely an instrument which serves"**: *Encyclopedia of Nineteenth-Century Photography*, edited by John Hannavy (New York: Routledge, 2013), 671.

158 **"image would become more important than the object"**: Oliver Wendell Holmes, "The Stereoscope and the Stereograph," *Atlantic*, June 1, 1859.

158 **"A revengeful God has given ear"**: Charles Baudelaire, "Salon of 1859," *Revue Française*, June 10–July 20, 1859. See also Charles Baudelaire, *The Mirror of Art*, edited and translated by Jonathan Mayne (London: Phaidon, 1955).

159 **"Knowing a great deal about what is in"**: Sontag, *On Photography*.

159 **"progressive reaction" . . . "reproducibility"**: Walter Benjamin, "The Work of Art in the Age of Mechanical Reproduction," in *Illuminations: Essays and Reflections*, edited by Hannah Arendt (New York: Schocken, 1968), 217–42.

161 **"Museum-going is turned into a computer game"**: Jed Perl, "Googled," *New Republic*, February 16, 2011.

162 **"Carsten Holler: Experience"**: Judith H. Dobrzynski, "High Culture Goes Hands-On," *New York Times*, August 11, 2013, SR1.

162 **"shift away from passive experiences"**: Steve Lohr, "Museums Morph Digitally," *New York Times*, October 26, 2014, F1.

162 **Cleveland Museum of Art**: Fred A. Bernstein, "Technology That Serves to Enhance, Not Distract," *New York Times*, March 21, 2013, F26.

162 **"digital first" . . . "You want the way"**: Lohr, "Museums Morph," F1.

163 **"restorative environments"**: Stephen Kaplan, Lisa V. Bardwell, and Deborah B. Slakter, "The Restorative Experience as a Museum Benefit," *Journal of Museum Education* 18, no. 3 (Fall 1993): 15–18.

163 **Another study by Daniel Fujiwara**: Daniel Fujiwara, "Museums and Happiness: The Value of Participating in Museums and the Arts," Happy Museum Project, April 2013.

163 **"Looking at great art"**: Judith H. Dobrzinski, "My Experience With, and Rationale For, 'Experience Museums,'" artinfo.com, blog post, August 13, 2013.

163 **"Cultivated philistines are in the habit"**: Theodore Adorno, *Minima Moralia: Reflections from Damaged Life* (New York: Verso, 1974), 216.

164 **In the image, the young couple stands**: *New York Times Magazine*, February 23, 2014, 35.

164 **most Googled question**: "A Little Look at a Big Year," Google Year in Search pamphlet, 2014.

164 **"ostensible immediacy of sexual contact"**: Richard Kearney, "Losing Our Touch," *New York Times*, August 31, 2014, SR4.
165 **"an acceptable way to express"**: Joseph Price, Rich Patterson, Mark Regnerus, and Jacob Walley, "How Much More XXX is Generation X Consuming? Evidence of Changing Attitudes and Behaviors Related to Pornography Since 1973," *Journal of Sex Research* 53, no. 1 (2016): 12–20.
165 **"real-life sex workers"**: Rob Henderson, "Shut Up and Drive," *Free Press*, April 17, 2023.
165 **"had a tendency to describe the act"**: Davy Rothbart," He's Just Not That into Anyone," *New York*, January 30, 2011.
166 **"It hardly seems fair to call that sex"**: Siobhan Rosen, "Dinner, Movie, and a Dirty Sanchez," *GQ*, February 2012.
166 **"sex doll brothels"**: E. J. Dickson, "Sex Doll Brothels Are Now a Thing. What Will Happen to Real-Life Sex Workers?," *Vox*, November 26, 2018.
166 **"We started our research seeking men"**: Jonathan Liew, "All Men Watch Porn, Scientists Find," *Telegraph*, December 2, 2009.
167 **"The machine-centered viewpoint"**: Donald Norman quoted in Nicholas Carr, *The Glass Cage: Automation and Us* (New York: W. W. Norton, 2014), 161.
167 **survey by the Japan Family Planning Association . . . "incredibly sophisticated virtual worlds"**: Abigail Haworth, "Why Have Young People in Japan Stopped Having Sex?," *Guardian*, October 20, 2013.
168 **"What if you never had to worry about food again?"**: Soylent website.
169 **"punishingly boring, joyless product"**: Farhad Manjoo, "The Soylent Revolution Will Not Be Pleasurable," *New York Times*, May 29, 2014, B1.
169 **Amazon's summary of thousands of reviews**: https://www.amazon.com/Soylent-Chocolate-Protein-Replacement-Bottles/dp/B08H6FB43L/ref=sr_1_5 (as of January 31, 2024; see paragraph opposite the listing of customer reviews).
169 **"a separation between our meals"**: Lizzie Widdicombe, "The End of Food," *New Yorker*, May 12, 2014.
169 **"Wi-Fi cuisine"**: Patricia Storace, "Seduced by the Food on Your Plate," *New York Review of Books*, December 18, 2014.
170 **Ibiza-based restaurant Sublimotion:** John O'Ceallaigh, "Is This the Most Expensive Restaurant in the World?," *Telegraph*, April 23, 2014.
171 **"The networked mediation of games"**: Rob Horning, "Dummy Discards a Heart," *New Inquiry*, May 22, 2012.
172 **"We have to have a very compelling reason"**: Ken Belson, "Going to the Game, to Watch Them All on TV," *New York Times*, September 15, 2013, A1.
172 **"to eliminate every last shred"**: Tim Heffernan, "The Deer Paradox," *Atlantic*, October 24, 2012.
172 **"When we're getting out, we're trying to become"**: Sarah Portlock, "Birders Use Smartphones to Play Bird Songs," *Wall Street Journal*, January 3, 2014.
173 **In *Anarchy, State, and Utopia*:** Robert Nozick, *Anarchy, State, and Utopia* (New York: Basic Books, 2013), 42–45.
175 **"a world where the recording of an event"**: Ian Kerr, "Review of *Delete*," *Surveillance and Society* 8, no. 2 (2010): 261–64.
175 **"A new kind of relationship between people"**: Christopher Bonanas, "It's Polaroid's World, We Just Live in It," *Wall Street Journal*, November 9, 2012.
176 **"the contamination of the pleasurable present"**: Stanley Milgram, "The Image Freezing Machine," in *The Individual in a Social World* (New York: Addison–Wesley, 1977).
176 **"creating new contexts for experience"**: Peter-Paul Verbeek, *Moralizing Tech-*

nology: Understanding and Designing the Morality of Things (Chicago: University of Chicago Press, 2011), 142.

176 **"good discipline for Americans"**: Dwight Macdonald, "The Triumph of the Fact," in *Masscult and Midcult*, edited by Louis Menand (New York: New York Review of Books, 2011) 231, 233, 235.

176 **"a user-experience researcher" at Facebook**: Robert Lane Green, "Facebook: Like?," *Intelligent Life*, May–June 2012.

177 **"the ersatz is so commonly accepted"**: Thomas Merton, *The Monastic Journey* (Collegeville, MN: Cistercian Publications, 1992), 75.

177 **"It won't matter where they are"**: Evgeny Morozov, *To Save Everything, Click Here* (New York: Public Affairs, 2013), 270–72.

177 **"virtual balconies"**: "An Inside Room with a View," Royal Caribbean website.

178 **"The visual simulations were meeting"**: Sue Thomas, "Technobiophilia," *Aeon*, September 24, 2013.

178 **"a life not really lived"**: Mark Slouka, *Essays from the Nick of Time: Reflections and Refutations* (Minneapolis: Graywolf Press, 2010), 78.

179 **"primary visceral consciousness"**: Aldous Huxley, "Meditation on El Greco," in *Collected Essays* (New York: Harper & Brothers, 1958), 150, 144, 377–78.

CHAPTER 7: PLACE, SPACE, AND SERENDIPITY

181 **McSorley's Old Ale House**: Joseph Mitchell, *McSorley's Wonderful Saloon* (New York: Pantheon, 2001).

181 **The owner did so "reluctantly"**: Dan Barry, "Dust Is Gone above the Bar, but a Legend Still Dangles," *New York Times*, April 7, 2011, A19.

182 **"Space is transformed into place"**: Yi-Fu Tuan, *Space and Place: The Perspective of Experience* (Minneapolis: University of Minnesota Press, 1977), 136, 54.

182 **James Joyce coined the word "iSpace"**: James Joyce, *Finnegans Wake* (London: Faber and Faber, 1975), 124.

183 **"We know roughly who you are"**: Scott Morrison, "Google CEO Envisions a Serendipity Engine," *Wall Street Journal*, September 29, 2010.

184 **"the industrialization of the ineffable"**: Nicholas Carr, "The Industrialization of the Ineffable," *Rough Type*, January 3, 2012.

184 **"seamlessly blend digital content"**: Apple website.

185 **"You have the space"**: Jeff Parsons, "Mark Zuckerberg Announces Wireless Oculus Rift Headset," *Daily Mirror*, October 7, 2016.

185 **"*Where* one is has less and less"**: Joshua Meyrowitz, *No Sense of Place: The Impact of Electronic Media on Social Behavior* (Oxford: Oxford University Press, 1986), viii.

186 **"third places"**: Ray Oldenburg, *The Great Good Place* (New York: DaCapo, 1989).

188 **"If you believe, as I do"**: Roland Kelts, "Private Worlds," *Adbusters* 86 (November–December 2009).

188 **"teaches people to bear the awful singing"**: Daisuke Inoue and Robert Scott, "Voice Hero: The Inventor of Karaoke Speaks," *Off the Map* 1, no. 4 (October 2013).

189 **"In growing up people learn literally thousands"**: Edward T. Hall, *The Silent Language* (New York: Anchor, 1990), 161.

190 **"only 43 percent of Americans know all"**: Charles M. Blow, "Friends, Neighbors, and Facebook," *New York Times*, June 12, 2010, A21.

190 **"social events among neighbors"**: Leslie Davis and Kim Parker, "A Half-Century after 'Mister Rogers' Debut, 5 Facts about Neighbors in U.S.," Pew Research Center, August 15, 2019.

190 **Research from the General Social Survey**: Conducted by NORC at the University of Chicago.
190 **"Our Epidemic of Loneliness and Isolation"**: "Our Epidemic of Loneliness and Isolation: The U.S. Surgeon General's Advisory on the Healing Effects of Social Connection and Community," 2023.
191 **"across age groups, people are spending less time"**: Juana Summers, Vincent Acovino, Christopher Intagliata, and Patrick Wood, "America Has a Loneliness Epidemic. Here Are 6 Steps to Address It," *All Things Considered*, National Public Radio, May 2, 2023.
191 **"The great bulk of human association"**: Oldenburg, *Great Good Place*, 24–25.
192 **"ranks those images based on their similarity"**: "What Is Google Lens?," Google website.
192 **"We lie in bed and listen to a broadcast"**: Wallace Stevens, *The Necessary Angel: Essays on Reality and the Imagination* (New York: Vintage, 1965), 18.
192 **"Moral psychology tells us"**: Bruce Jennings, "In Place," *Minding Nature* 5, no. 1 (May 2012).
193 **"We tracked people in scores"**: William H. Whyte, *The Social Life of Small Urban Spaces* (New York: Project for Public Spaces, 1980); the film is available on YouTube. See also Christine Rosen, "Technology, Mobility, and Community," in *Localism in the Mass Age*, edited by Mark T. Mitchell and Jason Peters (Eugene, OR: Front Porch Republic, 2018): 243–49; Christine Rosen, "The New Meaning of Mobility," in *Why Place Matters: Geography, Identity, and Civic Life*, edited by Wilfred M. McClay and Ted V. McAllister (New York: New Atlantis, 2014), 180–87.
193 **"With the advent of the Sony Walkman"**: Matt Alt, "The Walkman, Forty Years On," *New Yorker*, June 29, 2020.
195 **"were considerably less likely to participate"**: Keith N. Hampton, Oren Livio, and Lauren Sessions Goulet, "The Social Life of Wireless Urban Spaces: Internet Use, Social Networks, and the Public Realm," *Journal of Communication* 60, no. 4 (December 2010): 701–22.
195 **"are not alone in the true sense"**: Megan Gambino, "How Technology Makes Us Better Social Beings," *Smithsonian*, July 10, 2011.
196 **"sitting in the modern coffee shop"**: John Freeman, "Not So Fast," *Wall Street Journal*, August 21, 2009.
197 **"If people are not speaking to each other"**: Richard Sennett, *The Fall of Public Man* (New York: W. W. Norton, 1992), 222.
197 **"Communities are constituted by physical proximity"**: Sherry Turkle, "A Conversation with Sherry Turkle," *Hedgehog Review* 14, no. 1 (Spring 2012).
197 **"I would insist that real community is local"**: Virginia Sole-Smith, "Let's Get Together and Feel Alright," *Real Simple*, April 2015, 195–99.
197 **"Facebook can't substitute"**: Sole-Smith, "Let's Get Together."
198 **"I've spent many years studying"**: David Sax, "Why Strangers Are Good for Us," *New York Times*, June 17, 2022, A24. See also Gillian M. Sandstrom and Elizabeth W. Dunn, "Social Interactions and Well Being: The Surprising Power of Weak Ties," *Personality and Social Psychology Journal* 40, no. 7 (July 2014).
198 a **"very pretty capacity for dissociated vigilance"**: Erving Goffman, *Relations in Public: Microstudies of the Public Order* (New York: Basic Books, 1971), 238.
199 **"By defining the situation"**: Jackson Toby, "Some Variables in Role Conflict Analysis," *Social Forces* 30 (1962): 323–37.
199 **Researchers at Nagaoka University**: Hisashi Murakami, Claudio Feliciani, Yuta Nishinari, and Katsuhiro Nishinari, "Mutual Anticipation Can Contribute to Self-

Organization in Human Crowds," *Science Advances* 7, no. 12 (March 17, 2021). See also Matt Simon, "People Who Text While Walking Actually Do Ruin Everything," *Wired*, March 17, 2021.

199 **"The individual may desire, earn, and deserve"**: Erving Goffman, *Interaction Ritual: Essays on Face to Face Behavior* (New York: Pantheon, 1982), 58, 48–49.

200 **"the shielding of others"**: Sennett, *Fall of Public Man*, 264.

201 **"They reinforce the idea"**: Drew Austin, "Always In," *Real Life*, June 3, 2019.

201 **"In the street people astound and interest"**: Exhibition catalogue, *Alberto Giacometti: A Retrospective Exhibition* (New York: Praeger and the Solomon R. Guggenheim Museum, 1974), 31.

201 **"the greatest serendipity machine"**: Ian Leslie, "In Search of Serendipity," *Intelligent Life*, January–February 2012.

202 **"The funny thing about these cities"**: Will Doig, "Science Fiction No More: The Perfect City Is Under Construction," *Salon*, April 28, 2012.

202 **"People who think the Web is killing off"**: Steven Johnson, "Anatomy of an Idea," *Medium*, December 14, 2011.

202 **"You cannot have the joys"**: Anthony Daniels, "Loss and Gain," *New Criterion*, November 2012.

203 **"We discover who we are"**: Mark Vernon, "The Return of Virtue Ethics," Big Questions Online, January 25, 2011.

203 **"the only kind of public building"**: Oldenburg, *Great Good Place*, 47.

203 **"still in the very early stages"**: Greg Lindsay, "Engineering Serendipity," *New York Times*, April 7, 2013, SR12.

204 **"The environment in which we live"**: Oldenburg, *Great Good Place*, 85, 296.

204 **"Every cubic inch of space"**: Walt Whitman, *Leaves of Grass* (New York: Modern Library, 1993).

204 **and in some cases, entire cities**: Erin Griffith, "The Silicon Valley Elite Who Want to Build a City from Scratch," *New York Times*, August 25, 2023.

205 **"It is by knowing where you stand"**: Eudora Welty, *On Writing* (New York: Modern Library, 2002), 54.

CONCLUSION

207 **"Humane is an experience company"**: See also Humane News, press release, February 2024: "Humane is an experience company that creates the technologies and platforms for the intelligence age. Contextual computing, powered by AI, built on a foundation of trust and privacy. Humane believes in a future of technology that feels familiar, natural, and human."

207 **"A small percent of people live"**: Niccolo Soldo, "The Dubrovnik Interviews—Marc Andreessen, Interviewed by a Retard," *Fisted by Foucault*, Substack, May 31, 2021.

208 **"the less invasive an intervention is"**: Frank Hindriks and Igor Douven, "Nozick's Experience Machine: An Empirical Study," *Philosophical Psychology* 31, no. 2 (2018): 278–98.

209 **"We're going to make machines intelligent"**: Wendell Wallach, "Who Ultimately Will Have the Upper Hand? Machines or Humans?," *Washington Post*, January 8, 2016.

210 **"reading your soul"**: Jess Joho, "TikTok's algorithms knew I was bi before before I did. I'm not the only one," *Mashable*, September 18, 2022.

211 **"There was a lot of social pressure"**: Meera Navlakha, "Why Have Some People Stopped Using BeReal?," *Mashable*, February 23, 2023.

212 **American Time Use Survey**: Bryce Ward, "Americans Are Choosing to Be Alone. Here's Why We Should Reverse That," *Washington Post*, November 23, 2022.

212 **"Both Democrats and Republicans"**: Adrian J. Rivera and Patrick Healy, "We Asked 11 Americans Why It's So Difficult to Trust One Another," *New York Times*, June 15, 2023.

213 **"Online feels more peaceful"**: Ariel Kaminer and Adrian J. Rivera, "Listen to Us. What These 12 Kids Want Adults to Know," *New York Times*, March 21, 2023.

214 **According to Common Sense Media**: "The Common Sense Census: Media Use by Tweens and Teens, 2021," Common Sense Media, March 9, 2022.

214 **"spends more than two hours daily"**: "The TikTok Challenge: Curbing Social Media's Influence on Young Minds," Reboot Foundation, May 2023.

214 **"It is both an instrument of liberation"**: Lewis Mumford, *Technics and Civilization* (New York: Harcourt Brace, 1963), 283.

215 **Kate Gladstone of Albany**: Isabella Paoletto, "What Killed Penmanship?," *New York Times*, March 24, 2023.

215 **"I visualize the feeling of drowning"**: Teju Cole, "A Visual Remix," *New York Times Magazine*," April 19, 2015, 20. See also Erik Kessels, "24 Hours in Photos," erikkessels.com.

215 **human contact was becoming a "luxury good"**: Nellie Bowles, "Human Contact as a Luxury Good," *New York Times*, March 24, 2019, SR1.

216 **"a tablet [computer] on a motorized stand"**: Janie Hahr, "California Man Learns He's Dying from Doctor on Robot Video," Associated Press, March 18, 2019.

216 **"We've crossed into replacing the dead"**: Adrienne Matai, "The Contest over Our Data after We Die," *New York Times*, July 25, 2021, ST10. See also Patrick Stokes, *Digital Souls: A Philosophy of Online Death* (London: Bloomsbury Academic, 2021).

217 **"dawning of a new age of personalized robot"**: Farhad Manjoo, "A Carousel of Memories, with Google at the Controls," *New York Times*, November 15, 2018, B6.

218 **"Death will eventually be reduced"**: Ian Sample, "If They Could Turn Back Time: How tech billionaires are trying to reverse the ageing process," *Guardian*, February 17, 2022.

Index